Canadian Living
Make it Tonight

Canadian Living

Make It Tonight

Delicious, no-fuss
dinner solutions
for every cook

INTRODUCTION

What kind of cookbook do you want for weeknight meals? That's the question we recently posed to the readers of *Canadian Living Magazine*. And did they have answers!

- **Familiar.** Almost all of our readers asked for recipes that use simple, everyday ingredients that most of us have on hand. Certainly not ones that require hard-to-find funky ingredients, or instant this or that.

- **Quick.** The time factor is key to weeknight meals, and anything that makes the after-work-and-school craze easier is welcome. Our readers wanted homemade fast food that's nothing like its commercial counterpart.

- **Simple.** Many of our readers work outside the home, so when they arrive after a tough day, they don't have the time or energy to make a complicated dinner. Simple preparation and cooking methods are ideal.

- **Healthy.** Just because they want quick and easy recipes doesn't mean our readers aren't concerned about their health. They want to make dishes in a hurry that still give them the energy and nutrients they need.

- **Inspiring.** After years of bustling activity, readers say, they've run out of ideas for dinner. They want a book with lots of recipes that will give them a break from the perennial conundrum of "What am I going to cook tonight?"

Fortunately, these five points are already basic to the *Canadian Living* food philosophy, and they form the guidelines for our week-night family meals. We shop for ingredients in the supermarket across the street; use as few pots, pans, bowls and measuring cups as possible; and employ simple preparation and cooking techniques that don't require chef certification.

The timer's on for us, too. Rush hour is our reality, but healthy eating is never far from our minds. We focus on vegetables and fruits, whole grains over processed ones, proper portion sizes and the modest use of fats and sweeteners. We also make weeknight meals a reality with recipes that are ready in 15 to 30 minutes and ones that contain just five or so ingredients. To make life even easier, we also offer recipes that make the most of convenient appliances, such as toaster ovens, barbecues and slow cookers.

In this book, you'll find all these solutions and more. We've even thrown in inspiring sides, salads and a few sweet treats, along with tons of tips that will take the rush out of rush-hour cooking.

Happy cooking!

Elizabeth Baird

ACKNOWLEDGEMENTS

Cookbooks are just like recipes: they require a variety of ingredients to make a foolproof final product. And the vital ingredients of this cookbook are the people who put it together. Leave one out and the recipe just doesn't taste as good or work as well.

At the top of the ingredient list is the brilliant team of food specialists who create recipes in The Canadian Living Test Kitchen: food section editor Gabrielle Bright; senior home economist Heather Howe; senior food specialist Alison Kent; food specialists Kate Dowhan, Rheanna Kish and Adell Shneer; and contributing editor Andrew Chase.

Testing the recipes until they're perfect is just one part of the process. Senior editor Beverley Renahan, copy chief Wendy Graves, senior copy editor Miriam Osborne, copy editor Sarah Jane Silva and researcher Sarah Snowdon ensure that every recipe is clear, accurate and consistent. An extra thank-you goes to Miriam Osborne, who did a thorough final check for rogue typos. Thanks also to Gillian Watts, who created an index that will help you find whatever you're looking for. Nutritional analysis is entrusted to Sharyn Joliat of Info Access.

Directing the delicious visuals for *Canadian Living* Magazine is creative director Michael Erb, with senior associate art director June Anderson and former senior associate art director John Edney, who worked with many talented photographers and stylists (see page 239) to make the food on these pages look as mouth-watering on paper as it does in real life. Administrator Olga Goncalves Costa, editorial assistants Teresa Sousa and Patrick Flynn, and art production coordinator Erin Poetschke pulled together all the materials and visuals with precision and aplomb.

The project editor, the person who steered this cookbook through its various stages of doneness is superorganized managing editor Tina Anson Mine. She worked closely with production manager Marie-Suzanne Menier, our organizational whiz in Montreal, and eagle-eyed copy editor Valérie Quintal. Kudos also to book designers Mario Mercier and his team at orangetango, who created a lovely, easy-to-read design that home cooks will love.

Finally, generous helpings of appreciation are served to *Canadian Living* Magazine editor-in-chief Susan Antonacci and group publisher Lynn Chambers, Transcontinental Books publisher Jean Paré; and Duncan Shields, Frances Bedford and Janet Joy Wilson of Random House Canada. Without them, this project would never have made it to your table.

TABLE
OF
CONTENTS

CHAPTER 1

Make It Tonight... in 15 to 20 Minutes

Rainbow Trout with Dijon Mayonnaise

Trout is a healthy, fast choice for dinner. This method of coating fish with seasoned mayonnaise is so versatile. Try it with salmon, tilapia and catfish for equally easy prep and tasty results.

4	rainbow trout fillets (about 6 oz/175 g each)	4
2 tbsp	light mayonnaise	25 mL
2 tsp	Dijon mustard	10 mL
¼ tsp	each salt and pepper	1 mL
1 tbsp	chopped fresh parsley	15 mL
	Lemon wedges	

> Pat fish dry; place on greased rimmed baking sheet. In small bowl, combine mayonnaise, mustard, salt and pepper; spread on each fillet. Broil 6 inches (15 cm) from heat until fish flakes easily when tested, about 6 minutes.

> Sprinkle with parsley. Serve with lemon to squeeze over top.

Makes 4 servings. PER SERVING: about 226 cal, 29 g pro, 11 g total fat (3 g sat. fat), 1 g carb, 0 g fibre, 82 mg chol, 282 mg sodium. % RDI: 10% calcium, 4% iron, 11% vit A, 13% vit C, 14% folate.

VARIATIONS

Rainbow Trout with Curry Mayonnaise
● Replace mustard with mild curry paste.

Rainbow Trout with Thai Mayonnaise
● Replace mustard with 1 tsp (5 mL) Thai red curry paste.

Green Beans with Sun-Dried Tomatoes

1 lb	green beans, trimmed	500 g
2 tbsp	slivered oil-packed sun-dried tomatoes	25 mL
1 tsp	extra-virgin olive oil	5 mL
¼ tsp	dried oregano	1 mL

> In saucepan of boiling salted water, cover and cook beans until tender-crisp, about 7 minutes. Drain and toss with tomatoes, oil and oregano.

Makes 4 servings. PER SERVING: about 49 cal, 2 g pro, 2 g total fat (trace sat. fat), 8 g carb, 3 g fibre, 0 mg chol, 10 mg sodium. % RDI: 4% calcium, 5% iron, 7% vit A, 20% vit C, 14% folate.

Corned Beef and Avocado Rolls

An avocado needs three to five days to ripen. Set it on the counter and out of the sun, or seal it in a paper bag with an apple to speed up the process.

4	large flour tortillas	4
2 cups	torn mixed salad greens	500 mL
8 oz	sliced corned beef	250 g
1	avocado, halved, pitted and sliced	1
½ cup	thinly sliced red onion	125 mL
LIME MAYONNAISE:		
⅓ cup	light mayonnaise	75 mL
1 tbsp	water	15 mL
1 tbsp	lime or lemon juice	15 mL
2 tsp	chopped fresh coriander	10 mL
Dash	hot pepper sauce	Dash

❯ LIME MAYONNAISE: In bowl, combine mayonnaise, water, lime juice, coriander and hot pepper sauce; set aside.

❯ On work surface, spread tortillas with Lime Mayonnaise. Layer one-quarter each of the greens, corned beef, avocado and onion on bottom third of each. Fold bottom up; fold in sides and roll up. Cut each roll in half on the diagonal.

Makes 4 servings. PER SERVING: about 439 cal, 17 g pro, 24 g total fat (5 g sat. fat), 40 g carb, 5 g fibre, 62 mg chol, 1,090 mg sodium. % RDI: 5% calcium, 26% iron, 9% vit A, 15% vit C, 59% folate.

Carrot and Celery Slaw

2	carrots, coarsely grated	2
2	radishes, grated	2
1	stalk celery, grated	1
2 tsp	white wine vinegar	10 mL
2 tsp	vegetable oil	10 mL
2 tsp	prepared horseradish	10 mL
Pinch	each salt and pepper	Pinch

❯ In bowl, combine carrots, radishes and celery. Add vinegar, oil, horseradish, salt and pepper. Toss to combine.

Makes 4 servings. PER SERVING: about 41 cal, 1 g pro, 2 g total fat (trace sat. fat), 5 g carb, 1 g fibre, 0 mg chol, 26 mg sodium. % RDI: 2% calcium, 2% iron, 113% vit A, 10% vit C, 5% folate.

Bok Choy and Pork Stir-Fry

A stir-fry can be fast if the ingredient list is short – like this one. For our easy No-Fail Rice recipe, turn to page 26.

1	pork tenderloin (about 12 oz/375 g)	1
1 tbsp	cornstarch	15 mL
1 tbsp	each soy sauce and hoisin sauce	15 mL
2 tbsp	vegetable oil	25 mL
6	baby bok choy, halved lengthwise	6
3	green onions, sliced	3
2 tsp	grated gingerroot	10 mL
½ tsp	five-spice powder or grated gingerroot	2 mL
1	clove garlic, minced	1
Pinch	hot pepper flakes	Pinch
4 cups	cooked rice	1 L

❯ Thinly slice pork crosswise; set aside.

❯ In measuring cup, whisk together ¾ cup (175 mL) water, cornstarch, soy sauce and hoisin sauce; set aside.

❯ In wok or large skillet, heat half of the oil over high heat; stir-fry pork, in 2 batches, until browned, about 3 minutes. Transfer to bowl.

❯ Add remaining oil to wok. Stir-fry bok choy, green onions, ginger, five-spice powder, garlic and hot pepper flakes until greens are wilted, about 3 minutes.

❯ Return pork and accumulated juices to pan. Add soy sauce mixture; stir-fry until sauce is thickened, about 1 minute. Serve over rice.

Makes 4 servings. PER SERVING: about 473 cal, 28 g pro, 10 g total fat (1 g sat. fat), 66 g carb, 3 g fibre, 50 mg chol, 410 mg sodium. % RDI: 14% calcium, 22% iron, 31% vit A, 55% vit C, 30% folate.

Ham and Artichoke Panini

Any flat buns, even folded-over thick pocketless pitas, make fine toasted sandwiches. If you have a panini press, use it without adding the oil.

4	panini buns, halved	4
6 oz	shaved Black Forest ham	175 g
1	jar (6 oz/170 mL) marinated artichoke hearts, drained	1
12	leaves fresh basil	12
12	slices provolone cheese	12
1 tsp	vegetable oil	5 mL

❯ Cover cut side of panini bottoms with ham; divide artichoke hearts over top. Top with basil leaves then provolone cheese. Cover with panini tops, pressing to compress.

❯ In large nonstick skillet or grill pan, heat oil over medium heat; toast sandwiches, pressing with spatula and turning once, until crusty and golden and cheese is melted, about 8 minutes.

Makes 4 servings. PER SERVING: about 412 cal, 26 g pro, 17 g total fat (8 g sat. fat), 37 g carb, 3 g fibre, 49 mg chol, 1,411 mg sodium. % RDI: 36% calcium, 21% iron, 12% vit A, 5% vit C, 32% folate.

Roasted Salmon with Prosciutto

Salmon matched with prosciutto and mustard makes a luscious combination. Trout or any other firm-fleshed fish also works well. Wide slices of prosciutto guarantee maximum coverage and taste.

¼ cup	Dijon mustard	50 mL
2 tbsp	chopped fresh chives or green onions	25 mL
¼ tsp	pepper	1 mL
4	skinless salmon fillets (6 oz/175 g each)	4
4	thin slices prosciutto (about 2 oz/60 g)	4

❯ In small bowl, mix together mustard, chives and pepper; spread over both sides of salmon. Place fish, flat skinned side down, on prosciutto; wrap around fish.

❯ Arrange fish, prosciutto seam side up, on parchment paper–lined or greased rimmed baking sheet; roast in 400°F (200°C) oven until fish flakes easily when tested, about 10 minutes. (Or place on greased grill over medium heat; close lid and grill, turning once, until fish flakes easily when tested, about 10 minutes.)

Makes 4 servings. PER SERVING: about 311 cal, 33 g pro, 19 g total fat (4 g sat. fat), 1 g carb, 0 g fibre, 91 mg chol, 463 mg sodium. % RDI: 4% calcium, 6% iron, 3% vit A, 8% vit C, 21% folate.

HOW TO GET HELP IN THE KITCHEN

● Expect everyone to pitch in. When kids are little, take the time to teach them to set the table, peel carrots and potatoes, shake salad dressing and tear lettuce. As they grow, let them try new dishes, especially the ones they like.

● Keep a binder of favourite recipes, chosen by you and your family. Or keep them in a virtual recipe box on your computer. Enlist everyone's aid in planning weekly menus, building them around dishes they like (with your guidance, of course). Make the shopping list based on their choices.

● Shop from a list and bring along family members so you can pass on your wisdom about choosing the best fruits and vegetables. This encourages children to make wise choices with the amount of money the family has budgeted for food. And it means you can pass the shopping chores on to them later.

● Post the week's menu on the fridge or a kitchen whiteboard or blackboard. If kids are old enough, encourage them to start supper when they get home.

● Draw up a schedule and assign everyone a job. Rotate duties so no one is stuck making the salad – or taking out the garbage – every night.

● Cook together as a family. It provides lots of opportunities to hear about the day's events. This time can be just as valuable as the time you spend together at the table. Consider it a warmup!

● Make regular dinner together a priority in your family. Studies show that this pays off for kids, both in school and in relations with their peers.

Philly Cheese Steak Pizza

This pizza is perfect for leftover roast beef – homemade or purchased. You can spice it up with pickled hot peppers.

1 tbsp	extra-virgin olive oil	15 mL
1	sweet green pepper, sliced	1
2	cloves garlic, minced	2
Half	sweet onion, sliced	Half
2 cups	sliced mushrooms	500 mL
1 tsp	dried oregano	5 mL
¼ tsp	each salt and pepper	1 mL
1 lb	pizza dough	500 g
½ cup	pizza sauce	125 mL
8	slices provolone cheese	8
1 cup	thinly sliced roast beef	250 mL

> In large skillet, heat oil over medium-high heat; sauté green pepper, garlic, onion, mushrooms, oregano, salt and pepper until onion is golden and no liquid remains, about 5 minutes. Set aside.

> Lightly grease 12-inch (30 cm) pizza pan. On floured surface, roll out pizza dough to fit pan. Place on pan; spread with pizza sauce. Top with half of the cheese then vegetable mixture. Top with roast beef then remaining cheese.

> Bake in bottom third of 500°F (260°C) oven until crust is golden and cheese is bubbly, 10 minutes.

Makes 8 slices, or 4 servings. PER SLICE: about 390 cal, 25 g pro, 17 g total fat (8 g sat. fat), 33 g carb, 2 g fibre, 51 mg chol, 786 mg sodium. % RDI: 29% calcium, 21% iron, 13% vit A, 20% vit C, 15% folate.

TIP
• Sweet onions – with their low levels of the tear-causing chemical pyruvate – include Spanish, Vidalia, SuperSweet and others from Texas.

Steak and Mushroom Baguette

A steak sandwich is a real crowd-pleasing meal. Serve it with a salad or crudités and dip, such as Herbed Feta Dip (recipe, page 166) or Herb Dip (recipe, page 53).

2 tsp	vegetable oil (approx)	10 mL
1 lb	beef inside round fast-fry steak, cut into thin strips	500 g
1	onion, sliced	1
3 cups	sliced mushrooms (8 oz/250 g)	750 mL
3	cloves garlic, minced	3
1	sweet yellow pepper, sliced	1
½ tsp	dried oregano	2 mL
½ tsp	each salt and pepper	2 mL
1	baguette (about 24 inches/60 cm)	1
1	jar (6 oz/170 mL) marinated artichoke hearts, drained	1

❯ In large skillet, heat oil over medium-high heat; stir-fry beef, in 2 batches and adding more oil if necessary, until browned but still pink inside, about 3 minutes. Transfer to plate.

❯ Add onion, mushrooms, garlic, yellow pepper, oregano, salt and pepper to skillet; sauté until liquid is evaporated, about 5 minutes. Return beef and any accumulated juices to pan; heat through.

❯ Cut baguette lengthwise in half almost but not all the way through. If desired, remove some of the soft centre.

❯ Spoon half of the beef mixture onto bottom of baguette. Top with artichokes and remaining beef mixture. Cover with top. Cut into sections.

Makes 4 servings. PER SERVING: about 427 cal, 35 g pro, 10 g total fat (2 g sat. fat), 49 g carb, 5 g fibre, 49 mg chol, 838 mg sodium. % RDI: 8% calcium, 39% iron, 1% vit A, 83% vit C, 51% folate.

SUBSTITUTIONS

● Replace beef with sliced boneless skinless chicken breasts or sliced boneless pork chops.

● Replace marinated artichoke hearts with ½ cup (125 mL) sliced drained oil-packed sun-dried tomatoes.

EASY PIZZA CRUST

Fresh or frozen pizza dough is easy to find at the supermarket. But if you're a purist, it's a snap to make at home. While the dough is rising, get the toppings ready, fix a salad and set the table. And maybe pour yourself a glass of wine.

● In food processor, pulse together 2 cups (500 mL) all-purpose flour; 1½ tsp (7 mL) quick-rising (instant) dry yeast; and ¾ tsp (4 mL) salt. With motor running, whirl in ¾ cup (175 mL) hot water and 2 tsp (10 mL) olive oil. Whirl until dough forms ball, about 1 minute. Let dough rest in work bowl until doubled in bulk, about 40 minutes.

● Press dough into ball; on floured surface, roll out or press into circle big enough to fit 12-inch (30 cm) greased pizza pan. (If dough is too elastic, let relax for a few minutes.) Let rise for thick crust, or top and bake right away for thin crust. **Makes one 12-inch (30 cm) pizza crust.**

20-Minute Chicken Linguine

Pasta entrées are fast if you start by putting a big pot of water on to boil. Be sure to cover the pot, then salt the water once it comes to a boil.

2	boneless skinless chicken breasts	2
¾ tsp	each salt and pepper	4 mL
3 tbsp	extra-virgin olive oil	50 mL
2 cups	cherry tomatoes	500 mL
1	small onion, sliced	1
8	cloves garlic, sliced	8
1 tsp	dried oregano	5 mL
2 cups	firmly packed coarsely shredded radicchio (or firmly packed whole spinach leaves)	500 mL
4	green onions, sliced	4
12 oz	linguine	375 g
¼ cup	grated Parmesan cheese	50 mL

❯ Cut chicken crosswise into strips; season with half each of the salt and pepper. In large skillet, heat 1 tbsp (15 mL) of the oil over medium-high heat; sauté chicken until golden, about 3 minutes. Transfer to plate.

❯ Add tomatoes, onion, garlic, oregano and remaining oil, salt and pepper to skillet; sauté for 2 minutes. Add radicchio; sauté until tomatoes begin to split and soften, 2 minutes. Return chicken to skillet; add green onions and heat through.

❯ Meanwhile, in large pot of boiling salted water, cook linguine until tender but firm, about 10 minutes. Drain; return to pot. Add sauce; toss to coat. Serve sprinkled with Parmesan cheese.

Makes 4 servings. PER SERVING: about 546 cal, 30 g pro, 15 g total fat (3 g sat. fat), 72 g carb, 5 g fibre, 44 mg chol, 821 mg sodium. % RDI: 13% calcium, 22% iron, 6% vit A, 28% vit C, 65% folate.

VARIATION

20-Minute Tofu Linguine
● Substitute 1 block firm tofu (about 12 oz/375 g), cut into strips, for the chicken.

COOKING BASICS

● Read the recipe through before starting.

● The size of fresh food (such as fruits and vegetables), pans and dishes is medium unless specified.

● All foods requiring washing are washed before preparation or use.

● Fruits and vegetables such as apples, onions and bananas are peeled.

● Eggs are large and shelled.

● Butter is salted unless otherwise stated.

● Pepper is black and freshly ground.

● All-purpose flour, icing sugar and cocoa powder are not sifted before measuring.

● Dried herbs are crumbled, not ground.

● Ovens are preheated. Items are baked in the centre of the oven unless otherwise noted.

● Saucepans are uncovered unless noted.

● Generic names for ingredients (for example, hot pepper sauce for Tabasco) are used unless a specific brand is essential to the recipe.

Golden Haddock Fillets

Why not try this with other fish such as catfish, tilapia and trout fillets? Get the kids in the kitchen to help make the tangy slaw side dish – grating the carrots and whisking the dressing are good jobs for junior cooks.

1½ lb	haddock or cod fillets	750 g
2 tbsp	minced fresh parsley	25 mL
½ tsp	salt	2 mL
¼ tsp	pepper	1 mL
2 tbsp	vegetable oil	25 mL
	Lemon wedges	

> Sprinkle fish with parsley, salt and pepper.

> In large skillet, heat oil over medium-high heat; fry fish, turning once, until golden and fish flakes easily when tested, about 6 minutes. Serve with lemon wedges to squeeze over top.

Makes 4 servings. PER SERVING: about 212 cal, 32 g pro, 8 g total fat (1 g sat. fat), 1 g carb, trace fibre, 98 mg chol, 403 mg sodium. % RDI: 5% calcium, 14% iron, 3% vit A, 12% vit C, 7% folate.

Tartar Cabbage Slaw

¼ cup	light mayonnaise	50 mL
2 tbsp	cider vinegar	25 mL
2 tbsp	sweet green relish or chopped pickles	25 mL
¼ tsp	each salt and pepper	1 mL
2½ cups	thinly sliced cabbage	625 mL
1½ cups	grated carrots	375 mL
2	green onions, sliced	2

> In large bowl, whisk together mayonnaise, vinegar, relish, salt and pepper.

> Add cabbage, carrots and green onions; toss to coat.

Makes 4 servings. PER SERVING: about 84 cal, 1 g pro, 5 g total fat (1 g sat. fat), 10 g carb, 2 g fibre, 5 mg chol, 312 mg sodium. % RDI: 4% calcium, 5% iron, 117% vit A, 32% vit C, 13% folate.

Tuna Salad Potatoes

To make Tuna Salad Potato Melts, follow recipe but broil for only 2 minutes. Top each stuffed potato with 1 slice Cheddar cheese; broil until bubbly and golden, about 3 minutes.

4	large baking potatoes (about 2 lb/1 kg)	4
2	cans (each 170 g) solid white or chunk light tuna, drained	2
½ cup	diced roasted or fresh sweet red pepper	125 mL
¼ cup	sliced pitted black olives	50 mL
¼ cup	light mayonnaise	50 mL
¼ cup	light sour cream	50 mL
1	stalk celery, diced	1
¼ cup	diced red onion	50 mL
2 tbsp	chopped fresh parsley	25 mL
2 tbsp	lemon juice	25 mL
½ tsp	salt	2 mL
¼ tsp	pepper	1 mL

❯ Prick each potato several times; microwave on high, turning halfway through, until tender, about 12 minutes.

❯ Meanwhile, in bowl, combine tuna, red pepper, olives, mayonnaise, sour cream, celery, onion, parsley, lemon juice, salt and pepper; set aside.

❯ Cut X in top of each potato; squeeze to open and separate. Mound tuna mixture on potatoes.

❯ Place potatoes on rimmed baking sheet; broil 6 inches (15 cm) from heat until heated through and edges are crisp and darkened, about 5 minutes.

Makes 4 servings. PER SERVING: about 338 cal, 22 g pro, 8 g total fat (2 g sat. fat), 46 g carb, 4 g fibre, 28 mg chol, 776 mg sodium. % RDI: 7% calcium, 27% iron, 12% vit A, 107% vit C, 14% folate.

Squash, Lentil and Chickpea Soup

For a shortcut, use already peeled and cubed fresh butternut squash.

1 tbsp	vegetable oil	15 mL
1 tsp	cumin seeds or ground cumin	5 mL
2 cups	chopped peeled butternut squash	500 mL
1	onion, chopped	1
2	cloves garlic, minced	2
½ tsp	each chili powder and pepper	2 mL
¼ tsp	salt	1 mL
3 tbsp	tomato paste	50 mL
1	can (19 oz/540 mL) lentils, drained and rinsed	1
1	can (19 oz/540 mL) chickpeas, drained and rinsed	1
4 cups	vegetable stock	1 L
1	strip lemon rind	1
¼ cup	chopped fresh parsley	50 mL
	Lemon wedges	

❯ In Dutch oven, heat oil over medium heat; fry cumin seeds for 1 minute. Add squash, onion, garlic, chili powder, pepper and salt; fry, stirring occasionally, until onion is softened, 4 minutes. Add tomato paste; cook, stirring, for 1 minute.

❯ Add lentils, chickpeas, stock and lemon rind; cover and bring to boil over high heat. Reduce heat and simmer until squash is tender, about 12 minutes. Discard lemon rind. Sprinkle with parsley. Serve with lemon wedges.

Makes 4 servings. PER SERVING: about 349 cal, 16 g pro, 5 g total fat (1 g sat. fat), 62 g carb, 12 g fibre, 0 mg chol, 1,710 mg sodium. % RDI: 10% calcium, 44% iron, 67% vit A, 50% vit C, 123% folate.

Pan-Fried Tofu with Asian Garlic Sauce

Rice is a must-serve side dish for this recipe, and the secret to having everything on the table fast is to put the rice on first. See No-Fail Rice, below, for our tried-and-true method.

1	pkg (350 g) extra-firm tofu	1
2 tbsp	vegetable oil (approx)	25 mL
1	onion, chopped	1
3	cloves garlic, minced	3
1 tsp	minced gingerroot (or ½ tsp/2 mL ground ginger)	5 mL
¼ tsp	pepper	1 mL
¾ cup	vegetable stock or sodium-reduced chicken stock	175 mL
¼ cup	soy sauce	50 mL
1 tbsp	cornstarch	15 mL
2	green onions, diagonally sliced	2

❯ Pat tofu dry; cut crosswise into 4 slices. In large skillet, heat half of the oil over medium-high heat; fry tofu, turning once and adding more oil if necessary, until golden, about 8 minutes. Remove to plates and keep warm.

❯ Add remaining oil to pan; fry onion, garlic, ginger and pepper over medium heat, adding more oil if necessary, until onion is softened, about 3 minutes.

❯ Add stock and soy sauce; bring to boil. Stir cornstarch with 1 tbsp (15 mL) water; stir into pan and boil, stirring, until thickened, about 1 minute. Pour over tofu. Sprinkle with green onions.

Makes 4 servings. PER SERVING: about 181 cal, 11 g pro, 12 g total fat (1 g sat. fat), 9 g carb, 1 g fibre, 0 mg chol, 1,155 mg sodium. % RDI: 13% calcium, 15% iron, 7% vit C, 15% folate.

Sesame Green Bean Stir-Fry

1 tsp	vegetable oil	5 mL
1 lb	green beans, trimmed	500 g
1 tsp	sesame seeds	5 mL
1 tsp	sesame oil	5 mL

❯ In skillet, heat oil over medium-high heat; stir-fry green beans for 2 minutes. Add 1 tbsp (15 mL) water, sesame seeds and sesame oil. Cover and steam until green beans are tender-crisp, about 4 minutes.

Makes 4 servings. PER SERVING: about 56 cal, 2 g pro, 3 g total fat (trace sat. fat), 7 g carb, 3 g fibre, 0 mg chol, 1 mg sodium. % RDI: 4% calcium, 4% iron, 6% vit A, 15% vit C, 14% folate.

NO-FAIL RICE

● In covered saucepan, bring 2⅔ cups (650 mL) water and ¼ tsp (1 mL) salt to boil. Stir in 1⅓ cups (325 mL) rice; cover, reduce heat to low and simmer until rice is tender and liquid is absorbed, about 20 minutes for basmati, jasmine or other white long-grain rice, about 45 minutes for brown rice. Fluff with fork and serve.

FLAVOURING SUGGESTIONS

Add a strip of lemon peel, sprig of parsley, a bay leaf or a few slices of fresh ginger. Or simmer in chicken or vegetable stock instead of water.

Tomato Baguette Pizza

This pizza gets its smoky flavour from smoked mozzarella. You can use plain mozzarella or provolone – or a smoked Cheddar or Gouda.

1 tbsp	vegetable oil	15 mL
2	onions, sliced	2
2	cloves garlic, minced	2
3 cups	sliced mushrooms	750 mL
½ tsp	each salt and dried Italian herb seasoning	2 mL
¼ tsp	pepper	1 mL
1	baguette (about 24 inches/60 cm)	1
2 cups	shredded smoked mozzarella cheese	500 mL
⅔ cup	packed fresh basil leaves	150 mL
2	tomatoes, sliced	2

❯ In skillet, heat oil over medium-high heat; sauté onions, garlic, mushrooms, salt, Italian seasoning and pepper until golden, about 6 minutes.

❯ Halve baguette lengthwise then crosswise; place, cut side up, on rimmed baking sheet. Sprinkle with half of the cheese; top with ½ cup (125 mL) of the basil, mushroom mixture, then tomatoes. Sprinkle with remaining cheese.

❯ Bake in 400°F (200°C) oven until cheese is melted, about 10 minutes. Shred remaining basil; sprinkle over top. Cut into 8 pieces.

Makes 4 servings. PER SERVING: about 449 cal, 21 g pro, 20 g total fat (10 g sat. fat), 48 g carb, 5 g fibre, 51 mg chol, 956 mg sodium. % RDI: 37% calcium, 24% iron, 22% vit A, 30% vit C, 38% folate.

Romaine Wedges

1	romaine heart, quartered	1
4	radishes, sliced	4
1	piece (2 inches/5 cm) English cucumber, halved lengthwise and thinly sliced	1
2 tbsp	vegetable oil	25 mL
1 tbsp	chopped fresh parsley	15 mL
1 tbsp	red wine vinegar	15 mL
1 tsp	Dijon mustard	5 mL
Pinch	each salt and pepper	Pinch

❯ Place each romaine quarter on plate; top with radishes and cucumber. In bowl, whisk together vegetable oil, parsley, vinegar, mustard, salt and pepper. Drizzle over salads.

Makes 4 servings. PER SERVING: about 75 cal, 1 g pro, 7 g total fat (1 g sat. fat), 3 g carb, 2 g fibre, 0 mg chol, 24 mg sodium. % RDI: 2% calcium, 5% iron, 30% vit A, 27% vit C, 33% folate.

Juicy Portobello and White Bean Hummus Pitas

Choose your favourite sprouts – such as radish, sunflower, broccoli, corn, sweet pea or alfalfa – for this juicy sandwich. If you want to make a more traditional hummus, simply swap the white kidney beans for chickpeas and add 2 tbsp (25 mL) tahini.

4	portobello mushrooms, stems removed	4
1 tbsp	extra-virgin olive oil	15 mL
¼ tsp	each salt and pepper	1 mL
4	pitas	4
1 cup	White Bean Hummus (recipe, right)	250 mL
1 cup	sprouts	250 mL
1 cup	sliced cucumber	250 mL
1	large tomato, sliced	1

❯ Place mushrooms, gill side down, on rimmed baking sheet. Brush with oil; sprinkle with salt and pepper. Broil, turning once, until tender and browned, 4 minutes. Let cool slightly and slice.

❯ Broil pitas, turning once, until hot but still soft, about 1 minute. Cut in half and open up to create pockets; spread ¼ cup (50 mL) hummus inside each. Divide mushrooms, sprouts, cucumber and tomato among pockets.

Makes 4 servings. PER SERVING: about 374 cal, 16 g pro, 8 g total fat (1 g sat. fat), 62 g carb, 12 g fibre, 0 mg chol, 964 mg sodium. % RDI: 9% calcium, 30% iron, 5% vit A, 25% vit C, 56% folate.

White Bean Hummus

1	can (19 oz/540 mL) white kidney beans, drained and rinsed	1
1 tbsp	minced fresh parsley	15 mL
1 tbsp	lemon juice	15 mL
1 tbsp	extra-virgin olive oil	15 mL
¼ tsp	each ground cumin and chili powder	1 mL
¼ tsp	each salt and pepper	1 mL
2	cloves garlic, minced	2

❯ In food processor, purée together beans, parsley, lemon juice, oil, cumin, chili powder, salt and pepper until smooth. Stir in garlic; set aside.

Makes 1 cup (250 mL). PER 1 TBSP (15 mL): about 33 cal, 2 g pro, 1 g total fat (trace sat. fat), 5 g carb, 2 g fibre, 0 mg chol, 113 mg sodium. % RDI: 1% calcium, 3% iron, 2% vit C, 5% folate.

Gruyère and Ham Pasta

Any short pasta – macaroni, penne or shells – is suitable. Get the pasta water boiling before you make the sauce to ensure that everything's on the table in 20 minutes.

2 tbsp	butter	25 mL
1	onion, chopped	1
½ tsp	salt	2 mL
¼ tsp	each dried thyme and pepper	1 mL
2 tbsp	all-purpose flour	25 mL
2 cups	milk	500 mL
1½ cups	shredded Gruyère or Cheddar cheese	375 mL
1 tsp	Dijon mustard	5 mL
4 cups	Scoobi-Do pasta	1 L
2 cups	chopped fresh spinach	500 mL
2 cups	cubed ham	500 mL
1 cup	halved grape tomatoes	250 mL

❯ In saucepan, melt butter over medium heat; fry onion, salt, thyme and pepper until onion is softened, about 5 minutes.

❯ Sprinkle with flour; cook, stirring, for 1 minute. Whisk in milk; cook, whisking, until thick enough to coat spoon, about 7 minutes. Stir in cheese and mustard; cook, stirring, until cheese is melted.

❯ Meanwhile, in large pot of boiling salted water, cook pasta until tender but firm, about 8 minutes. Drain and return to pot. Add sauce, spinach, ham and tomatoes; toss to combine.

Makes 4 servings. PER SERVING: about 738 cal, 47 g pro, 28 g total fat (15 g sat. fat), 76 g carb, 5 g fibre, 112 mg chol, 1,732 mg sodium. % RDI: 59% calcium, 38% iron, 49% vit A, 20% vit C, 105% folate.

Spaghetti Carbonara

When it's almost time to go grocery shopping, this is an entrée you can pull off with refrigerator staples. Serve with extra grated Parmesan cheese to sprinkle over top.

4	slices bacon, chopped	4
1	small onion, chopped	1
2	cloves garlic, minced	2
4	eggs	4
¼ cup	grated Parmesan cheese	50 mL
2 tbsp	chopped fresh parsley	25 mL
¼ tsp	each salt and pepper	1 mL
12 oz	spaghetti	375 g

❯ In large skillet, fry bacon over medium heat until crisp, about 5 minutes. Drain off fat. Add onion and garlic to pan. Fry until softened, about 4 minutes.

❯ Meanwhile, in bowl, whisk together eggs, cheese, parsley, salt and pepper. Set aside.

❯ Meanwhile, in large pot of boiling salted water, cook spaghetti until tender but firm, about 8 minutes. Drain and return to pot over low heat.

❯ Immediately stir in bacon and egg mixtures; heat, stirring, until pasta is coated, about 30 seconds.

Makes 4 servings. PER SERVING: about 482 cal, 22 g pro, 14 g total fat (5 g sat. fat), 66 g carb, 4 g fibre, 200 mg chol, 628 mg sodium. % RDI: 11% calcium, 29% iron, 9% vit A, 5% vit C, 92% folate.

CHAPTER 2

Make It Tonight... in 30 Minutes

Tomato-Topped Beef Patties

If anyone in the family doesn't like onions in patties or burgers, try grating them instead of chopping. It's a little more work, but the onion cooks more evenly, and onion haters won't find any little raw bits.

1	egg	1
¼ cup	dry bread crumbs	50 mL
1	small onion, grated	1
2	cloves garlic, minced	2
2 tbsp	chopped fresh parsley	25 mL
½ tsp	each salt and pepper	2 mL
¼ tsp	each hot pepper sauce and Worcestershire sauce	1 mL
1 lb	lean ground beef	500 g
2	plum tomatoes, thinly sliced	2
¼ tsp	each dried thyme and oregano	1 mL

❯ In bowl, beat egg; mix in bread crumbs, onion, garlic, parsley, salt, pepper, hot pepper sauce and Worcestershire sauce. Mix in beef. Shape into four ½-inch (1 cm) thick patties. Place on foil-lined rimmed baking sheet. Top with tomato slices; sprinkle with thyme and oregano.

❯ Roast in 400°F (200°C) oven until meat thermometer inserted sideways registers 160°F (71°C), about 25 minutes.

Makes 4 servings. PER SERVING: about 293 cal, 25 g pro, 17 g total fat (7 g sat. fat), 8 g carb, 1 g fibre, 114 mg chol, 442 mg sodium. % RDI: 4% calcium, 22% iron, 5% vit A, 15% vit C, 10% folate.

Sweet-and-Sour Coleslaw

1 tbsp	light mayonnaise	15 mL
1 tbsp	vegetable oil	15 mL
1 tbsp	cider vinegar	15 mL
1 tsp	granulated sugar	5 mL
½ tsp	celery seeds	2 mL
¼ tsp	each salt and pepper	1 mL
3 cups	coleslaw mix or shredded cabbage	750 mL
⅓ cup	thinly sliced red onion	75 mL

❯ In large bowl, whisk together mayonnaise, oil, vinegar, sugar, celery seeds, salt and pepper. Add coleslaw mix and onion; toss to coat.

Makes 4 servings. PER SERVING: about 65 cal, 1 g pro, 5 g total fat (trace sat. fat), 6 g carb, 1 g fibre, 1 mg chol, 182 mg sodium. % RDI: 3% calcium, 4% iron, 12% vit A, 30% vit C, 10% folate.

Lazy Shepherd's Pie

It's not the shepherd who's lazy – it's the smart cook who puts this comforting dish together fast.

4	large potatoes (unpeeled), cubed (2 lb/1 kg)	4
¼ cup	milk or buttermilk	50 mL
1	green onion, sliced	1
1 lb	lean ground beef	500 g
1 tbsp	vegetable oil	15 mL
2½ cups	small mushrooms (about 8 oz/250 g)	625 mL
1	onion, diced	1
1 tsp	dried thyme	5 mL
¼ tsp	each salt and pepper	1 mL
1½ cups	sodium-reduced beef stock	375 mL
1 tbsp	cornstarch	15 mL
1 tbsp	Dijon mustard	15 mL
1 cup	frozen peas	250 mL

❯ In large saucepan of boiling salted water, cover and cook potatoes until tender, about 12 minutes. Drain and return to pan; shaking pan, dry over low heat, about 1 minute. Mash coarsely; stir in milk and green onion.

❯ Meanwhile, heat skillet over medium-high heat; sauté beef, breaking up with fork, until no longer pink, about 5 minutes. Transfer to plate. Drain fat from skillet.

❯ In same skillet, heat oil over medium heat; fry mushrooms, onion, thyme, salt and pepper, stirring occasionally, until mushrooms are golden, about 8 minutes.

❯ Whisk together stock, cornstarch and mustard; stir into skillet. Add beef and peas; bring to boil. Reduce heat and simmer until thickened and heated through, 5 minutes. Serve over potatoes.

Makes 4 servings. PER SERVING: about 492 cal, 30 g pro, 19 g total fat (7 g sat. fat), 51 g carb, 6 g fibre, 65 mg chol, 1,045 mg sodium. % RDI: 7% calcium, 39% iron, 8% vit A, 48% vit C, 24% folate.

Beef and Sweet Potato Stir-Fry

When making a stir-fry sauce, stir it together in a 2-cup (500 mL) glass measuring cup. Then it's easy to pour the well-mixed sauce into the pan when you're ready.

2 tbsp	vegetable oil	25 mL
1 lb	beef stir-fry strips	500 g
1	onion, sliced	1
3	cloves garlic, minced	3
2 cups	cubed peeled sweet potatoes (2 small)	500 mL
1	sweet yellow or green pepper, sliced	1
½ cup	beef stock	125 mL
¼ cup	oyster sauce	50 mL
1 tbsp	cornstarch	15 mL
1 tbsp	rice vinegar or cider vinegar	15 mL
1 tsp	sesame oil	5 mL
2	green onions, thinly sliced	2

❯ In wok or large skillet, heat 1 tbsp (15 mL) of the oil over high heat. Stir-fry beef, in 2 batches, until browned but still pink inside, about 2 minutes. Transfer to plate.

❯ Drain fat from pan; add remaining oil. Fry onion and garlic over medium heat until onion is softened, about 2 minutes.

❯ Stir in sweet potatoes, yellow pepper and ½ cup (125 mL) water; cover and steam until sweet potatoes are tender, about 10 minutes.

❯ Meanwhile, in measuring cup, whisk together beef stock, oyster sauce, cornstarch, vinegar and sesame oil. Return beef and any accumulated juices to pan.

❯ Add oyster sauce mixture and bring to boil; boil, stirring, until thickened and glossy, about 1 minute. Sprinkle with green onions.

Makes 4 servings. PER SERVING: about 316 cal, 29 g pro, 11 g total fat (2 g sat. fat), 26 g carb, 2 g fibre, 49 mg chol, 658 mg sodium. % RDI: 4% calcium, 22% iron, 114% vit A, 98% vit C, 16% folate.

EQUIPMENT
WOK 101

For stir-frying, nothing beats the wok. Its unique bowl shape ensures even heat distribution for faster cooking, while sloping sides keep food in the pan (and off the stove). Plus, you can stir-fry, steam, braise, fry and smoke all in one pan.

SIZE AND SHAPE
Size Matters: Wok sizes vary. For home use, we recommend a standard 14-inch (35 cm) wok, which is a manageable weight with enough surface area for cooking three or four portions at once.

Nice Bottoms: Traditional round-bottom woks are unstable on western stove tops, so flat-bottom woks were designed to sit directly on electric coils (ceramic cooktops and gas burners, too).
Handles: Traditional woks have two metal handles, making it easy to lift the pan on and off the stove. Most modern household woks have only one long handle (like a skillet), eliminating the need for a pot holder while providing excellent leverage for tilting. Many also have a small grip at the front, providing better balance when lifting.

→

Sweet-and-Sour Halibut with Vegetable Noodle Stir-Fry

This is a lovely layered supper – noodles and vegetables underneath, glazed fish on top.

Half	pkg (1-lb/454 g pkg) rice stick noodles	Half
1 cup	chicken stock	250 mL
¼ cup	orange juice	50 mL
3 tbsp	granulated sugar	50 mL
2 tbsp	each red wine vinegar and tomato paste	25 mL
2 tsp	cornstarch	10 mL
2 tsp	soy sauce	10 mL
1 tsp	ground ginger	5 mL
2	cloves garlic, minced	2
2 tbsp	vegetable oil (approx)	25 mL
4	halibut, tilapia or catfish fillets (1½ lb/750 g total)	4
1	sweet red pepper, diced	1
2 cups	quartered mushrooms (about 5 oz/150 g)	500 mL
1	zucchini, diced	1

❯ In bowl of boiling water, soak noodles until pliable and tender, about 6 minutes. Drain and chill in cold water; drain and set aside.

❯ Meanwhile, in large measuring cup, whisk together stock, orange juice, sugar, vinegar, tomato paste, cornstarch, soy sauce, ginger and garlic; set aside.

❯ In large skillet, heat 2 tsp (10 mL) of the oil over medium-high heat; fry tilapia, turning once and adding more oil if necessary, until golden and fish flakes easily when tested, about 6 minutes. Add stock mixture and bring to boil; boil until thickened, about 2 minutes.

❯ Meanwhile, in separate skillet, heat remaining oil over medium-high heat; stir-fry red pepper, mushrooms and zucchini, adding more oil if necessary, until tender-crisp, about 2 minutes. Add noodles; stir-fry until hot, about 1 minute. Serve in bowls topped with fish and sauce.

Makes 4 servings. PER SERVING: about 566 cal, 40 g pro, 12 g total fat (1 g sat. fat), 72 g carb, 4 g fibre, 54 mg chol, 506 mg sodium. % RDI: 10% calcium, 21% iron, 21% vit A, 100% vit C, 19% folate.

MATERIALS
Cast Iron/Enamel: Cast-iron woks have been used in China for centuries. They retain heat evenly and cook quickly. Before using, season to prevent sticking. Here's how.
• Using sponge, scrub inside of wok with hot water and a bit of liquid detergent; scrub exterior with scouring pad. Rinse and dry well.
• Using paper towel, rub about 2 tbsp (25 mL) vegetable oil over wok surface. Heat over medium-low heat for about 10 minutes. Wipe off black residue. Let cool.
• Repeat until no black remains (about 3 times).

Preseasoned Carbon Steel: This natural nonstick surface is easy to clean up and is a good choice for novice wokers. Hand-wash.

WOK ACCESSORIES
If you do a lot of frying, a skimmer-strainer made of brass wire mesh with a long bamboo handle is essential. For stir-frying, a shovel-shaped wok spatula is handy. Its curved bowl matches the contours of the wok, and it has a long handle to keep your hands safe.

35

Fish Tacos

High in protein, fish is a healthy dinner choice. Lots of vegetable toppings only add to the good nutrition.

½ cup	shredded carrot	125 mL
¼ cup	thinly sliced red onion	50 mL
1 tsp	lime juice	5 mL
¼ cup	light sour cream or plain yogurt	50 mL
1 tbsp	minced fresh coriander	15 mL
1	green onion, minced	1
8	small flour or corn tortillas	8
1	plum tomato, diced	1
Half	avocado, peeled, pitted and diced	Half
FISH:		
1 lb	tilapia or rainbow trout fillets	500 g
1 tbsp	vegetable oil	15 mL
1 tsp	chili powder	5 mL
½ tsp	dried oregano	2 mL
¼ tsp	each salt and pepper	1 mL

❯ FISH: Pat fish dry; arrange on foil-lined or greased rimmed baking sheet. Brush with oil. In small bowl, combine chili powder, oregano, salt and pepper; sprinkle over fish. Broil until fish flakes easily when tested, about 5 minutes.

❯ Meanwhile, in small bowl, combine carrot, red onion and lime juice. In separate small bowl, combine sour cream, coriander and green onion.

❯ Break fish into chunks; divide among tortillas. Top with sour cream mixture, carrot mixture, tomato and avocado.

Makes 4 servings. PER SERVING: about 417 cal, 27 g pro, 15 g total fat (3 g sat. fat), 42 g carb, 4 g fibre, 54 mg chol, 570 mg sodium. % RDI: 7% calcium, 20% iron, 56% vit A, 13% vit C, 49% folate.

Edamame Vegetable Soup

Edamame is the Japanese name for green soybeans, also known as sweet beans, vegetable soybeans and beer beans. They are sold frozen both in the pod and shelled. The shelled version is the most convenient.

1 tbsp	vegetable oil	15 mL
3	carrots, sliced	3
2	stalks celery, sliced	2
1	onion, chopped	1
2	cloves garlic, minced	2
½ tsp	dried thyme	2 mL
¼ tsp	pepper	1 mL
4 cups	vegetable stock	1 L
1	red-skinned potato (unpeeled), cubed	1
Half	pkg (454 g pkg) medium-firm tofu	Half
1½ cups	frozen shelled soybeans (edamame)	375 mL
Dash	hot pepper sauce	Dash
1 tbsp	minced fresh chives or green onion	15 mL

❯ In large saucepan, heat oil over medium heat; fry carrots, celery, onion, garlic, thyme and pepper, stirring occasionally, until onion is softened, about 5 minutes.

❯ Add stock and potato; bring to boil. Reduce heat, cover and simmer until carrots and potato are tender, about 15 minutes.

❯ Cut tofu into ½-inch (1 cm) cubes. Add to soup along with soybeans and hot pepper sauce; heat through.

❯ Serve sprinkled with chives.

Makes 4 servings. PER SERVING: about 291 cal, 18 g pro, 12 g total fat (1 g sat. fat), 32 g carb, 8 g fibre, 0 mg chol, 1,053 mg sodium. % RDI: 22% calcium, 29% iron, 145% vit A, 47% vit C, 71% folate.

Jerk Pork Chops

For this menu, start the rice first, then season and roast the chops. Allspice and thyme are the signature flavours of any jerk dish.

4	pork loin centre chops	4
1 tbsp	each soy sauce, orange juice and extra-virgin olive oil	15 mL
2	cloves garlic, minced	2
3	green onions, minced	3
1 tsp	each ground allspice and dried thyme	5 mL
¼ tsp	each salt and pepper	1 mL
¼ tsp	ground ginger	1 mL
Pinch	cayenne pepper	Pinch

❯ Slash fat around pork at 1-inch (2.5 cm) intervals; set aside.

❯ In bowl, combine soy sauce, orange juice, oil, garlic, green onions, allspice, thyme, salt, pepper, ginger and cayenne; rub on both sides of chops.

❯ In small roasting pan, roast chops in 375°F (190°C) oven, turning halfway through, until browned, juices run clear when pork is pierced and just a hint of pink remains inside, about 18 minutes.

Makes 4 servings. PER SERVING: about 190 cal, 21 g pro, 10 g total fat (3 g sat. fat), 3 g carb, 1 g fibre, 58 mg chol, 453 mg sodium. % RDI: 3% calcium, 10% iron, 1% vit A, 7% vit C, 5% folate.

Peas, Pepper and Rice

1 tbsp	vegetable oil	15 mL
1	small onion, chopped	1
1	sweet red pepper, chopped	1
¾ cup	parboiled rice	175 mL
1½ cups	chicken stock	375 mL
¼ tsp	each cinnamon, salt and pepper	1 mL
¾ cup	frozen peas	175 mL

❯ In saucepan, heat oil over medium-high heat; fry onion until softened. Add red pepper and rice; stir for 1 minute.

❯ Add stock, cinnamon, salt and pepper; bring to boil. Reduce heat, cover and simmer until rice is tender and liquid is absorbed, about 20 minutes. With fork, stir in peas; heat through.

Makes 4 servings. PER SERVING: about 207 cal, 6 g pro, 4 g total fat (1 g sat. fat), 35 g carb, 2 g fibre, 0 mg chol, 460 mg sodium. % RDI: 4% calcium, 7% iron, 12% vit A, 87% vit C, 12% folate.

Chicken and Gnocchi Soup

This soup has the kind of grandmother (*nonna, oma,* fill in whatever word you like) touch we crave on a cold evening. It's a very up-to-date grandmother, though, who adds the spinach topping.

8 oz	boneless skinless chicken breast	250 g
1 tbsp	vegetable oil	15 mL
1	small onion, diced	1
1	each small carrot and stalk celery, diced	1
2	cloves garlic, minced	2
1 tsp	dried oregano	5 mL
Pinch	each salt and pepper	Pinch
1	bay leaf	1
1	pkg (900 mL) sodium-reduced chicken stock	1
1	pkg (1 lb/500 g) fresh gnocchi	1
RUSTIC SPINACH GREMOLADA:		
1 cup	fresh spinach, chopped	250 mL
½ tsp	grated lemon rind	2 mL
2 tsp	lemon juice	10 mL
2 tsp	extra-virgin olive oil	10 mL
1	clove garlic, minced	1

❯ Cut chicken into cubes. In large saucepan, heat oil over medium heat; fry chicken, onion, carrot, celery, garlic, oregano, salt, pepper and bay leaf, stirring occasionally, until onion is softened, about 5 minutes.

❯ Add chicken stock and 1½ cups (375 mL) water; bring to boil. Reduce heat to medium; cover and simmer for 10 minutes. Add gnocchi; simmer, uncovered, until gnocchi float to top and are firm to the touch, about 5 minutes. Discard bay leaf.

❯ RUSTIC SPINACH GREMOLADA: Meanwhile, in bowl, combine spinach, lemon rind and juice, oil and garlic. Sprinkle onto bowls of soup.

Makes 4 servings. PER SERVING: about 399 cal, 22 g pro, 7 g total fat (1 g sat. fat), 63 g carb, 6 g fibre, 34 mg chol, 765 mg sodium. % RDI: 6% calcium, 13% iron, 38% vit A, 95% vit C, 26% folate.

WHAT DO I COOK FIRST?

"It all depends" isn't much help, but it does all depend on what you're cooking. Start by reading the recipes you're serving, then:

• Start with the dish that takes the longest time. This is often the starch. To make pasta, for example, it takes about 10 minutes for the covered pot of water to come to a boil. Then it takes up to 10 minutes for most pastas to soften to the al dente stage. Rice and potatoes take about 25 minutes from start to finish.

• Move on to the quick stuff. While the starches are cooking, get to work on the quicker dishes: grilled or roasted fish, sautéed chops or chicken, or sauce to serve over pasta.

• Toss the salad or make veggies and dip. Serve them while the rest of dinner cooks. It's a healthy first course and kills hunger pangs while you wait.

Pork Chops with Cranberry Glaze

Dried cranberries make this a year-round dish.

4	pork loin centre chops, boneless (1 lb/500 g) or bone in (1½ lb/750 g)	4
½ tsp	each salt and pepper	2 mL
2 tbsp	vegetable oil	25 mL
2	shallots or half small onion, finely diced	2
2	cloves garlic, minced	2
⅓ cup	sodium-reduced chicken stock	75 mL
⅓ cup	dried cranberries	75 mL
¼ cup	apple jelly	50 mL
3 tbsp	cider vinegar	50 mL
1 tsp	chopped fresh rosemary (or ½ tsp/2 mL crumbled dried)	5 mL

❯ Sprinkle pork chops with half each of the salt and pepper.

❯ In large skillet, heat 1 tbsp (15 mL) of the oil over medium-high heat; brown pork chops, turning once, until golden. Transfer to plate. Drain fat from pan.

❯ Add remaining oil to pan; fry shallots, garlic and remaining salt and pepper over medium heat, stirring occasionally, until shallots are softened, about 2 minutes.

❯ Add stock, cranberries, jelly, vinegar and rosemary. Stir until jelly is melted and cranberries are softened, about 4 minutes.

❯ Return pork and any accumulated juices to pan, turning to coat. Reduce heat, cover and simmer, turning once, until juices run clear when pork is pierced and just a hint of pink remains inside, about 5 minutes. Transfer pork to platter; keep warm.

❯ Boil sauce until syrupy, about 1 minute. Pour over pork.

Makes 4 servings. PER SERVING: about 317 cal, 23 g pro, 14 g total fat (3 g sat. fat), 25 g carb, 1 g fibre, 63 mg chol, 396 mg sodium. % RDI: 3% calcium, 8% iron, 1% vit A, 3% vit C, 2% folate.

Chicken Breasts with Spinach Salad

Cherry tomatoes, halved if they are large, are a good substitute for chopped tomatoes.

4	boneless skinless chicken breasts	4
4 cups	lightly packed torn fresh spinach	1 L
2 cups	cubed English cucumber	500 mL
1 cup	chopped tomatoes	250 mL
⅓ cup	crumbled feta cheese	75 mL
¼ cup	pitted black olives, halved	50 mL
DRESSING:		
¼ cup	red wine vinegar	50 mL
¼ cup	extra-virgin olive oil	50 mL
2 tbsp	lemon juice	25 mL
2 tsp	granulated sugar	10 mL
3	cloves garlic, minced	3
½ tsp	each dried oregano and mint	2 mL
¼ tsp	each salt and pepper	1 mL

❯ Place chicken in small roasting pan; set aside.

❯ DRESSING: In measuring cup, whisk together vinegar, oil, lemon juice, sugar, garlic, oregano, mint, salt and pepper; pour ⅓ cup (75 mL) over chicken. Roast in 400°F (200°C) oven, turning once, until no longer pink inside, about 10 minutes. Broil until golden, about 2 minutes.

❯ Meanwhile, in large bowl, toss together spinach, cucumber, tomatoes, feta cheese, olives and remaining dressing until coated. Divide salad among plates.

❯ Thinly slice chicken; arrange over salad.

Makes 4 servings. PER SERVING: about 351 cal, 35 g pro, 19 g total fat (4 g sat. fat), 11 g carb, 3 g fibre, 87 mg chol, 458 mg sodium. % RDI: 13% calcium, 22% iron, 44% vit A, 53% vit C, 60% folate.

Asparagus Ricotta Frittata

Ricotta is a handy ingredient to keep in the fridge, not only for this fresh-tasting frittata but also to top fruit or spoon over chili, vegetable soups or spaghetti sauce.

8 oz	asparagus	250 g
1 tbsp	butter	15 mL
2	green onions, thinly sliced	2
1	clove garlic, minced	1
¼ tsp	each salt and pepper	1 mL
¼ tsp	dried thyme	1 mL
1 cup	ricotta cheese	250 mL
4	eggs	4
¼ cup	shredded Gruyère cheese	50 mL
2 tbsp	chopped fresh parsley	25 mL

❯ Snap woody ends off asparagus; cut asparagus into 2-inch (5 cm) lengths to make about 2 cups (500 mL).

❯ In 9-inch (23 cm) ovenproof skillet, melt butter over medium heat; fry green onions, garlic, salt, pepper, thyme and asparagus until asparagus is tender-crisp, about 5 minutes.

❯ Meanwhile, in bowl, whisk ricotta with eggs until smooth; stir in Gruyère and parsley. Pour into skillet, smoothing top.

❯ Bake in 400°F (200°C) oven until puffed and golden and knife inserted in centre comes out clean, about 20 minutes. Let stand for 5 minutes before inverting onto platter.

Makes 4 to 6 servings. PER EACH OF 6 SERVINGS: about 165 cal, 11 g pro, 12 g total fat (7 g sat. fat), 3 g carb, 1 g fibre, 155 mg chol, 205 mg sodium. % RDI: 15% calcium, 7% iron, 17% vit A, 7% vit C, 29% folate.

Spinach Pesto Fusilli with Peppers

If you don't have any fusilli pasta on hand, you can use penne, rotini or radiatore instead.

1	pkg (300 g) frozen spinach, thawed	1
3	cloves garlic, minced	3
1 tbsp	pine nuts	15 mL
1 tsp	dried basil	5 mL
½ tsp	each salt and pepper	2 mL
¼ cup	extra-virgin olive oil	50 mL
¼ cup	grated Parmesan cheese	50 mL
4 tsp	balsamic vinegar	20 mL
5 cups	fusilli (12 oz/375 g)	1.25 L
1	small red onion	1
1	each sweet red and yellow pepper	1

❯ Squeeze spinach to remove moisture. In food processor, purée together spinach, garlic, pine nuts, basil, salt and pepper until smooth. Pulse in 3 tbsp (45 mL) of the oil; pulse in Parmesan cheese and vinegar. Set aside.

❯ In large pot of boiling salted water, cook pasta until tender but firm, about 8 minutes. Reserving 1½ cups (375 mL) pasta cooking liquid, drain and return to pot. Add spinach pesto and reserved cooking liquid; simmer over medium heat until hot, about 3 minutes.

❯ Meanwhile, thinly slice onion and red and yellow peppers. In skillet, heat remaining oil over medium heat; fry onion and peppers until tender-crisp, about 4 minutes.

❯ Serve pasta topped with pepper mixture.

Makes 4 servings. PER SERVING: about 531 cal, 17 g pro, 18 g total fat (3 g sat. fat), 76 g carb, 7 g fibre, 5 mg chol, 813 mg sodium. % RDI: 18% calcium, 25% iron, 51% vit A, 168% vit C, 85% folate.

Chickpea Ragout with Polenta

Polenta may be unfamiliar, but it's worth trying. This dish uses prepared polenta available in many supermarkets. You can serve the ragout on rice or pasta if that's what you have in the house.

2 tbsp	extra-virgin olive oil	25 mL
Half	small eggplant, diced (2 cups/500 mL)	Half
1	small zucchini, diced	1
1	sweet red pepper, diced	1
1	onion, diced	1
2	cloves garlic, minced	2
1 tsp	dried oregano	5 mL
Pinch	each salt and hot pepper flakes	Pinch
1	can (28 oz/796 mL) diced tomatoes	1
1	can (19 oz/540 mL) chickpeas, drained and rinsed	1
2 tbsp	tomato paste	25 mL
¼ cup	chopped fresh parsley	50 mL
1	tube (17 oz/500 g) prepared polenta, cut into 8 rounds	1
2 tbsp	grated Parmesan cheese (optional)	25 mL

➤ In shallow Dutch oven, heat 1 tbsp (15 mL) of the oil over medium heat; fry eggplant, zucchini, red pepper, onion, garlic, oregano, salt and hot pepper flakes, stirring occasionally, until vegetables are tender, about 8 minutes.

➤ Stir in tomatoes, chickpeas and tomato paste; cover and simmer until sauce is thickened, about 15 minutes. Stir in parsley.

➤ Meanwhile, brush polenta with remaining oil; sprinkle with cheese (if using). Arrange on rimmed baking sheet; broil, 6 inches (15 cm) from heat, until edges are golden, about 6 minutes. Arrange on plates and top with ragout.

Makes 4 servings. PER SERVING: about 373 cal, 11 g pro, 9 g total fat (1 g sat. fat), 66 g carb, 11 g fibre, 0 mg chol, 1,003 mg sodium. % RDI: 12% calcium, 33% iron, 22% vit A, 147% vit C, 69% folate.

QUICK FIXES
IF YOUR SAUCE OR GRAVY IS TOO THIN
• Uncover pan and boil over medium-high heat for a few minutes. If meat or vegetables are already tender, remove with a slotted spoon and keep warm in the serving bowl.

• If the sauce has a salted base, boiling it down can make it too salty. Try one of the following:

• Stir in beurre manié, 1 tbsp (15 mL) at a time. What's beurre manié? Simply equal parts soft butter and all-purpose flour mashed together until smooth. Keep a jar of it in the fridge to thicken soups, sauces, stews or anything braised.

• Shake or whisk 2 tbsp (25 mL) all-purpose flour with ⅓ cup (75 mL) cold water. Whisk or stir into liquid and simmer until thickened. This amount should thicken 2 cups (500 mL) sauce or gravy.

IF YOUR SAUCE OR GRAVY IS TOO THICK
• Add a little more of the liquid called for in the recipe. If you've run out of stock or tomato juice or wine, just use water.

Fish and Chips

The roasted potato wedges – so much healthier than french fries – are possible in this 30-minute supper thanks to a quick pre-cooking stint in the microwave.

4	potatoes (about 2 lb/1 kg)	4
2 tbsp	vegetable oil (approx)	25 mL
1 tsp	ground cumin	5 mL
½ tsp	each salt and pepper	2 mL
¼ tsp	turmeric	1 mL
2	cloves garlic, minced	2
¼ cup	all-purpose flour	50 mL
½ tsp	paprika	2 mL
4	tilapia or catfish fillets	4
4 cups	packed baby spinach	1 L
	Lemon wedges	

❯ Scrub potatoes; prick in several places. Microwave on high for 4 minutes or until tender-firm. Let cool for 5 minutes. Cut lengthwise into wedges.

❯ In large bowl, toss together potato wedges, half each of the oil, cumin, salt and pepper, the turmeric and garlic; arrange on greased rimmed baking sheet. Bake in 450°F (230°C) oven, turning once, until crispy and golden brown, about 20 minutes.

❯ Meanwhile, in shallow dish, whisk together flour, paprika and remaining cumin, salt and pepper. Press fish into flour mixture, turning to coat; shake off excess.

❯ In large skillet, heat remaining oil over medium-high heat; fry fish in 2 batches, turning once and adding more oil if necessary, until golden and fish flakes easily when tested, about 7 minutes.

❯ Add spinach; cover and steam until wilted, about 2 minutes. Serve with potato wedges and lemon wedges to squeeze over fish.

Makes 4 servings. PER SERVING: about 417 cal, 39 g pro, 11 g total fat (2 g sat. fat), 44 g carb, 5 g fibre, 71 mg chol, 366 mg sodium. % RDI: 8% calcium, 33% iron, 32% vit A, 38% vit C, 51% folate.

CHAPTER 3

Make It Tonight... with Five or So Ingredients

Beef and Broccoli Stir-Fry

Instead of flank steak, choose a piece of top sirloin grilling steak and slice thinly across the grain, or use beef stir-fry strips available at the meat counter. This recipe can be your template for other stir-fries. Try lean pork – tenderloin is best – or chicken breasts instead of the beef. Another option is to replace the broccoli with an equal amount of other quick-cooking green vegetables: sugar snap peas, green beans, halved brussels sprouts, halved baby bok choy or coarsely shredded cabbage are all excellent.

12 oz	flank marinating steak	375 g
3 tbsp	oyster sauce	50 mL
1 tbsp	cornstarch	15 mL
4 cups	broccoli florets	1 L
2	cloves garlic, minced	2
1 tbsp	minced gingerroot	15 mL

> Slice beef thinly across the grain; sprinkle with ¼ tsp (1 mL) pepper; set aside.

> In small bowl, whisk together ¾ cup (175 mL) water, oyster sauce and cornstarch; set aside.

> In wok or skillet, heat 1 tbsp (15 mL) vegetable oil over medium-high heat; stir-fry beef until browned but still pink inside, about 3 minutes. Transfer to plate.

> Add 1 tbsp (15 mL) vegetable oil to wok; stir-fry broccoli, garlic and ginger for 1 minute. Cover and steam for 2 minutes.

> Return beef and any accumulated juices to wok. Add oyster sauce mixture; stir-fry until slightly thickened, about 3 minutes.

Makes 4 servings. PER SERVING: about 253 cal, 21 g pro, 15 g total fat (4 g sat. fat), 8 g carb, trace fibre, 36 mg chol, 436 mg sodium. % RDI: 4% calcium, 16% iron, 20% vit A, 67% vit C, 19% folate.

TECHNIQUE
STIR-FRYING

1. Heat wok over medium-high to high heat for at least 1 minute; add oil, drizzling over side and bottom of wok. To ensure tender, flavourful meat, sear only small amounts (about 1 cup/250 mL) at a time.

TIPS
• Have all ingredients prepped and at hand.
• Cut all ingredients about the same size.
• Stir-fry hard vegetables (broccoli, carrots and eggplant) first, followed by softer vegetables (zucchini, snow peas and bean sprouts) and leafy greens (bok choy).

2. When adding sauce, form a well by pushing meat and vegetables up the side of the wok. Pour sauce in the middle, stirring to thicken before tossing with other ingredients.

Beef and Pepper Kabobs

Here's a barbecue dish you can grill outside or inside under the broiler or on an electric grill.

1 lb	top sirloin grilling steak (about 1 inch/2.5 cm thick)	500 g
1 tbsp	lemon juice	15 mL
½ tsp	dried rosemary	2 mL
1	large sweet red pepper (or 2 small)	1

❯ Trim fat from steak; cut into 1-inch (2.5 cm) cubes.

❯ In glass bowl, whisk together 3 tbsp (50 mL) extra-virgin olive oil, lemon juice, rosemary and ½ tsp (2 mL) each salt and pepper; add beef and stir to coat. Cover and marinate for 10 minutes. *(Make-ahead: Refrigerate for up to 8 hours.)*

❯ Meanwhile, core and cut red pepper into 1-inch (2.5 cm) squares. Alternately thread marinated beef and red pepper loosely onto metal or soaked wooden skewers.

❯ Place skewers on greased grill over medium-high heat or under broiler; close lid and grill or broil, turning 3 times, until beef is browned but still pink inside, about 10 minutes.

Makes 4 servings. PER SERVING: about 189 cal, 21 g pro, 10 g total fat (3 g sat. fat), 3 g carb, 1 g fibre, 51 mg chol, 185 mg sodium. % RDI: 2% calcium, 18% iron, 15% vit A, 113% vit C, 6% folate.

Parsley Rice

¾ cup	parboiled rice	175 mL
¼ cup	finely chopped fresh parsley	50 mL

❯ In saucepan, bring 1½ cups (375 mL) water and ¼ tsp (1 mL) salt to boil over medium-high heat; stir in rice. Cover and reduce heat to medium-low; simmer until tender, about 20 minutes.

❯ Remove from heat; let stand until liquid is absorbed, about 5 minutes. Fluff with fork. Stir in parsley.

Makes 4 servings. PER SERVING: about 130 cal, 3 g pro, trace total fat (0 g sat. fat), 28 g carb, 1 g fibre, 0 mg chol, 151 mg sodium. % RDI: 3% calcium, 4% iron, 2% vit A, 7% vit C, 4% folate.

WHAT DOES FIVE OR SO INGREDIENTS MEAN?

The ingredient lists for the recipes in this chapter include about five (sometimes four, sometimes up to seven) ingredients. The only other things you'll need to make them are your pantry staples of oil, salt and pepper. It's that simple!

Pork with Lemon Caper Sauce

This restaurant-style dish known as *piccata* is one you can whip up at home. Don't be afraid to dazzle your family and friends!

8	pork loin centre cut chops, boneless fast fry (about 1 lb/500 g)	8
¼ cup	all-purpose flour	50 mL
3	cloves garlic, minced	3
1 tbsp	rinsed drained capers	15 mL
½ cup	sodium-reduced chicken stock	125 mL
2 tbsp	lemon juice	25 mL

❯ Between sheets of plastic wrap, pound pork to scant ¼-inch (5 mm) thickness. In bag, shake together flour and ¼ tsp (1 mL) each salt and pepper. One piece at a time, shake pork in flour mixture to coat.

❯ In large skillet, heat 1 tbsp (15 mL) extra-virgin olive oil over medium-high heat; fry pork, turning once, in 2 batches and adding more oil if necessary, until golden, juices run clear when pork is pierced and just a hint of pink remains inside, about 3 minutes. Transfer to platter; keep warm.

❯ Add 1 tbsp (15 mL) extra-virgin olive oil to pan; fry garlic and capers over medium heat for 1 minute. Add stock and lemon juice; boil for 1 minute, scraping up any brown bits from bottom of pan. Serve over pork.

Makes 4 servings. PER SERVING: about 302 cal, 26 g pro, 18 g total fat (4 g sat. fat), 7 g carb, trace fibre, 73 mg chol, 357 mg sodium. % RDI: 3% calcium, 10% iron, 5% vit C, 7% folate.

Chili-Rubbed Pork Chops

Just wait for a harried suppertime, when this simple recipe will come to your rescue. Check out other rubs you can make at home (see Make-Your-Own Seasonings, opposite) that taste just as delicious on these succulent chops.

4	pork rib chops	4
1 tbsp	packed brown sugar	15 mL
2 tsp	ground cumin	10 mL
2 tsp	chili powder	10 mL

❯ Trim fat from chops; slash edges at 1-inch (2.5 cm) intervals to prevent curling. In small bowl, combine sugar, cumin, chili powder and 1 tsp (5 mL) salt; stir in 1 tbsp (15 mL) vegetable oil. Rub all over chops. *(Make-ahead: Cover and refrigerate for up to 24 hours.)*

❯ Place chops in greased grill pan or on greased grill over medium-high heat; close lid (if using barbecue) and grill, turning once, until juices run clear when pork is pierced and just a hint of pink remains inside, about 8 minutes.

Makes 4 servings. PER SERVING: about 227 cal, 23 g pro, 13 g total fat (4 g sat. fat), 4 g carb, trace fibre, 56 mg chol, 626 mg sodium. % RDI: 3% calcium, 12% iron, 5% vit A, 2% vit C, 2% folate.

TIP
● Try buying a family pack of chops. Season and enclose the number you need for each meal in freezer bags. Packed in a single layer, four chops will defrost in the fridge in a day.

MAKE-YOUR-OWN SEASONINGS

Use these as rubs for fish, chops and chicken, or add them to soups, salad dressings, dips and stews. Store in airtight jars in a cool, dark drawer for up to 1 month.

HERB SEASONING MIX
• In small bowl, mix together ½ cup (125 mL) dried chopped chives; 2 tbsp (25 mL) dried parsley flakes; 2 tsp (10 mL) each dried basil, dried thyme, garlic powder and onion powder; and 1 tsp (5 mL) pepper. **Makes 1 cup (250 mL).**

LEMON DILL SEASONING MIX
• Mix together ⅓ cup (75 mL) each dried dillweed and parsley flakes; 4 tsp (20 mL) lemon-and-pepper seasoning; and 1 tbsp (15 mL) each celery salt, dry mustard and garlic salt. **Makes about 1 cup (250 mL).**

CURRY SEASONING MIX
• Mix together ½ cup (125 mL) dried minced onion; 2 tbsp (25 mL) curry powder; 4 tsp (20 mL) each ground cumin and salt; and 2 tsp (10 mL) each turmeric and pepper. **Makes 1 cup (250 mL).**

QUICK DIPS

HERB DIP
• In bowl, whisk together ½ cup (125 mL) plain yogurt; ½ cup (125 mL) cream cheese; ¼ cup (50 mL) light mayonnaise; and 4 tsp (20 mL) Herb Seasoning Mix (recipe, left). Cover and refrigerate for at least 2 hours. *(Make-ahead: Cover and refrigerate for up to 3 days.)* Garnish with 2 tbsp (25 mL) chopped fresh chives. **Makes 1¼ cups (300 mL).**

PER 1 TBSP (15 mL): about 35 cal, 1 g pro, 3 g total fat (2 g sat. fat), 1 g carb, 0 g fibre, 8 mg chol, 44 mg sodium. % RDI: 1% calcium, 1% iron, 3% vit A, 1% folate.

VARIATIONS

Lemon Dill Dip
• Replace Herb Seasoning Mix with 2 tsp (10 mL) Lemon Dill Seasoning Mix (recipe, left). Replace chives with chopped fresh dill.

Curry Dip
• Replace Herb Seasoning Mix with 2 tsp (10 mL) Curry Seasoning Mix (recipe, left). Add 1 tbsp (15 mL) mango chutney. Replace chives with chopped fresh coriander.

Pork Chops with Balsamic Glaze

The sweet-and-sour taste of balsamic vinegar really tarts up everyday pork chops.

2 tsp	dried Italian herb seasoning	10 mL
4	pork loin centre chops	4
2 tbsp	balsamic vinegar	25 mL
¾ cup	sodium-reduced chicken stock	175 mL
1 tsp	cornstarch	5 mL

❯ In small bowl, mix together 2 tbsp (25 mL) extra-virgin olive oil, Italian herb seasoning and pinch salt; brush over chops. In large skillet, fry chops over medium-high heat, adding more oil if necessary, until browned, juices run clear when pork is pierced and just a hint of pink remains inside, about 4 minutes per side. Transfer to plate; keep warm. Drain off any fat in pan.

❯ Add vinegar to pan; simmer over medium heat for 30 seconds. Whisk stock with cornstarch; add to pan and bring to boil, stirring and scraping up any brown bits. Reduce heat and simmer until thickened, about 1 minute. Return chops and any accumulated juices to pan; heat through, turning to coat and glaze.

Makes 4 servings. PER SERVING: about 385 cal, 24 g pro, 16 g total fat (4 g sat. fat), 35 g carb, 3 g fibre, 66 mg chol, 231 mg sodium. % RDI: 6% calcium, 14% iron, 223% vit A, 42% vit C, 10% folate.

SUBSTITUTION

● Wine, cider vinegar and rice vinegar are equally good for glazing the chops. If you substitute one of these, add a pinch of sugar to the cornstarch mixture to make up for the natural sweetness of the balsamic vinegar.

Mashed Sweet Potatoes

4	sweet potatoes, peeled and cubed	4
¼ cup	sodium-reduced chicken stock	50 mL
2	green onions, sliced	2

❯ In large saucepan of boiling salted water, cover and cook potatoes until tender, about 10 minutes. Drain and return to pot. Add chicken stock and ½ tsp (2 mL) pepper; mash until smooth. Serve sprinkled with green onions.

Makes 4 servings. PER SERVING: about 141 cal, 2 g pro, trace total fat (0 g sat. fat), 32 g carb, 3 g fibre, 0 mg chol, 56 mg sodium. % RDI: 3% calcium, 6% iron, 222% vit A, 40% vit C, 9% folate.

Five-Spice Roasted Chicken

To protect a skillet that has a wooden or plastic handle in the oven, wrap the handle in foil.

2 tbsp	lemon juice	25 mL
2 tsp	liquid honey	10 mL
1 tsp	five-spice powder	5 mL
8	chicken pieces	8

➤ In large bowl, whisk together lemon juice, 1 tbsp (15 mL) vegetable oil, honey, five-spice powder and ¼ tsp (1 mL) each salt and pepper. Remove skin from chicken, if desired. Add chicken to marinade, turning to coat; let stand for 5 minutes. *(Make-ahead: Cover and refrigerate for up to 8 hours.)*

➤ In ovenproof skillet, heat 1 tbsp (15 mL) vegetable oil over medium-high heat; brown chicken, in batches and adding more oil if necessary. Drain fat from skillet.

➤ Return all chicken to skillet. Roast in 425°F (220°C) oven until juices run clear when chicken is pierced, about 30 minutes.

Makes 4 servings. PER SERVING (WITHOUT SKIN): about 275 cal, 26 g pro, 17 g total fat (3 g sat. fat), 5 g carb, trace fibre, 94 mg chol, 226 mg sodium. % RDI: 1% calcium, 9% iron, 3% vit A, 2% vit C, 3% folate.

Ginger Rice

1 cup	jasmine or other long-grain rice	250 mL
6	slices gingerroot	6
1	green onion (green part only), minced	1

➤ In saucepan, bring 1½ cups (375 mL) water, rice, ginger and ¼ tsp (1 mL) salt to boil. Reduce heat to low; cover and simmer until rice is tender and no liquid remains, 20 minutes. Stir in onion.

Makes 4 servings. PER SERVING: about 172 cal, 4 g pro, trace total fat (trace sat. fat), 37 g carb, 1 g fibre, 0 mg chol, 147 mg sodium. % RDI: 2% calcium, 2% iron, 2% vit C, 3% folate.

THE TOP 10 RECIPES TO KNOW BY HEART

1. Best-Ever Burgers **(recipe, page 150)**

2. Spaghetti Sauce **(recipe, page 120)**

3. Beef and Broccoli Stir-Fry **(recipe, page 50)**

4. Chunky Beef Chili **(recipe, page 113)**

5. Pork Chops with Balsamic Glaze **(recipe, opposite)**

6. Saucy Chicken with Tomatoes **(recipe, page 72)**

7. Chicken Fingers with Honey Mustard Sauce **(recipe, page 144)**

8. Rainbow Trout with Dijon Mayonnaise **(recipe, page 12)**

9. Mac and Cheese **(recipe, page 119)**

10. Easy-as-Pie Frittata **(recipe, page 109)**

Crispy Cornmeal Chicken

You don't need to buy coating mixes to create crusty, moist chicken. Cornmeal and a few seasonings are the secret.

½ cup	cornmeal	125 mL
½ tsp	dried thyme	2 mL
¼ cup	buttermilk	50 mL
4	boneless skinless chicken breasts	4

> In shallow dish, whisk together cornmeal, thyme, ½ tsp (2 mL) salt and ¼ tsp (1 mL) pepper. Pour buttermilk into separate shallow dish. Dip chicken into buttermilk then cornmeal mixture, turning and pressing to coat.

> In large skillet, heat 1 tbsp (15 mL) vegetable oil over medium heat; fry chicken, turning once and adding up to 1 tbsp (15 mL) more vegetable oil if necessary, until crisp, golden and no longer pink inside, about 14 minutes.

Makes 4 servings. PER SERVING: about 279 cal, 32 g pro, 9 g total fat (1 g sat. fat), 14 g carb, 1 g fibre, 78 mg chol, 377 mg sodium. % RDI: 3% calcium, 6% iron, 1% vit A, 2% vit C, 5% folate.

Sautéed Cherry Tomatoes

2	cloves garlic, minced	2
2 cups	cherry or grape tomatoes	500 mL
1 tbsp	chopped fresh parsley or chives	15 mL

> In skillet, heat 1 tbsp (15 mL) vegetable oil over medium-high heat; sauté garlic and ¼ tsp (1 mL) each salt and pepper until fragrant, about 30 seconds. Add tomatoes; sauté until beginning to soften, about 5 minutes. Sprinkle with parsley.

Makes 4 servings. PER SERVING: about 44 cal, 1 g pro, 4 g total fat (trace sat. fat), 3 g carb, 1 g fibre, 0 mg chol, 150 mg sodium. % RDI: 1% calcium, 3% iron, 4% vit A, 22% vit C, 4% folate.

Roasted Chicken Breasts with Sage and Prosciutto

Instead of sage, you can take your pick of herbs to season this chicken; thyme, basil and marjoram are delicious choices.

2 tbsp	Dijon mustard	25 mL
Dash	hot pepper sauce	Dash
4	boneless skinless chicken breasts	4
1 tsp	crumbled dried sage	5 mL
8	thin slices prosciutto (5 oz/150 g)	8

> Combine mustard and hot pepper sauce; brush all over chicken. Sprinkle with sage and ¼ tsp (1 mL) pepper.

> Wrap prosciutto around chicken, covering as much as possible. Place on foil-lined rimmed baking sheet; brush tops with 1 tsp (5 mL) vegetable oil. *(Make-ahead: Cover and refrigerate for up to 2 hours.)*

> Bake in 375°F (190°C) oven until prosciutto is crispy and chicken is no longer pink inside, about 20 minutes.

Makes 4 servings. PER SERVING: about 226 cal, 38 g pro, 7 g total fat (2 g sat. fat), 2 g carb, trace fibre, 99 mg chol, 649 mg sodium. % RDI: 2% calcium, 8% iron, 1% vit A, 2% folate.

TIP
● In warm weather, cook these breasts on the barbecue. Instead of using crumbled dried sage, place whole fresh sage leaves on the chicken before wrapping the prosciutto around it.

Pork Chops with Mustard Crumb Crust

With a crunchy golden coating, these chops are pleasing to everyone, especially children. Serve with mashed potatoes and green beans or broccoli.

1 tbsp	Dijon mustard	15 mL
1 tbsp	light mayonnaise	15 mL
2	green onions, minced	2
½ cup	fresh bread crumbs	125 mL
2 tbsp	minced fresh parsley (optional)	25 mL
2	cloves garlic, minced	2
4	pork loin centre chops, boneless or bone in, trimmed	4

> In bowl, combine mustard, mayonnaise and green onions. In another bowl, combine bread crumbs, parsley (if using), 1 tbsp (15 mL) vegetable oil and garlic.

> Slash edges of pork chops to prevent curling; sprinkle with ¼ tsp (1 mL) each salt and pepper. In large ovenproof skillet, heat 1 tbsp (15 mL) vegetable oil over medium-high heat; brown chops. Drain off fat, leaving chops in pan.

> Spread mayonnaise mixture over chops; top with bread crumb mixture, pressing to adhere. Roast in 425°F (220°C) oven until juices run clear when pork is pierced and just a hint of pink remains inside, and bread crumbs are golden, about 15 minutes.

Makes 4 servings. PER SERVING: about 260 cal, 27 g pro, 15 g total fat (3 g sat. fat), 4 g carb, trace fibre, 72 mg chol, 312 mg sodium. % RDI: 4% calcium, 11% iron, 1% vit A, 7% vit C, 6% folate.

Vaguely Coq au Vin

Impressive enough for your favourite people, this browned then wine-simmered chicken is a dish every cook should have in his or her repertoire.

8	chicken thighs (2 lb/1 kg total)	8
¼ cup	all-purpose flour	50 mL
2¼ tsp	dried thyme	11 mL
6	small onions, quartered	6
1 cup	dry white wine	250 mL

> Pull skin off chicken. In bag, shake together flour, 2 tsp (10 mL) of the thyme and ½ tsp (2 mL) each salt and pepper. Add chicken, in batches, and shake to coat.

> In large skillet or Dutch oven, heat 1 tbsp (15 mL) extra-virgin olive oil over medium-high heat; brown chicken on both sides, adding more oil if necessary. Transfer to plate.

> Drain off fat in skillet; reduce heat to medium. Cook onions, stirring occasionally and adding more oil if necessary, until golden and softened, about 5 minutes.

> Return chicken to skillet; pour wine over top. Cover and simmer, turning once, until juices run clear when chicken is pierced, about 20 minutes. Transfer to platter and keep warm.

> Add remaining thyme and ¼ tsp (1 mL) each salt and pepper to pan juices; boil until thickened, about 5 minutes. Pour over chicken.

Makes 4 servings. PER SERVING: about 262 cal, 24 g pro, 10 g total fat (2 g sat. fat), 16 g carb, 2 g fibre, 95 mg chol, 534 mg sodium. % RDI: 5% calcium, 20% iron, 2% vit A, 13% vit C, 17% folate.

TIP
• While the taste will not be exactly the same, you can replace the wine with chicken stock, sodium-reduced if possible, and a splash of vinegar to simulate the taste of grapes. Pour 1 tbsp (15 mL) white or red wine vinegar or cider vinegar into liquid measure; fill to 1 cup (250 mL) with chicken stock.

Teriyaki-Glazed Wings

Get the wings in the oven first, then put the rice on to simmer.

2½ lb	chicken wings (about 15)	1.25 kg
¾ cup	thick teriyaki sauce	175 mL
1	clove garlic, minced	1
1 tsp	grated orange rind	5 mL
2 tbsp	thinly sliced green onion	25 mL

> Cut off wing tips at joint; freeze tips for stock (see Slow Cooker Chicken Stock, page 130). Separate wings at remaining joint; trim off excess skin. Place wings on rack on foil-lined rimmed baking sheet. Bake in 400°F (200°C) oven, turning once, for 20 minutes.

> Meanwhile, in large bowl, combine teriyaki sauce, garlic and orange rind; set ¼ cup (50 mL) aside for basting. Add wings to remaining sauce in large bowl; toss to coat well. Return to rack; bake, turning once, until juices run clear when wings are pierced, about 25 minutes. Brush with reserved sauce. Broil, turning once, until browned, about 4 minutes. Sprinkle with onion.

Makes 4 servings. PER SERVING: about 361 cal, 32 g pro, 21 g total fat (6 g sat. fat), 9 g carb, trace fibre, 91 mg chol, 2,163 mg sodium. % RDI: 3% calcium, 17% iron, 5% vit A, 2% vit C, 7% folate.

Rice with Peas and Bamboo Shoots

1½ cups	chicken stock	375 mL
2 tbsp	soy sauce	25 mL
2 cups	short-grain rice	500 mL
1	can (8 oz/227 mL) sliced bamboo shoots, drained and rinsed	1
½ cup	frozen peas	125 mL
1	green onion, thinly sliced	1
2 tbsp	toasted sesame seeds	25 mL

> In saucepan, bring stock, ¾ cup (175 mL) water and soy sauce to boil. Add rice and bamboo shoots. Cover and simmer over medium-low heat until rice is tender but still firm, about 15 minutes. Turn off heat.

> With fork, gently stir in peas, green onion and sesame seeds. Let stand, covered, until liquid is absorbed and rice is completely tender, about 8 minutes.

Makes 4 servings. PER SERVING: about 425 cal, 12 g pro, 4 g total fat (1 g sat. fat), 84 g carb, 3 g fibre, 0 mg chol, 827 mg sodium. % RDI: 2% calcium, 12% iron, 1% vit A, 3% vit C, 11% folate.

Zucchini Toss with Penne

Year round, zucchini is inexpensive, and in the summer there are countless ways to enjoy this colourful vegetable.

4	cloves garlic, slivered	4
1 tsp	dried Italian herb seasoning	5 mL
2	sweet red peppers, chopped	2
3	zucchini (1 lb/500 g total)	3
4 cups	penne	1 L
½ cup	freshly grated pecorino, Asiago or feta cheese	125 mL

❯ In skillet, heat 2 tbsp (25 mL) extra-virgin olive oil over medium heat; fry garlic, Italian herb seasoning and ¼ tsp (1 mL) coarsely ground pepper for 4 minutes, stirring occasionally.

❯ Add chopped red peppers; fry for 4 minutes, stirring occasionally.

❯ Meanwhile, shred zucchini coarsely. Increase heat to medium-high; add zucchini to pan and sauté until heated through, about 2 minutes.

❯ Meanwhile, in pot of boiling salted water, cook penne until tender but firm, 8 minutes. Drain.

❯ In large warmed pasta bowl, combine zucchini mixture, penne and cheese; toss to coat.

Makes 4 servings. PER SERVING: about 460 cal, 15 g pro, 13 g total fat (4 g sat. fat), 72 g carb, 6 g fibre, 12 mg chol, 340 mg sodium. % RDI: 14% calcium, 29% iron, 38% vit A, 173% vit C, 90% folate.

BREADS ON THE DOUBLE

Who doesn't like delicious, warm, crusty bread? Here are a couple of quick versions to serve with dinner tonight.

QUICK AND FRESH FLATBREAD

● Pat out 1 lb (500 g) fresh pizza dough onto 12-inch (30 cm) greased pizza pan or small rimmed baking sheet. Brush with extra-virgin olive oil and season as desired below. Bake in centre of 425°F (220°C) oven until golden, about 12 minutes.

● Herb Flatbread: Sprinkle with chopped fresh rosemary or dried rosemary (or oregano or dried Italian herb seasoning). If you like, dust with a generous sprinkle of freshly grated Parmesan, Asiago or Romano cheese.

● Simple Salt-and-Pepper Flatbread: Sprinkle with coarse sea salt and cracked pepper.

● Seeded Flatbread: Sprinkle with sesame, poppy or flaxseeds. A touch of salt is good with the seeds, too.

ROASTED GARLIC BAGUETTE

● In small saucepan, combine 6 cloves garlic with a few drops of oil. Cover and "roast" over low heat, swirling pan occasionally, until garlic is soft, about 15 minutes. Transfer to bowl and let cool.

● Mash garlic with ¼ cup (50 mL) butter, generous sprinkle dried thyme and rosemary or oregano, and quick grate of pepper.

● Slit baguette lengthwise almost all the way through. Spread cut sides with butter mixture; sprinkle with freshly grated Parmesan, Asiago or Romano cheese if you like. Wrap in foil.

● Bake in 350°F (180°C) oven, turning once, until crust is crisped and butter is melted, about 10 minutes. (Or place on barbecue; close lid and grill over medium heat.)

Bean Burgers with Coriander Cream

When it comes to cooking for a vegetarian and burgers are on the menu, nothing is easier than these bean-based patties. Mild or medium salsa is plenty hot for most people, especially when salsa is not just a condiment but also the central ingredient that adds moisture and flavour to the patties.

1	can (19 oz/540 mL) red kidney, romano or black beans	1
½ cup	dry bread crumbs	125 mL
½ cup	mild or medium salsa	125 mL
⅓ cup	light sour cream	75 mL
2 tbsp	minced fresh coriander	25 mL

› Drain and rinse beans; place in bowl. With potato masher or fork, mash beans until fairly smooth but still with some small lumps.

› Stir in bread crumbs and salsa to make fairly firm mixture. With wet hands, form into four ½-inch (1 cm) thick patties; set aside on waxed paper–lined baking sheet.

› In small bowl, stir together sour cream and coriander. *(Make-ahead: Cover patties and cream separately and refrigerate for up to 4 hours.)*

› In large skillet, heat 2 tsp (10 mL) vegetable oil over medium-high heat; fry patties, turning once and adding more oil if necessary, until crusty outside and piping hot inside, about 10 minutes. Serve topped with coriander cream.

Makes 4 servings. PER SERVING: about 203 cal, 10 g pro, 4 g total fat (1 g sat. fat), 32 g carb, 9 g fibre, 3 mg chol, 654 mg sodium. % RDI: 9% calcium, 15% iron, 2% vit A, 3% vit C, 30% folate.

TIP
• Experiment with all sorts of toppings, such as diced avocado, a generous mound of shredded romaine lettuce or sprouts, or a little cheese, such as Monterey Jack or creamy Fontina.

Pasta with White Beans and Rapini

Pasta and beans provide this vegetarian dish with complete protein. It's also a tasty way to introduce rapini, also known as broccoli rabe, which is related to the cabbage and turnip families. Serve with grated cheese.

1	bunch rapini or broccoli	1
4 cups	whole wheat penne	1 L
1½ cups	fresh bread crumbs	375 mL
4	cloves garlic, minced	4
Pinch	hot pepper flakes	Pinch
1	can (19 oz/540 mL) romano beans, drained and rinsed	1

❯ Trim base of rapini stalks. In large pot of boiling salted water, cover and cook rapini until tender, about 2 minutes. With slotted spoon, transfer to colander to drain. Chop into 1-inch (2.5 cm) pieces; set aside.

❯ In same pot of boiling salted water, cook penne until tender but firm, 8 to 10 minutes. Reserving ½ cup (125 mL) of the cooking liquid, drain and return to pot.

❯ Meanwhile, in large skillet, heat 1 tsp (5 mL) extra-virgin olive oil over medium heat; fry bread crumbs with one-quarter of the garlic, stirring, until golden, about 3 minutes. Transfer to bowl; set aside.

❯ In same skillet, heat ¼ cup (50 mL) extra-virgin olive oil over medium heat; fry remaining garlic and hot pepper flakes, stirring, until golden, about 1 minute. Stir in rapini and beans; heat through, about 3 minutes. Add to pasta and toss to coat, adding some of the reserved cooking liquid, if desired. Serve sprinkled with bread crumb mixture.

Makes 4 servings. PER SERVING: about 591 cal, 24 g pro, 17 g total fat (2 g sat. fat), 92 g carb, 17 g fibre, 0 mg chol, 978 mg sodium. % RDI: 20% calcium, 51% iron, 28% vit A, 30% vit C, 82% folate.

Havarti Cheese and Pepper Panini

While arugula is usually a salad ingredient, here it lends its appealing bitterness to hot, crusty grilled sandwiches.

4	panini buns, halved	4
8	slices Havarti or jalapeño Havarti cheese	8
1½ cups	arugula or spinach leaves	375 mL
1 cup	sliced roasted red peppers	250 mL

> Brush cut sides of panini bottoms with 1 tbsp (15 mL) extra-virgin olive oil; cover with half of the cheese. Top with arugula, red peppers then remaining cheese. Cover with panini top.

> Cook in panini press on medium-low until buns are toasted and cheese is melted, 6 minutes. (Or cook in skillet, turning once and pressing to flatten.)

Makes 4 servings. PER SERVING: about 403 cal, 17 g pro, 22 g total fat (11 g sat. fat), 37 g carb, 2 g fibre, 51 mg chol, 648 mg sodium. % RDI: 33% calcium, 18% iron, 34% vit A, 100% vit C, 39% folate.

VARIATION

Grilled Havarti Cheese and Pepper Sandwiches
• Substitute 8 slices whole grain bread for the panini buns. Brush vegetable oil or butter over bottom of large skillet or grill pan; heat over medium-low heat. Cook sandwiches, pressing with spatula and turning once, until bread is crusty and cheese is melted.

Yogurt Dill Dip with Carrots and Radishes

½ cup	plain Balkan-style yogurt	125 mL
2 tbsp	light mayonnaise	25 mL
1 tbsp	chopped fresh dill (or 1 tsp/5 mL dried dillweed)	15 mL
1	clove garlic, minced	1
	Carrot sticks and radishes	

> In small bowl, mix together yogurt, mayonnaise, dill, garlic, and ¼ tsp (1 mL) each salt and pepper. Serve with carrot sticks and radishes.

Makes ⅔ cup (150 mL) dip. PER 1 TBSP (15 ML) DIP: about 21 cal, 1 g pro, 2 g total fat (1 g sat. fat), 1 g carb, 0 g fibre, 3 mg chol, 81 mg sodium. % RDI: 2% calcium, 1% vit A.

Make It Tonight... in One Pot

Meatball Noodle Soup

Have a bowl of cold water handy when forming any raw meat into patties or balls – dipping your hands in the water helps unstick them.

1 lb	lean ground beef	500 g
2	cloves garlic, minced	2
1 tsp	each dried thyme, salt and pepper	5 mL
2 tsp	vegetable oil	10 mL
1	each onion and sweet red pepper, chopped	1
2	carrots, halved lengthwise and sliced	2
2 tbsp	tomato paste	25 mL
4 cups	beef stock	1 L
1½ cups	thinly sliced broccoli florets	375 mL
1 cup	egg noodles	250 mL

> In bowl, combine beef, garlic, thyme and ½ tsp (2 mL) each of the salt and pepper; roll by scant 1 tbsp (15 mL) into balls.

> In large saucepan, heat oil over medium-high heat; brown meatballs, in batches and turning often, about 5 minutes. Transfer to plate. Drain fat from pan.

> Add onion, red pepper, carrots and remaining salt and pepper to pan; fry over medium heat, stirring occasionally, until softened, about 3 minutes. Stir in tomato paste; cook for 2 minutes. Add stock and bring to boil, stirring and scraping up brown bits from bottom of pan. Return meatballs to pan; reduce heat and simmer for 5 minutes.

> Add broccoli and noodles; simmer until noodles are tender and digital thermometer inserted into meatballs reads 160°F (71°C), about 5 minutes.

Makes 4 servings. PER SERVING: about 305 cal, 27 g pro, 14 g total fat (5 g sat. fat), 18 g carb, 3 g fibre, 69 mg chol, 1,450 mg sodium. % RDI: 6% calcium, 28% iron, 106% vit A, 115% vit C, 18% folate.

TIP
● During the winter, you can use frozen broccoli. For variety, change the pasta; alphabet pasta is a favourite with kids.

Sausage, Potato and Swiss Chard Soup

If you like it hot, use hot Italian sausage, or use another favourite fresh sausage, such as farmer's or chorizo. Spinach can substitute for the Swiss chard, but heat it just until wilted.

1 lb	Italian sausage	500 g
1 tbsp	extra-virgin olive oil	15 mL
1	onion, chopped	1
2	cloves garlic, minced	2
3 cups	cubed peeled potatoes	750 mL
½ tsp	dried Italian herb seasoning	2 mL
½ tsp	pepper	2 mL
¼ tsp	hot pepper flakes	1 mL
3 cups	water	750 mL
1 cup	sodium-reduced chicken stock	250 mL
2 cups	packed coarsely chopped Swiss chard leaves	500 mL
½ cup	shaved Parmesan cheese	125 mL

> Cut sausage into 1-inch (2.5 cm) pieces. In large saucepan, heat oil over medium-high heat; brown sausage. Transfer to bowl. Drain fat from pan.

> Add onion, garlic, potatoes, Italian herb seasoning, pepper and hot pepper flakes to pan; fry over medium heat, stirring occasionally, until onion is softened, about 5 minutes.

> Add water and stock; bring to boil. Return sausage to pan; reduce heat, cover and simmer until potatoes are almost tender, about 7 minutes.

> Add Swiss chard; simmer, covered, until tender, about 5 minutes. Top with Parmesan cheese.

Makes 8 servings. PER SERVING: about 203 cal, 12 g pro, 12 g total fat (4 g sat. fat), 13 g carb, 1 g fibre, 29 mg chol, 508 mg sodium. % RDI: 6% calcium, 8% iron, 3% vit A, 10% vit C, 4% folate.

EQUIPMENT
ESSENTIAL KITCHEN TOOLS

ON A DESERT ISLAND, YOU CAN GET BY WITH:
- Paring knife and chef's knife
- Cutting board
- Large and small saucepan
- Skillet (seasoned cast-iron is best)

IF YOU AREN'T PLANNING A ROBINSON CRUSOE EXISTENCE, ADD THE FOLLOWING:
- Dry and liquid measuring cups
- Salad spinner and colander
- Lifter
- Tongs – about 9 inches (23 cm) long
- Pepper mill
- Butcher's steel
- Large sieve for draining and straining
- Wooden spoons
- Silicone spatulas
- Skewers
- Meat thermometer (digital instant-read recommended for ground meats and poultry)
- Rimmed baking sheet
- Small roasting pan with rack
- Grill pan
- Steamer insert
- Kitchen scissors and vegetable peeler
- Dutch oven
- Wok or large, deep skillet

FOR A LITTLE LUXURY, ADD:
- Immersion blender
- Food processor
- Toaster oven
- Slow cooker
- Muffin and cake pans
- Rice cooker
- Panini press

Spiced Beef Skillet Dinner

While the beef and vegetables are simmering, prepare the couscous. For our foolproof preparation method, see Fluffy Couscous, below.

1 lb	lean ground beef	500 g
1 tbsp	vegetable oil	15 mL
1	onion, chopped	1
2	cloves garlic, minced	2
2	carrots, julienned	2
Half	sweet red pepper, thinly sliced	Half
1 tbsp	sweet or smoked sweet paprika	15 mL
1 tsp	each ground ginger, cumin and cinnamon	5 mL
¼ tsp	each salt and hot pepper flakes	1 mL
1	can (28 oz/796 mL) diced tomatoes	1
2 tbsp	tomato paste	25 mL
¾ cup	sliced pitted green olives	175 mL
2 tbsp	chopped fresh coriander or green onion	25 mL
2 cups	hot cooked couscous	500 mL

❯ In large skillet, sauté beef over medium-high heat, breaking up with fork, until no longer pink, about 5 minutes. Using slotted spoon, transfer to plate. Drain fat from skillet.

❯ Add oil to pan; fry onion and garlic over medium heat until fragrant, about 1 minute. Add carrots, red pepper, 2 tbsp (25 mL) water, paprika, ginger, cumin, cinnamon, salt and hot pepper flakes; fry, stirring often, until vegetables are tender-crisp, about 3 minutes.

❯ Return beef and any accumulated juices to skillet. Add tomatoes and tomato paste; bring to boil. Reduce heat and simmer until vegetables are tender, about 10 minutes. Stir in olives and coriander; heat through, about 1 minute. Serve over couscous.

Makes 4 servings. PER SERVING: about 450 cal, 29 g pro, 20 g total fat (6 g sat. fat), 41 g carb, 5 g fibre, 61 mg chol, 1,089 mg sodium. % RDI: 12% calcium, 40% iron, 122% vit A, 100% vit C, 19% folate.

TIP
● The selection of paprika available today has expanded with the arrival of smoked paprika from Spain. Sweet or mild paprika is ideal for this dish, and you can use either smoked or regular, depending on your preference.

FLUFFY COUSCOUS
● Measure 1 cup (250 mL) couscous (whole wheat recommended) into heatproof bowl. Stir in ½ tsp (2 mL) salt; stir in 1½ cups (375 mL) boiling water or sodium-reduced chicken or vegetable stock. Cover and let stand for 5 minutes. Fluff with fork and serve.

FLAVOURING SUGGESTIONS
Add chopped fresh herbs, such as parsley or chives, a few currants and/or slivered almonds or other nuts.

Pork Chops with Puttanesca Sauce

Serve this hearty dish over pasta, Creamy Polenta (see page 73) or Fluffy Couscous (see page 69).

4	pork loin centre chops, boneless or bone in, trimmed	4
2 tbsp	vegetable oil	25 mL
1	onion, chopped	1
2	cloves garlic, minced	2
½ tsp	each pepper and hot pepper flakes	2 mL
¼ tsp	salt	1 mL
1	can (19 oz/540 mL) tomatoes	1
¼ cup	tomato paste	50 mL
½ cup	chopped pitted black olives	125 mL
1 tbsp	drained capers	15 mL
¼ cup	minced fresh basil or parsley	50 mL

❯ Slash edges of pork chops to prevent curling. In large skillet, heat 1 tbsp (15 mL) of the oil over medium-high heat; brown pork chops. Transfer to plate.

❯ Drain fat from pan; add remaining oil. Fry onion, garlic, pepper, hot pepper flakes and salt over medium heat until softened, about 4 minutes.

❯ Add tomatoes and tomato paste; mash with potato masher. Add olives and capers; bring to boil, stirring and scraping up brown bits. Reduce heat and simmer for 10 minutes or until spoon drawn across bottom of pan leaves space that fills in slowly.

❯ Return chops and any accumulated juices to pan; add basil. Cover and simmer until juices run clear when pork is pierced and just a hint of pink remains inside, about 10 minutes.

Makes 4 servings. PER SERVING: about 292 cal, 25 g pro, 16 g total fat (2 g sat. fat), 14 g carb, 3 g fibre, 60 mg chol, 980 mg sodium. % RDI: 9% calcium, 19% iron, 14% vit A, 48% vit C, 10% folate.

VARIATION

Veal Chops with Puttanesca Sauce
● Replace pork with veal rib or loin chops. Increase tomato paste to ⅓ cup (75 mL). Increase cooking time to 15 minutes.

Herbed Lamb Chops with Tuscan Beans

Pairing lamb with seasoned white beans is a French classic. Canned white kidney beans make this dish doable on a weeknight.

8	lamb loin chops (about 1½ lb/750 g)	8
1 tsp	crumbled dried rosemary (or 1 sprig fresh)	5 mL
½ tsp	each salt and pepper	2 mL
2 tbsp	extra-virgin olive oil	25 mL
1	onion, chopped	1
2	cloves garlic, minced	2
2 tsp	all-purpose flour	10 mL
1¼ cups	sodium-reduced chicken stock	300 mL
1	can (19 oz/540 mL) white kidney beans, drained and rinsed	1
1 tbsp	chopped fresh parsley	15 mL
1 tbsp	lemon juice	15 mL
	Lemon wedges	

➤ Sprinkle lamb chops with half each of the rosemary, salt and pepper. In skillet, heat half of the oil over medium-high heat; fry chops, turning once, until medium-rare, about 5 minutes. Transfer to plate and keep warm. Drain fat from pan.

➤ Add remaining oil to pan; fry onion, garlic and remaining rosemary, salt and pepper, stirring occasionally, until onion is softened, about 5 minutes. Sprinkle flour into pan; whisk in stock and bring to boil over medium heat, whisking and scraping up brown bits, until thickened, about 1 minute.

➤ Add beans; heat through. Mash about ⅓ cup (75 mL) bean mixture in skillet. Stir in parsley and lemon juice; spoon onto plates. Top with lamb chops; drizzle any remaining sauce around beans. Garnish with lemon wedges.

Makes 4 servings. PER SERVING: about 539 cal, 30 g pro, 36 g total fat (13 g sat. fat), 23 g carb, 8 g fibre, 93 mg chol, 895 mg sodium. % RDI: 5% calcium, 27% iron, 1% vit A, 10% vit C, 34% folate.

EQUIPMENT
SEASONING A CAST-IRON SKILLET

Seasoning creates a natural nonstick surface. Do this before you use the pan for the first time and reseason if food starts to stick.
- Lightly rub interior of pan with lard or vegetable oil; bake in 300°F (150°C) oven for 1 hour. Repeat process several times.
- Cast iron absorbs grease from fatty foods, creating a patina that strengthens the seasoning.

Saucy Chicken with Tomatoes

This is your basic browned-then-skillet-stewed chicken. If you have a handful of fresh mushrooms in the crisper, chop them and fry them up with the green pepper. Serve over pasta, rice or Creamy Polenta (opposite).

8	boneless skinless chicken thighs	8
2 tbsp	all-purpose flour	25 mL
½ tsp	salt	2 mL
¼ tsp	pepper	1 mL
2 tbsp	vegetable oil (approx)	25 mL
1	onion, diced	1
2	cloves garlic, minced	2
1	sweet green pepper, chopped	1
1 tsp	dried Italian herb seasoning	5 mL
1	can (28 oz/796 mL) diced tomatoes	1
½ cup	sodium-reduced chicken stock	125 mL
⅓ cup	tomato paste	75 mL
2 tbsp	chopped fresh parsley	25 mL

➤ Toss chicken with flour, salt and pepper. In large shallow Dutch oven, heat half of the oil over medium-high heat; brown chicken, in 2 batches and adding more oil if necessary. Transfer to plate. Drain fat from pan.

➤ Heat remaining oil in pan over medium heat; fry onion, garlic, green pepper and Italian herb seasoning until onion is softened, about 4 minutes. Stir in tomatoes, stock and tomato paste; bring to boil.

➤ Return chicken and any accumulated juices to pan; reduce heat and simmer until thickened and juices run clear when chicken is pierced, about 20 minutes. Sprinkle with parsley.

Makes 4 servings. PER SERVING: about 298 cal, 26 g pro, 13 g total fat (2 g sat. fat), 21 g carb, 4 g fibre, 95 mg chol, 743 mg sodium. % RDI: 9% calcium, 32% iron, 10% vit A, 98% vit C, 18% folate.

TIP

• Save a few dollars by buying bone-in skin-on chicken thighs. It's easy to pull off the skin and trim off any fat. Bone-in thighs need to be cooked for about 40 minutes in the sauce.

Paprika Chicken and Rice

Chicken thighs are always the best choice for braising. They stay moist and are more flavourful than breasts. Trim any fat from thighs before browning.

1	large onion	1
1 lb	boneless skinless chicken thighs, or chicken breasts, halved	500 g
½ tsp	each salt and pepper	2 mL
2 tbsp	vegetable oil	25 mL
2 cups	halved white or cremini mushrooms	500 mL
2 tbsp	sweet paprika	25 mL
½ tsp	dried dillweed	2 mL
1¾ cups	sodium-reduced chicken stock	425 mL
1 cup	parboiled rice	250 mL
1	large Cubanelle or sweet green pepper, chopped	500 mL
⅓ cup	light sour cream	75 mL

> Cut onion into ½-inch (1 cm) wide strips; set aside.

> Sprinkle chicken with half each of the salt and pepper. In large skillet, heat 1 tbsp (15 mL) of the oil over medium-high heat; brown chicken, about 6 minutes. Transfer to plate. Drain fat from pan.

> Add remaining oil to pan; sauté onion and mushrooms until onion is softened and no liquid remains, about 3 minutes. Reduce heat to medium-low. Add paprika, dillweed and remaining salt and pepper; cook, stirring, until fragrant, about 1 minute.

> Stir in chicken stock and rice; bring to boil. Return chicken and any accumulated juices to pan, stirring to coat. Reduce heat, cover and simmer until almost all liquid is absorbed, about 12 minutes.

> Stir in pepper; simmer, covered, until juices run clear when chicken is pierced and pepper is tender, about 4 minutes. Serve with sour cream.

Makes 4 servings. PER SERVING: about 451 cal, 29 g pro, 15 g total fat (3 g sat. fat), 50 g carb, 4 g fibre, 98 mg chol, 675 mg sodium. % RDI: 10% calcium, 26% iron, 20% vit A, 57% vit C, 14% folate.

CREAMY POLENTA

• In large saucepan, bring 4 cups (1 L) water to boil. Stir in ½ tsp (2 mL) salt. Reduce heat to low; whisk in 1 cup (250 mL) cornmeal. Simmer, whisking almost constantly, until polenta is thick enough to mound on spoon, about 20 minutes.

TIP
For the silkiest texture, use medium cornmeal, not coarse.

Halibut and Clam Chowder

If you like, you can top each serving with a toasted baguette slice rubbed with a halved clove of garlic then lightly brushed with olive oil.

1 tbsp	vegetable oil	15 mL
1	onion, chopped	1
1	clove garlic, minced	1
2	tender stalks celery, diced	2
1	large potato, peeled and diced	1
1 tsp	dried thyme	5 mL
¼ tsp	salt	1 mL
1	can (19 oz/540 mL) stewed tomatoes	1
1⅓ cups	sodium-reduced chicken stock	325 mL
¼ cup	tomato paste	50 mL
12 oz	halibut or tilapia fillets	375 g
1	can (5 oz/142 g) whole baby clams	1
1	sweet green pepper, diced	1
1 cup	frozen corn kernels	250 mL

❯ In large saucepan, heat oil over medium heat; fry onion, garlic, celery, potato, thyme and salt, stirring occasionally, until vegetables are softened and slightly golden, about 10 minutes.

❯ Add tomatoes, stock and tomato paste; bring to boil. Reduce heat, cover and simmer until potato is tender, about 12 minutes.

❯ Meanwhile, cut fish into 1-inch (2.5 cm) pieces; add to pan. Add clams, green pepper and corn; simmer, covered, over medium-low heat until fish flakes easily when tested, about 5 minutes.

Makes 4 servings. PER SERVING: about 271 cal, 26 g pro, 6 g total fat (1 g sat. fat), 30 g carb, 4 g fibre, 37 mg chol, 617 mg sodium. % RDI: 12% calcium, 52% iron, 13% vit A, 87% vit C, 24% folate.

Chicken and Kielbasa Rice Dinner

A good Dutch oven has a thick bottom and a lid that fits snugly. Any large saucepan that fits that description is useful for brown-and-braise dishes like this.

8	boneless skinless chicken thighs	8
½ tsp	each salt and pepper	2 mL
1 tbsp	vegetable oil	15 mL
1	onion	1
1	sweet red or green pepper	1
¾ cup	cubed kielbasa or ham (about 4 oz/125 g)	175 mL
1 tsp	dried thyme	5 mL
¾ cup	long-grain rice	175 mL
1½ cups	sodium-reduced chicken stock	375 mL
1 cup	frozen peas	250 mL
2	green onions, sliced	2

❯ Sprinkle chicken with half each of the salt and pepper. In Dutch oven, heat oil over medium-high heat; brown chicken, about 4 minutes. Transfer to plate and set aside. Drain fat from pan.

❯ Meanwhile, cut onion and red pepper lengthwise into ¼-inch (5 mm) wide slices.

❯ In same pan, fry kielbasa, onion, red pepper, thyme and remaining salt and pepper over medium heat, stirring occasionally, until onion is softened, about 5 minutes.

❯ Add rice; fry, stirring, for 1 minute to coat. Add chicken stock. Nestle chicken into rice and bring to boil. Reduce heat to low; cover and simmer until almost no liquid remains and juices run clear when chicken is pierced, about 15 minutes.

❯ Stir in peas; heat through, about 2 minutes. Sprinkle with green onions.

Makes 4 servings. PER SERVING: about 413 cal, 32 g pro, 14 g total fat (3 g sat. fat), 38 g carb, 3 g fibre, 113 mg chol, 887 mg sodium. % RDI: 6% calcium, 21% iron, 15% vit A, 98% vit C, 20% folate.

Chicken with Green Beans and Cherry Tomatoes

Here's a dish you can make in your wok or Dutch oven. It follows a simple pattern – brown, add liquid and simmer – with the added advantage of letting the simmering stock steam the beans.

8	boneless skinless chicken thighs	8
2 tbsp	vegetable oil	25 mL
1	onion, chopped	1
3	cloves garlic, minced	3
1 tsp	dried oregano	5 mL
¼ tsp	each salt and pepper	1 mL
1 cup	chicken stock	250 mL
2 cups	green beans, trimmed	500 mL
2 tsp	cornstarch	10 mL
1 cup	cherry tomatoes, halved	250 mL
2	green onions, thinly sliced	2

❯ Cut chicken into 2-inch (5 cm) pieces. In large deep skillet, heat 1 tbsp (15 mL) of the oil over medium-high heat; brown chicken. Transfer to plate. Drain off fat in pan.

❯ Heat remaining oil in pan over medium heat; fry onion, garlic, oregano, salt and pepper until onion is softened, about 3 minutes.

❯ Add chicken stock, chicken and any accumulated juices; bring to boil. Reduce heat, cover and simmer until juices run clear when chicken is pierced, about 10 minutes.

❯ Meanwhile, cut beans into 1-inch (2.5 cm) long pieces; add to pan. Cover and cook until beans are tender-crisp, about 5 minutes.

❯ Whisk cornstarch with 1 tbsp (15 mL) water; stir into pan. Stir in tomatoes. Simmer, stirring, until thickened, 1 minute. Sprinkle with green onions.

Makes 4 servings. PER SERVING: about 242 cal, 25 g pro, 11 g total fat (2 g sat. fat), 11 g carb, 2 g fibre, 95 mg chol, 443 mg sodium. % RDI: 5% calcium, 18% iron, 8% vit A, 28% vit C, 18% folate.

TIP
• Substitute 4 boneless skinless chicken breasts for the thighs; cook until no longer pink inside, about 10 minutes.

Chicken Cauliflower Curry

While fresh jalapeño peppers are often available, you can replace them with a pinch of hot pepper flakes or a pickled jalapeño pepper when a dish needs a touch of heat and your crisper registers zero fresh jalapeños.

12 oz	boneless skinless chicken breasts	375 g
2 tbsp	vegetable oil (approx)	25 mL
1	onion, chopped	1
1	jalapeño pepper, seeded and minced (optional)	1
¼ tsp	salt	1 mL
2 tbsp	mild curry paste	25 mL
1	can (28 oz/796 mL) diced tomatoes	1
2 cups	cauliflower florets	500 mL
1	Granny Smith apple, cored and diced	1
¼ cup	golden raisins	50 mL
1 cup	frozen peas	250 mL
¼ cup	chopped fresh coriander	50 mL

> Cut chicken crosswise into strips. In large skillet, heat 1 tbsp (15 mL) of the oil over medium-high heat; brown chicken, in 2 batches and adding more oil if necessary. Transfer to bowl. Drain fat from skillet.

> In same pan, heat remaining oil over medium heat; fry onion, jalapeño pepper (if using) and salt, stirring occasionally, until onion is softened, about 3 minutes.

> Add curry paste; cook, stirring, until fragrant, about 1 minute. Drain tomatoes, reserving juice for another use (see Tip, below). Add diced tomatoes to skillet.

> Return chicken to pan. Stir in cauliflower, apple and raisins; cover and simmer until cauliflower is tender, about 10 minutes.

> Add peas and half of the coriander. Simmer, covered, until steaming, about 5 minutes. Sprinkle with remaining coriander.

Makes 4 servings. PER SERVING: about 313 cal, 24 g pro, 13 g total fat (1 g sat. fat), 28 g carb, 6 g fibre, 49 mg chol, 610 mg sodium. % RDI: 7% calcium, 19% iron, 9% vit A, 77% vit C, 25% folate.

TIP
• When the juice from a can of tomatoes is not needed for a recipe, you can refrigerate or freeze it to use in spaghetti sauce or soup. You can even freeze it in ice-cube trays for quick melting.

Skillet Fish with Tomato Zucchini Sauce

Red-skinned new potatoes are a delicious accompaniment. No need to peel them – just scrub, quarter if large and cook in covered saucepan of boiling salted water until tender, about 15 minutes. That means getting the potatoes going before tackling the fish.

2 tbsp	butter or vegetable oil	25 mL
1	onion, chopped	1
2	cloves garlic, minced	2
2 cups	thinly sliced zucchini (about 2 small)	500 mL
½ cup	diced sweet red pepper	125 mL
2 tbsp	chopped fresh oregano (or 1 tsp/5 mL dried)	25 mL
¾ tsp	each salt and pepper	4 mL
¼ tsp	hot pepper sauce	1 mL
1	can (14 oz/398 mL) stewed tomatoes	1
4	fish fillets (such as tilapia or catfish), about 6 oz (175 g) each	4
1	lemon, thinly sliced	1

❯ In large skillet, melt butter over medium-high heat; sauté onion, garlic, zucchini, red pepper, oregano, ½ tsp (2 mL) each of the salt and pepper and hot pepper sauce until onion is softened, about 5 minutes.

❯ Add tomatoes; break up large pieces with potato masher. Bring to boil; reduce heat and simmer, stirring often, until thick enough to mound on spoon, about 10 minutes.

❯ Place fish in single layer on vegetables; sprinkle with remaining salt and pepper. Cover and simmer until fish flakes easily when tested, 8 minutes.

❯ Transfer fish to plate; keep warm. Simmer sauce until thickened again, about 2 minutes. Spoon over fish; serve with lemon slices.

Makes 4 servings. PER SERVING: about 275 cal, 32 g pro, 10 g total fat (4 g sat. fat), 15 g carb, 3 g fibre, 96 mg chol, 875 mg sodium. % RDI: 6% calcium, 11% iron, 36% vit A, 87% vit C, 14% folate.

THE WELL-STOCKED KITCHEN
ESSENTIAL FLAVOURINGS

• <u>Sauces:</u> soy, oyster, hoisin, black bean and garlic, ketchup, salsa, Worcestershire, barbecue and hot pepper

• <u>Pastes and butters:</u> Indian curry paste (mild or hot), Thai red curry paste, anchovy paste, tahini and nut butters (peanut, almond and others)

• <u>Mustards:</u> Dijon, Russian, honey and grainy

• <u>Prepared horseradish</u>

Kale and Chickpea Soup

Hearty and satisfying, this is a first-rate dinnertime soup. Serve with whole grain rolls or baguette.

2 tbsp	extra-virgin olive oil	25 mL
1	onion, chopped	1
2	cloves garlic, minced	2
½ tsp	each salt and pepper	2 mL
¼ tsp	crumbled dried sage	1 mL
3 cups	sodium-reduced chicken stock	750 mL
2 cups	cubed peeled sweet potato (1 large)	500 mL
1½ cups	cubed Black Forest ham (about 6 oz/175 g)	375 mL
1	sweet red pepper, chopped	1
1	can (19 oz/540 mL) chickpeas, drained and rinsed	1
3 cups	chopped kale	750 mL

> In large saucepan, heat oil over medium heat; fry onion, garlic, salt, pepper and sage, stirring occasionally, until onion is softened, about 5 minutes.

> Add stock, 3 cups (750 mL) water, sweet potato, ham, red pepper and chickpeas; bring to boil. Reduce heat, cover and simmer until potatoes are tender, about 15 minutes.

> Add kale; simmer until tender, about 5 minutes. *(Make-ahead: Let cool for 30 minutes; refrigerate until cold. Refrigerate in airtight container for up to 3 days.)*

Makes 6 servings. PER SERVING: about 260 cal, 14 g pro, 8 g total fat (1 g sat. fat), 34 g carb, 5 g fibre, 14 mg chol, 830 mg sodium. % RDI: 8% calcium, 17% iron, 110% vit A, 130% vit C, 30% folate.

VARIATION

Spinach and Chickpea Soup
● Substitute spinach for kale; cook until wilted, about 1 minute.

Grilled Rosemary Garlic Flank Steak with Potatoes and Carrots

The one pot this time is the barbecue. Nothing could be simpler.

¼ cup	vegetable oil	50 mL
2 tbsp	balsamic or wine vinegar	25 mL
1 tbsp	chopped fresh rosemary (or ¾ tsp / 4 mL crumbled dried)	15 mL
2 tsp	Dijon mustard	10 mL
2	cloves garlic, minced	2
1 tsp	packed brown sugar	5 mL
1 tsp	each salt and pepper	5 mL
1	flank steak (about 1½ lb/750 g)	1
4	potatoes (about 1 lb/500 g), peeled	4
4	carrots	4

❯ In shallow glass dish, whisk together oil, vinegar, rosemary, mustard, garlic, brown sugar, salt and pepper; remove half and set aside. Add steak to remaining marinade in dish; turn to coat. Let stand for 10 minutes. *(Make-ahead: Cover and refrigerate for up to 12 hours.)*

❯ Meanwhile, cut potatoes into ¼-inch (5 mm) thick rounds. Cut carrots diagonally into ½-inch (1 cm) thick slices. In microwaveable bowl, combine potatoes, carrots and ⅓ cup (75 mL) hot water; cover and microwave at high until tender-crisp, about 5 minutes. Drain. Add reserved marinade; toss together.

❯ Arrange steak, potatoes and carrots on greased grill over medium-high heat; close lid and grill, turning once, until steak is medium-rare and vegetables are tender and grill-marked, about 12 minutes.

❯ Transfer steak to cutting board; tent with foil and let stand for 5 minutes. Transfer potatoes and carrots to plates; keep warm. Thinly slice steak across the grain; serve with potatoes and carrots.

Makes 4 servings. PER SERVING: about 497 cal, 42 g pro, 24 g total fat (6 g sat. fat), 28 g carb, 4 g fibre, 69 mg chol, 593 mg sodium. % RDI: 4% calcium, 28% iron, 182% vit A, 27% vit C, 14% folate.

CHAPTER 5

Make It Tonight...
from the Pantry

Artichoke Chicken Flatbread

The cooked chicken called for in this recipe could be leftovers from the night before, the remains of a rotisserie chicken from the supermarket or a 284-gram tin of seasoned chicken chunks.

1	jar (370 mL) roasted red peppers, drained	1
2	cloves garlic, smashed	2
2 tbsp	extra-virgin olive oil	25 mL
½ tsp	salt	2 mL
1	thin-crust 12-inch (30 cm) flatbread or pizza crust	1
1 cup	shredded mozzarella cheese or crumbled goat cheese	250 mL
1¾ cups	sliced cooked chicken	425 mL
Half	red onion, thinly sliced	Half
1	jar (6 oz/170 mL) marinated artichoke hearts	1
¼ cup	sliced black olives (optional)	50 mL
½ tsp	dried oregano	2 mL

> In food processor, purée together roasted red peppers, smashed garlic, olive oil and salt; spread evenly over flatbread.

> Sprinkle with half of the cheese. Scatter chicken, onion, artichokes, olives (if using) and oregano over top; sprinkle with remaining cheese.

> Bake in bottom third of 500°F (260°C) oven until golden and bubbly, 15 minutes. (Or bake according to flatbread manufacturer's instructions.)

Makes 4 servings. PER SERVING: about 486 cal, 31 g pro, 23 g total fat (7 g sat. fat), 39 g carb, 4 g fibre, 80 mg chol, 947 mg sodium. % RDI: 19% calcium, 22% iron, 27% vit A, 162% vit C, 16% folate.

Tex-Mex Tomato Rice Soup

Garnish this kid-friendly soup with shredded Cheddar cheese and sour cream. Serve with warmed wheat or corn tortillas.

2 tbsp	vegetable oil	25 mL
1	onion, chopped	1
2	cloves garlic, minced	2
1	fresh or pickled jalapeño pepper, seeded and minced	1
½ tsp	each salt, pepper and ground cumin	2 mL
¼ tsp	chili powder	1 mL
2	carrots, chopped	2
¼ cup	long-grain rice	50 mL
1	can (28 oz/796 mL) diced tomatoes	1
¼ cup	minced fresh coriander (optional)	50 mL
1 tbsp	lime juice	15 mL

> In large saucepan, heat oil over medium heat; fry onion, garlic, jalapeño, salt, pepper, cumin and chili powder, stirring occasionally, until onion is softened, about 5 minutes.

> Add carrots, rice, tomatoes and 4 cups (1 L) water; bring to boil. Reduce heat and simmer until rice and carrots are tender, about 20 minutes. *(Make-ahead: Let cool for 30 minutes; refrigerate until cold. Refrigerate in airtight container for up to 3 days.)* Add coriander (if using) and lime juice.

Makes 6 servings. PER SERVING: about 116 cal, 2 g pro, 5 g total fat (trace sat. fat), 17 g carb, 2 g fibre, 0 mg chol, 409 mg sodium. % RDI: 5% calcium, 9% iron, 70% vit A, 40% vit C, 7% folate.

Salmon Wraps

It takes just 10 minutes to put these fresh-tasting wraps together.

¼ cup	minced fresh mint (or ½ tsp/2 mL dried)	50 mL
¼ cup	light mayonnaise	50 mL
1 tbsp	lime or lemon juice	15 mL
1 tsp	minced gingerroot (or ¾ tsp/4 mL ground ginger)	5 mL
1	green onion, minced	1
¼ tsp	each salt and pepper	1 mL
2	cans (each 7½ oz/213 g) sockeye salmon, drained	2
4	large whole wheat tortillas	4
2 cups	shredded lettuce	500 mL

➤ In bowl, stir together mint, mayonnaise, lime juice, ginger, green onion, salt and pepper. Add salmon; mash to combine.

➤ Place tortillas on work surface; top with lettuce. Spoon one-quarter of the salmon mixture onto centre of each tortilla. Fold in sides and roll up from bottom; cut in half, if desired.

Makes 4 servings. PER SERVING: about 352 cal, 27 g pro, 12 g total fat (2 g sat. fat), 44 g carb, 5 g fibre, 43 mg chol, 913 mg sodium. % RDI: 21% calcium, 22% iron, 7% vit A, 5% vit C, 21% folate.

TIME-SAVING TIPS

● Plan a week's worth of menus at one time. Try two weeks if that suits you better.

● Make a shopping list from your menus and organize it according to the store's layout (produce, dairy, meat – you get the picture). This cuts back on missed items and return visits to the supermarket.

● Shop when the store is not busy and stick with the supermarket you like so you're not constantly looking for items in a new layout.

● Grocery shop online. It's a great time saver, especially for items you regularly purchase.

● Make at least one meal a week that creates leftovers. Reheat them or get creative: roasted chicken one night, then chicken pizza the next.

● Double and freeze your favourite dishes. Don't forget to label them with name, date and reheating instructions – otherwise, you'll be facing a freezer full of UFOs (unidentified frozen objects).

● Try prepared items in the produce department. More and more come peeled (pineapple), destalked (broccoli), premixed (salad greens) and cubed (squash).

● Don't freeze out frozen vegetables and fruit. They are just as nutritious as fresh, and you'll save a bundle of time not having to scrape the kernels off the cob, trim the beans or broccoli, or shell the peas.

● Wash greens and herbs as soon as you get home (see How to Wash and Store Greens, Herbs and Vegetables, page 193).

● Organize the week's food in a way that other family members find easy to understand. That means no excuses for not taking their turn with the cooking or prep.

Soy-Braised Tofu

A well-stocked Asian pantry and fridge set you up for a dish that's faster to the table than takeout or delivery. To make it even easier, buy minced ginger and garlic in jars and keep them at the ready in the fridge.

2 tbsp	cornstarch	25 mL
2 tbsp	sodium-reduced soy sauce	25 mL
2 tbsp	black bean garlic sauce	25 mL
2 tbsp	oyster or hoisin sauce	25 mL
¼ tsp	hot pepper sauce	1 mL
1 tbsp	vegetable oil	15 mL
2	carrots, diced	2
6	green onions (green and white parts separated), sliced	6
3	cloves garlic, minced	3
1 tbsp	minced gingerroot	15 mL
⅛ tsp	each ground cloves and pepper	0.5 mL
1	pkg (12 oz/340 g) precooked ground soy protein mixture	1
1	pkg (454 g) medium-firm tofu, drained and cut into ¾-inch (2 cm) cubes	1
1	can (10 oz/300 g) sliced mushrooms, drained	1
¾ cup	frozen peas or cut green beans	175 mL

❯ In small bowl, whisk together cornstarch, soy sauce, black bean sauce, oyster sauce and hot pepper sauce; set aside.

❯ In wok, heat oil over medium-high heat; stir-fry carrots, white parts of green onions, garlic, ginger, cloves and pepper until vegetables are tender, about 6 minutes. Add soy protein; heat through, about 1 minute.

❯ Stir in cornstarch mixture and 1¾ cups (425 mL) water; bring to boil. Add tofu and mushrooms; cover and cook over low heat until thickened, about 10 minutes.

❯ Stir in peas and green parts of green onions; cook for 1 minute.

Makes 4 servings. PER SERVING: about 289 cal, 27 g pro, 8 g total fat (1 g sat. fat), 28 g carb, 10 g fibre, 0 mg chol, 1,280 mg sodium. % RDI: 21% calcium, 49% iron, 71% vit A, 13% vit C, 40% folate.

Tortellini Casserole

Even a baked casserole is possible if you stock your fridge or freezer with a package or two of cheese- or meat-filled tortellini.

12 oz	fresh or frozen cheese or meat tortellini	375 g
1 tbsp	butter	15 mL
¼ cup	all-purpose flour	50 mL
3 cups	1% milk, warmed	750 mL
1 cup	grated Parmesan cheese	250 mL
¼ tsp	each salt and pepper	1 mL
Pinch	ground nutmeg	Pinch
½ cup	fresh bread crumbs (or ⅓ cup/75 mL dry bread crumbs)	125 mL
¼ cup	chopped fresh parsley	50 mL

❯ In pot of boiling salted water, cook tortellini until tender, about 8 minutes; drain.

❯ Meanwhile, in saucepan, melt butter over medium heat; stir in flour and cook, stirring, until light golden, about 1 minute. Gradually whisk in milk; simmer, stirring constantly, just until thick enough to coat back of spoon, about 7 minutes.

❯ Stir in ¾ cup (175 mL) of the Parmesan cheese, salt, pepper and nutmeg. Stir in tortellini. Scrape into 8-inch (2 L) square glass baking dish.

❯ In small bowl, mix together bread crumbs, parsley and remaining cheese; sprinkle over tortellini mixture. Bake in 400°F (200°C) oven until bubbly and browned, about 10 minutes.

Makes 4 servings. PER SERVING: about 504 cal, 29 g pro, 18 g total fat (10 g sat. fat), 56 g carb, 2 g fibre, 91 mg chol, 1,249 mg sodium. % RDI: 64% calcium, 17% iron, 22% vit A, 8% vit C, 19% folate.

Spinach Salad

¼ cup	coarsely chopped roasted red peppers	50 mL
2 tbsp	each extra-virgin olive oil and wine vinegar	25 mL
¼ tsp	each salt and pepper	1 mL
4 cups	baby spinach	1 L
1 cup	sliced mushrooms	250 mL

❯ In large bowl, whisk together red peppers, oil, vinegar, salt and pepper. Add spinach and mushrooms; toss to coat.

Makes 4 servings. PER SERVING: about 75 cal, 2 g pro, 7 g total fat (1 g sat. fat), 3 g carb, 1 g fibre, 0 mg chol, 195 mg sodium. % RDI: 3% calcium, 8% iron, 33% vit A, 48% vit C, 29% folate.

MAKE-YOUR-OWN HERB BLENDS

Add personality to stuffings, vinaigrettes, soups, dips, burgers, meat loaf, pizzas and sauces with these blends. Mix them with vegetable or olive oil and rub into chops, roasts or steaks. Note: Use dried herb leaves, not powdered herbs. Store in airtight jars in a cool, dark drawer for up to 3 months.

HERBES DE PROVENCE

● Mix together ¼ cup (50 mL) each dried oregano, thyme and savory; 1 tsp (5 mL) each basil and rosemary; and ½ tsp (2 mL) sage. **Makes about ¾ cup (175 mL).**

POULTRY SEASONING

● Mix together ¼ cup (50 mL) each dried sage, thyme and oregano. **Makes about ¾ cup (175 mL).**

ITALIAN HERB SEASONING

● Mix together 2 tbsp (25 mL) each dried basil, thyme, marjoram, oregano, sage and rosemary. **Makes about ¾ cup (175 mL).**

Sun-Dried Tomato and White Bean Risotto

While short-grain rice is essential for risotto, the beans are changeable. So if your cupboard contains kidney beans or chickpeas instead of white beans, don't be afraid to use them.

1 tbsp	extra-virgin olive oil	15 mL
1	onion, chopped	1
2	cloves garlic, minced	2
1 tsp	dried Italian herb seasoning	5 mL
¼ tsp	pepper	1 mL
1 cup	arborio or other short-grain rice	250 mL
2½ cups	hot vegetable stock	625 mL
1	can (19 oz/540 mL) navy (white pea) beans, drained and rinsed	1
½ cup	chopped drained oil-packed sun-dried tomatoes	125 mL
½ cup	grated Parmesan cheese	125 mL

❯ In large saucepan, heat oil over medium heat; fry onion, garlic, Italian herb seasoning and pepper, stirring occasionally, until softened, about 3 minutes.

❯ Add rice, stirring to coat. Add stock and bring to boil. Reduce heat to low; cover and simmer, stirring once, for 10 minutes. Stir vigorously for 15 seconds. Simmer, covered, for 5 minutes.

❯ Stir in beans; simmer, covered, until rice is creamy and slightly firm to the bite, about 2 minutes.

❯ Stir in sun-dried tomatoes and Parmesan cheese.

Makes 4 servings. PER SERVING: about 490 cal, 20 g pro, 10 g total fat (3 g sat. fat), 81 g carb, 10 g fibre, 11 mg chol, 1,184 mg sodium. % RDI: 21% calcium, 26% iron, 7% vit A, 25% vit C, 32% folate.

VARIATION
Sun-Dried Tomato and Two-Bean Risotto
● Add ½ cup (125 mL) chopped green beans along with the navy beans.

Red Pepper Pasta

A pasta shape such as radiatore or rotini is best because it will hold every last bit of this robust sauce. Sprinkle each serving with a little freshly grated hard cheese such as Parmesan, grana Padano, pecorino or Asiago.

2 tbsp	extra-virgin olive oil	25 mL
4	cloves garlic, minced	4
1	small onion, finely chopped	1
1	jar (313 mL) roasted red peppers	1
1	can (19 oz/540 mL) tomatoes	1
2 tsp	crumbled dried basil or mint	10 mL
½ tsp	each salt and pepper	2 mL
5 cups	radiatore or rotini (1 lb/500 g)	1.25 L

❯ In large skillet, heat oil over medium heat; fry garlic and onion, stirring occasionally, until softened, about 3 minutes.

❯ Reserving liquid, drain peppers. In food processor or blender, purée peppers with tomatoes until almost smooth.

❯ Add pepper mixture to pan along with basil, salt and pepper; bring to boil. Reduce heat and simmer, stirring often, until thick enough to mound on spoon, about 10 minutes.

❯ Meanwhile, in large pot of boiling salted water, cook pasta until tender but firm, about 8 minutes. Drain and return to pot. Add sauce and toss, adding some of the reserved pepper liquid, if desired.

Makes 4 servings. PER SERVING: about 532 cal, 16 g pro, 9 g total fat (1 g sat. fat), 97 g carb, 8 g fibre, 0 mg chol, 891 mg sodium. % RDI: 8% calcium, 44% iron, 22% vit A, 188% vit C, 114% folate.

THE WELL-STOCKED KITCHEN
ESSENTIAL PANTRY STAPLES

• Legumes: beans, lentils and chickpeas (always drain and rinse before using)

• Sodium-reduced stocks: chicken, beef and vegetable

• Tomatoes: whole, diced and stewed (try healthy no-salt-added varieties)

• Tomato paste: freeze any extra in ice-cube trays; wrap cubes separately and bag

• Pasta sauce: tomato-based (freeze leftovers in handy amounts; for example, 2 cups/500 mL for a pizza) and pesto

• Antipasti: roasted peppers and artichoke hearts (plain or marinated)

• Meat and fish: salmon, tuna, sardines, anchovies, clams, and chicken and turkey chunks

• Milks: dairy (evaporated, dried or ultra-high temperature – UHT – pasteurized) and nondairy (soy, rice and coconut milk)

• Veggies: baby beets and corn

• Oils: canola and extra-virgin olive

• Vinegars: red or white wine, balsamic, cider and rice

• Sun-dried tomatoes: packed in oil (use the oil in dressings or marinades) and made into pesto; dried are OK if they're pliable and softened in hot water for 20 minutes before using

Fettuccine with Green Olives, Capers and Parsley

A few pantry staples and just 10 minutes of cooking give you this stellar pasta dish.

10 oz	fettuccine or spaghetti	300 g
2 tbsp	extra-virgin olive oil	25 mL
2	cloves garlic, thinly sliced	2
¼ tsp	hot pepper flakes	1 mL
1 cup	sliced pitted green olives	250 mL
⅓ cup	chopped fresh parsley	75 mL
2 tbsp	capers, drained, rinsed and coarsely chopped	25 mL
1 tsp	grated orange rind	5 mL
1 tbsp	orange juice	15 mL
1 tsp	anchovy paste (optional)	5 mL

TIP
● If you're avoiding gluten in your diet, it's easy to substitute gluten-free alternatives to regular wheat-flour pasta in your favourite dishes. For this recipe, try brown rice fettuccine or white or brown rice spaghetti.

❯ In large pot of boiling salted water, cook pasta until tender but firm, about 8 minutes. Reserving ½ cup (125 mL) of the cooking liquid, drain and return to pot.

❯ Meanwhile, in large skillet, heat oil over medium heat; fry garlic and hot pepper flakes until fragrant, about 1 minute.

❯ Add olives, half of the parsley, the capers, orange rind and juice, and anchovy paste (if using); cook, stirring, until heated through, about 2 minutes. Add to pasta and toss to coat, adding enough of the reserved cooking liquid to moisten, if necessary. Stir in remaining parsley.

Makes 4 servings. PER SERVING: about 378 cal, 10 g pro, 13 g total fat (2 g sat. fat), 56 g carb, 5 g fibre, 0 mg chol, 834 mg sodium. % RDI: 4% calcium, 23% iron, 6% vit A, 13% vit C, 70% folate.

Whole Wheat Pasta with Peppers, Tomatoes and Olives

Pantry ingredients plus fresh sweet peppers add up to a colourful must-have dish for bustling weeknights. Serve with Parmesan cheese to sprinkle over top.

2 tbsp	extra-virgin olive oil	25 mL
3	sweet red or yellow peppers (or a combination), thinly sliced	3
1	small onion, thinly sliced	1
2	cloves garlic, minced	2
1 tsp	dried thyme	5 mL
¼ tsp	each salt and pepper	1 mL
Pinch	hot pepper flakes	Pinch
2	canned or fresh plum tomatoes, diced	2
¼ cup	oil-cured black olives, halved and pitted	50 mL
2 tbsp	cider vinegar or wine vinegar	25 mL
8 oz	whole wheat spaghettini	250 g
¼ cup	chopped fresh parsley	50 mL

❯ In large skillet, heat oil over medium heat; fry peppers, onion, garlic, thyme, salt, pepper and hot pepper flakes, stirring often, until very tender, about 18 minutes.

❯ Add tomatoes, olives and vinegar; cook, stirring, until heated through, about 1 minute.

❯ Meanwhile, in large pot of boiling salted water, cook pasta until tender but firm, about 8 minutes. Reserving ½ cup (125 mL) of the cooking liquid, drain and return to pot. Add pepper mixture and parsley; toss to coat, adding enough of the reserved cooking water to moisten, if necessary.

Makes 4 servings. PER SERVING: about 328 cal, 10 g pro, 11 g total fat (2 g sat. fat), 53 g carb, 7 g fibre, 0 mg chol, 638 mg sodium. % RDI: 5% calcium, 20% iron, 18% vit A, 242% vit C, 16% folate.

PERFECT PASTA

• It's important to have enough boiling water in the pot that it circulates freely around the pasta. For 1 lb (500 g) pasta, bring 20 cups (5 L) water to boil in large pot, covered. Add 2 tbsp (25 mL) salt, letting it dissolve for about 2 minutes. Add pasta; stir gently with wooden spoon. Boil until tender but firm (al dente). Drain; return to pot and add the sauce; heat through if necessary.

TIP
For 12 oz (375 g) pasta, reduce water to 16 cups (4 L) and salt to 4 tsp (20 mL).

No-Fail Cheddar Soufflé

Soufflés look hard, but looks can be deceiving. They're one of the easiest pantry suppers ever.

¼ cup	butter	50 mL
2 tbsp	grated Parmesan cheese	25 mL
⅓ cup	all-purpose flour	75 mL
½ tsp	salt	2 mL
¼ tsp	cayenne pepper	1 mL
1½ cups	milk	375 mL
6	egg yolks	6
1½ cups	shredded old Cheddar cheese	375 mL
2 tbsp	chopped green onions	25 mL
8	egg whites	8
¼ tsp	cream of tartar (optional)	1 mL

❯ Grease 8- x 3¾-inch (2.5 L) soufflé dish with 1 tsp (5 mL) of the butter; sprinkle evenly with Parmesan cheese. Set aside.

❯ In saucepan, melt remaining butter over medium heat. Stir in flour, salt and cayenne pepper; cook, stirring, for 2 minutes. Whisk in milk in 3 additions; cook, whisking, until as thick as paste, about 4 minutes. Remove from heat; whisk in egg yolks, Cheddar cheese and green onions. Transfer to large bowl; let cool for 10 minutes.

❯ In separate large bowl, beat egg whites with cream of tartar (if using) until stiff peaks form. Fold one-third into cheese mixture; fold in remaining whites. Scrape into prepared dish. Bake on baking sheet in centre of 375°F (190°C) oven until puffed and golden, about 55 minutes. Serve immediately.

Makes 4 servings. PER SERVING: about 494 cal, 27 g pro, 37 g total fat (20 g sat. fat), 14 g carb, trace fibre, 395 mg chol, 885 mg sodium. % RDI: 46% calcium, 13% iron, 42% vit A, 2% vit C, 30% folate.

Spaghetti with Tuna and Tomatoes

Canned tuna gets a dash of Italian flair in a simple homemade spaghetti sauce.

1 tbsp	extra-virgin olive oil	15 mL
1	onion, chopped	1
2	cloves garlic, minced	2
1 tsp	dried oregano	5 mL
½ tsp	pepper	2 mL
1	can (28 oz/796 mL) tomatoes	1
2 tbsp	tomato paste	25 mL
½ tsp	grated lemon rind	2 mL
2	cans (each 170 g) solid white or chunk light tuna, drained	2
⅓ cup	oil-cured black olives, pitted and quartered (approx)	75 mL
12 oz	spaghetti	375 g
¼ cup	chopped fresh parsley	50 mL
¼ tsp	hot pepper flakes (optional)	1 mL

❯ In large skillet, heat oil over medium heat; fry onion, garlic, oregano and pepper, stirring occasionally, until onion is softened, about 3 minutes.

❯ Mash in tomatoes, tomato paste and rind. Reduce heat; simmer until thickened, 14 minutes. With fork, break tuna into chunks; add to sauce along with olives. Heat through, about 2 minutes.

❯ Meanwhile, in large pot of boiling salted water, cook spaghetti until tender but firm, about 8 minutes; drain and return to pot. Add sauce and parsley; toss to coat. Sprinkle with hot pepper flakes (if using) and more olives (if desired).

Makes 4 servings. PER SERVING: about 529 cal, 30 g pro, 11 g total fat (2 g sat. fat), 78 g carb, 7 g fibre, 28 mg chol, 1,085 mg sodium. % RDI: 10% calcium, 41% iron, 16% vit A, 63% vit C, 89% folate.

Garlic Bread Crumb Pasta

Here's the perfect dish for leftover baguette.

8 oz	spaghetti	250 g
1	piece (6 inches/15 cm) baguette, cubed	1
¼ cup	extra-virgin olive oil	50 mL
3	cloves garlic, minced	3
¼ cup	chopped drained capers	50 mL
¼ cup	chopped fresh parsley	50 mL
2 tbsp	lemon juice	25 mL
½ cup	grated Parmesan cheese	125 mL

❯ In large pot of boiling salted water, cook spaghetti until tender but firm, about 8 minutes. Reserving ½ cup (125 mL) of the cooking liquid, drain and return to pot.

❯ Meanwhile, in food processor, chop baguette until in pea-size pieces; set aside.

❯ In skillet, heat oil over medium heat; fry crumbs and garlic until garlic is golden, about 4 minutes. Stir in capers, parsley and lemon juice. Add to pasta along with reserved cooking liquid; heat through. Sprinkle with cheese.

Makes 4 servings. PER SERVING: about 456 cal, 15 g pro, 19 g total fat (4 g sat. fat), 57 g carb, 4 g fibre, 11 mg chol, 788 mg sodium. % RDI: 16% calcium, 24% iron, 5% vit A, 10% vit C, 64% folate.

CHAPTER 6

Make It Tonight...
in the Toaster Oven

Sun-Dried Tomato Meat Loaf

A classic favourite gets updated with shiitake mushrooms and sun-dried tomatoes. Leftovers make great sandwiches.

1 tbsp	vegetable oil	15 mL
1½ cups	thinly sliced shiitake mushroom caps or white mushrooms	375 mL
½ cup	minced onion	125 mL
1	stalk celery, finely chopped	1
2	cloves garlic, minced	2
2 tbsp	balsamic or wine vinegar	25 mL
1	egg	1
½ cup	dry bread crumbs	125 mL
⅓ cup	chopped drained oil-packed sun-dried tomatoes	75 mL
½ tsp	dried thyme	2 mL
¼ tsp	each salt and pepper	1 mL
1 lb	lean ground pork or beef	500 g
TOPPING:		
3 tbsp	chili sauce or ketchup	50 mL
1 tbsp	Dijon mustard	15 mL
¼ tsp	dried thyme	1 mL

❯ In skillet, heat oil over medium-high heat; fry mushrooms, onion, celery and garlic, stirring occasionally, until softened, about 5 minutes. Stir in vinegar; cook until evaporated, about 30 seconds. Let cool slightly.

❯ Meanwhile, in large bowl and using fork, beat egg; blend in bread crumbs, tomatoes, thyme, salt and pepper. Mix in mushroom mixture and pork. Pack into 8- x 4-inch (1.5 L) loaf pan, mounding top.

❯ TOPPING: In small bowl, combine chili sauce, mustard and thyme; spread over loaf. *(Make-ahead: Cover and refrigerate for up to 12 hours.)*

❯ Bake in 350°F (180°C) toaster oven or oven until meat thermometer registers 170°F (75°C), 45 to 50 minutes. Let stand for 5 minutes. Drain off fat.

Makes 4 servings. PER SERVING: about 382 cal, 26 g pro, 21 g total fat (6 g sat. fat), 21 g carb, 3 g fibre, 116 mg chol, 592 mg sodium. % RDI: 7% calcium, 22% iron, 4% vit A, 23% vit C, 15% folate.

EASY BOILED OR MASHED POTATOES

• Count on 1 potato per person and an extra for the pan. Peel, if desired, or scrub and trim; cut into quarters. Place in saucepan; cover with boiling water and add 1 tsp (5 mL) salt. Cover and bring to boil. Reduce heat and simmer until fork-tender, about 15 minutes. Drain and return to pan; dry briefly over low heat.

SERVING SUGGESTIONS

Serve as is with a drizzle of olive oil or melted butter and a good grate of pepper. Or, for 4 large potatoes (about 2 lb/1 kg), mash or smash until creamy, adding 1 tbsp (15 mL) butter and up to 1 cup (250 mL) hot milk or cold buttermilk. Season with salt and pepper.

Baked Curried Chicken

You can also use bone-in chicken breasts or legs; increase baking time to 45 minutes.

⅓ cup	2% plain yogurt	75 mL
3 tbsp	liquid honey	50 mL
2 tbsp	mild or medium curry paste	25 mL
2 tbsp	soy sauce	25 mL
1 tbsp	vegetable oil	15 mL
2 tsp	Dijon mustard	10 mL
¼ tsp	pepper	1 mL
4	boneless skinless chicken breasts	4

➤ In large bowl, whisk together yogurt, honey, curry paste, soy sauce, oil, mustard and pepper. Add chicken and turn to coat all over. Scrape into toaster oven pan or 11- x 7-inch (2 L) glass baking dish.

➤ Bake in 375°F (190°C) toaster oven or oven, basting occasionally, until sauce is thickened and chicken is browned and no longer pink inside, about 30 minutes.

Makes 4 servings. PER SERVING: about 288 cal, 32 g pro, 10 g total fat (1 g sat. fat), 16 g carb, 1 g fibre, 79 mg chol, 846 mg sodium. % RDI: 4% calcium, 6% iron, 1% vit A, 3% vit C, 3% folate.

Green Beans with Almonds

1 lb	green beans, trimmed	500 g
1 tbsp	butter	15 mL
2 tbsp	slivered almonds	25 mL
1 tbsp	lemon juice	15 mL

➤ In large saucepan of boiling salted water, cook beans until tender-crisp, about 7 minutes. Drain well.

➤ Meanwhile, in skillet, melt butter over medium heat; fry almonds until light brown, about 3 minutes. Add lemon juice and beans; toss to coat.

Makes 4 servings. PER SERVING: about 87 cal, 3 g pro, 5 g total fat (2 g sat. fat), 9 g carb, 4 g fibre, 9 mg chol, 273 mg sodium. % RDI: 5% calcium, 6% iron, 10% vit A, 18% vit C, 16% folate.

Broiled Cumin Chicken with Zucchini and Carrot Salad

This recipe is loosely based on one chicken breast per person. However, one chicken breast is often more than a 4-oz (125 g) serving. If you get only two or three breasts to a pound (500 g), just slice the chicken after cooking and divide it into four portions.

1 tbsp	lemon juice	15 mL
2 tsp	vegetable oil	10 mL
1 tsp	ground cumin	5 mL
1 tsp	chili powder	5 mL
½ tsp	salt	2 mL
¼ tsp	pepper	1 mL
1 lb	boneless skinless chicken breasts	500 g
1½ cups	each shredded zucchini and carrots (2 each)	375 mL
1	green onion, finely chopped	1

❯ In small bowl, mix 1 tsp (5 mL) each of the lemon juice and oil; stir in cumin, chili powder and half each of the salt and pepper to form thin paste.

❯ Place chicken on greased toaster oven or oven broiler pan; brush with half of the paste. Turn and brush with remaining paste. Broil, turning once, until burnished brown outside and no longer pink inside, about 12 minutes. Transfer to cutting board and tent with foil; let stand for 10 minutes before slicing.

❯ In large bowl, combine remaining lemon juice, oil, salt and pepper. Add zucchini, carrots and green onion; toss to coat. Mound on plates; top with chicken.

Makes 4 servings. PER SERVING: about 175 cal, 27 g pro, 4 g total fat (1 g sat. fat), 7 g carb, 2 g fibre, 67 mg chol, 369 mg sodium. % RDI: 3% calcium, 10% iron, 120% vit A, 17% vit C, 10% folate.

EQUIPMENT
TOASTER OVEN 101

CAPACITY
As well as the usual toast capacity, large models can cook a chicken or 12-inch (30 cm) pizza. The larger the unit, the more room it will occupy, so choose the size that suits your needs and space.

SETTINGS
Most ovens bake, toast and keep food warm, but some don't broil. Often newer models are convection, which circulates heat for even temperature and fast results.

TIMER
Some models turn off automatically when the timer bell sounds.

TRAYS AND PANS
Most ovens come with trays and pans, but additional toaster-oven-size pans are available in houseware stores.

RACKS
Adjustable, multiposition and reversible racks accommodate everything from roasts to cookies. Some models have an auto-advance feature, which means that the rack slides out when the door opens.

COOL TOUCH
Many models have the safety feature of insulated walls so handles and exterior surfaces stay cool.

Penne Vegetable Bake

Individual baking dishes are just right for a meal for two. Double the recipe for four, with the option of making the casserole in an 8-inch (2 L) square glass baking dish.

1 cup	penne	250 mL
2 tsp	extra-virgin olive oil	10 mL
1	small onion, chopped	1
1 cup	chopped carrot	250 mL
1 cup	cauliflower florets	250 mL
¼ tsp	each salt and pepper	1 mL
3 tbsp	prepared pesto	50 mL
1	egg	1
1	tub (250 g) 2% cottage cheese	1
1	plum tomato, sliced	1
2 tbsp	grated Parmesan cheese	25 mL

> In pot of boiling salted water, cook pasta until tender but firm, about 10 minutes. Drain; set aside.

> In same pot, heat oil over medium heat; fry onion, carrot, cauliflower, salt and pepper, stirring occasionally, until vegetables are tender-crisp, about 5 minutes. Add pasta and pesto; toss to coat.

> In bowl, whisk egg with cottage cheese; stir into pasta mixture and toss to coat. Divide between two 2-cup (500 mL) baking dishes; press gently. Arrange tomato over top; sprinkle with cheese. Bake in 375°F (190°C) toaster oven or oven until golden and bubbly, about 30 minutes.

Makes 2 servings. PER SERVING: about 512 cal, 31 g pro, 22 g total fat (7 g sat. fat), 49 g carb, 6 g fibre, 117 mg chol, 1,296 mg sodium. % RDI: 26% calcium, 24% iron, 151% vit A, 53% vit C, 68% folate.

THE WELL-STOCKED KITCHEN
ESSENTIAL GRAINS

- Rice: parboiled long grain (white and whole grain), basmati and short grain (arborio or other kinds)

- Cornmeal: medium and coarse

- Couscous: regular and whole wheat

- Pasta: short (macaroni, fusilli, rigatoni and penne) and long (spaghetti, linguine and fettuccine) – try whole wheat for a nutritional boost

- Bread products: croutons, dry bread crumbs and crackers

Roasted Lemon Rosemary Cornish Hens

Cornish hens make the basis of a simple yet elegant dinner for two.

2 tsp	chopped fresh rosemary (or ½ tsp/2 mL dried)	10 mL
1 tsp	finely grated lemon rind	5 mL
¼ tsp	each salt and pepper	1 mL
2	small Cornish hens (about 1 lb/500 g each)	2
Half	lemon, cut into 4 wedges	Half
2 tbsp	butter, melted	25 mL

> In small bowl, mix together rosemary, lemon rind, salt and pepper; set aside.

> Remove giblets from hens (save for another use). Using fingers, gently loosen skin over breasts to create pockets; spread rosemary mixture under skin to cover breasts. Insert 2 lemon wedges into each cavity. Tuck wings under back; tie legs together with kitchen string, if desired. Brush hens with butter. *(Make-ahead: Cover and refrigerate for up to 24 hours; add 5 minutes to roasting time.)*

> Place hens, breast side up, on greased toaster oven broiler pan or small roasting pan. Roast in 400°F (200°C) toaster oven or oven until juices run clear when thigh is pierced, 55 to 60 minutes. Cover loosely with foil if browning too much. Transfer to serving platter. Tent with foil; let stand for 10 minutes. Cut in half or quarters with kitchen shears.

Makes 2 servings. PER SERVING: about 321 cal, 38 g pro, 18 g total fat (9 g sat. fat), trace carb, trace fibre, 208 mg chol, 507 mg sodium. % RDI: 3% calcium, 10% iron, 14% vit A, 3% vit C, 2% folate.

COOKING FOR TWO

THERE ARE TWO SCHOOLS OF THOUGHT:

1. Make family-size amounts. **Enjoy a portion or two, then divide and freeze what's left in one- or two-serving amounts. This works well for saucy dishes, marinating meat or chicken, or burgers.**

2. Make just enough for one or two. **If you shop for one or two, this already sets the limit for amounts. Keep leftovers at bay by cooking in smaller saucepans, skillets and roasting pans and using smaller appliances (a toaster oven instead of a regular oven) or smaller versions of appliances (such as a slow cooker).**

Lemon Dill Trout

Other mild fish, such as catfish or tilapia, are also excellent for this dish.

1 tbsp	extra-virgin olive oil	15 mL
1	shallot, minced (or 2 tbsp/25 mL minced onion)	1
1 tbsp	minced fresh dill (or 1 tsp/5 mL dried dillweed)	15 mL
1 tsp	finely grated lemon rind	5 mL
2 tsp	lemon juice	10 mL
1 tsp	chopped drained capers (optional)	5 mL
Pinch	each salt and pepper	Pinch
2	rainbow trout fillets (about 12 oz/375 g total)	2

> In small bowl, combine oil, shallot, dill, lemon rind and juice, capers (if using), salt and pepper.

> Arrange fish, skin side down, on greased toaster oven or oven broiler pan; brush with lemon mixture. Broil, watching closely, until fish is golden and flakes easily when tested, about 10 minutes.

Makes 2 servings. PER SERVING: about 263 cal, 29 g pro, 15 g total fat (3 g sat. fat), 1 g carb, trace fibre, 80 mg chol, 50 mg sodium. % RDI: 10% calcium, 4% iron, 11% vit A, 13% vit C, 14% folate.

BROCCOLI BASICS

• Serve the fish with nutritious broccoli. Trim and peel stalks; in saucepan, cover and cook broccoli in about 1 inch (2.5 cm) of boiling water for 4 minutes or steam for 7 minutes or until vivid green and tender-crisp. Drain; toss with extra-virgin olive oil or oil from a jar of sun-dried tomatoes.

Roasted Fish with Artichokes and Sun-Dried Tomatoes

You can use dry-packed sun-dried tomatoes instead of oil-packed. Just soak in boiling water for 20 minutes, then drain, slice and use as for the oil-packed variety.

4	halibut or tilapia fillets (about 1½ lb/750 g)	4
2	cloves garlic, minced	2
¼ tsp	each salt and pepper	1 mL
⅓ cup	drained oil-packed sun-dried tomatoes	75 mL
1	jar (6 oz/170 mL) marinated artichoke hearts, drained	1
1 tbsp	extra-virgin olive oil	15 mL
1 tbsp	chopped fresh parsley	15 mL
1	lemon, cut into wedges	1

> Place fish on greased toaster oven pan, in small roasting pan or on parchment paper–lined rimmed baking sheet. Spread garlic over top of fish; sprinkle with salt and pepper. Finely slice tomatoes; arrange over each fillet. Cut artichokes in half; place on tomatoes. Drizzle with oil.

> Roast in 400°F (200°C) toaster oven or oven until fish flakes easily when tested, about 12 minutes. Sprinkle with parsley. Serve with lemon wedges.

Makes 4 servings. PER SERVING: about 276 cal, 37 g pro, 11 g total fat (2 g sat. fat), 7 g carb, 2 g fibre, 54 mg chol, 288 mg sodium. % RDI: 9% calcium, 16% iron, 9% vit A, 32% vit C, 17% folate.

Glazed Catfish

Mayonnaise, like oil or butter, lends tons of taste to mild fish, keeps the fillets moist and effortlessly creates a glaze.

4	catfish or tilapia fillets (about 6 oz/175 g each)	4
2 tbsp	light mayonnaise	25 mL
2 tsp	lemon juice	10 mL
1 tsp	dried Italian herb seasoning	5 mL
¼ tsp	each salt and pepper	1 mL

> Pat fish dry; place on greased toaster oven or oven broiler pan.

> In small bowl, combine mayonnaise, lemon juice, Italian herb seasoning, salt and pepper; spread over fillets.

> Broil until fish flakes easily when tested, about 8 minutes.

Makes 4 servings. PER SERVING: about 204 cal, 21 g pro, 13 g total fat (3 g sat. fat), 1 g carb, trace fibre, 65 mg chol, 264 mg sodium. % RDI: 2% calcium, 6% iron, 2% vit A, 2% vit C, 5% folate.

Boston Lettuce and Radicchio Salad

2 tbsp	extra-virgin olive oil	25 mL
1 tbsp	red wine vinegar	15 mL
½ tsp	Dijon mustard	2 mL
Pinch	each granulated sugar, salt and pepper	Pinch
6 cups	torn Boston lettuce leaves	1.5 L
1 cup	torn radicchio leaves	250 mL
½ cup	sliced celery	125 mL

> In large bowl, whisk together oil, vinegar, mustard, sugar, salt and pepper.

> Add lettuce, radicchio and celery; toss to coat.

Makes 4 servings. PER SERVING: about 76 cal, 1 g pro, 7 g total fat (1 g sat. fat), 3 g carb, 1 g fibre, 0 mg chol, 27 mg sodium. % RDI: 3% calcium, 3% iron, 9% vit A, 13% vit C, 33% folate.

Lemon Parsley Roasted Fish

Simple preparations like this one are a healthful and delicious way to incorporate fish into your diet.

¼ cup	finely chopped fresh parsley	50 mL
2 tbsp	extra-virgin olive oil	25 mL
1 tsp	grated lemon rind	5 mL
1 tbsp	lemon juice	15 mL
½ tsp	salt	2 mL
¼ tsp	hot pepper flakes (or dash hot pepper sauce)	1 mL
3	cloves garlic, minced	3
4	fish fillets (such as tilapia or catfish), about 1½ lb (750 g)	4

❯ In large bowl, combine parsley, oil, lemon rind and juice, salt, hot pepper flakes and garlic. Pat fish dry; add to parsley mixture and turn to coat.

❯ Arrange fish on greased toaster oven or oven broiler pan; scrape any remaining parsley mixture over top. Roast in 450°F (230°C) toaster oven or oven until fish flakes easily when tested, about 10 minutes.

Makes 4 servings. PER SERVING: about 229 cal, 30 g pro, 11 g total fat (2 g sat. fat), 1 g carb, trace fibre, 78 mg chol, 434 mg sodium. % RDI: 2% calcium, 4% iron, 19% vit A, 12% vit C, 6% folate.

Red Potatoes and Sugar Snap Peas

8	small red-skinned potatoes, quartered	8
8 oz	sugar snap peas or snow peas, trimmed	250 g
1 tbsp	extra-virgin olive oil	15 mL
1 tbsp	lemon juice	15 mL
¼ tsp	each salt and pepper	1 mL
2	green onions, sliced	2

❯ In pot of boiling salted water, cover and cook potatoes just until tender, about 15 minutes.

❯ Add peas; cook for 2 minutes. Drain and place in bowl. Add oil, lemon juice, salt, pepper and green onions. Toss to coat.

Makes 4 servings. PER SERVING: about 135 cal, 4 g pro, 4 g total fat (1 g sat. fat), 22 g carb, 4 g fibre, 0 mg chol, 500 mg sodium. % RDI: 3% calcium, 12% iron, 2% vit A, 53% vit C, 19% folate.

Easy-as-Pie Frittata

Just mix, pour and bake. Serve this crustless quichelike dish hot, cold or even reheated alongside a simple green salad.

5	eggs	5
½ cup	milk or 10% cream	125 mL
1 tbsp	Dijon mustard	15 mL
1 cup	prepared croutons	250 mL
½ cup	shredded Fontina or provolone cheese	125 mL
¼ cup	chopped prosciutto or ham (about 2 oz/60 g)	50 mL
¼ cup	chopped roasted red pepper	50 mL
1	green onion, finely chopped	1

❯ Grease 9-inch (23 cm) pie plate or 8-inch (2 L) square metal cake pan; set aside.

❯ In bowl, whisk together eggs, milk and mustard; stir in croutons, half of the cheese, the prosciutto and half each of the red pepper and green onion. Pour into prepared pie plate; sprinkle with remaining cheese, red pepper and green onion.

❯ Bake in 350°F (180°C) toaster oven or oven until golden and set, about 20 minutes. If using metal pan, switch setting to broil; broil, watching closely, until golden and slightly puffy, about 2 minutes. Let cool on rack for 5 minutes. Run spatula around edge; cut into wedges. *(Make-ahead: Let cool completely. Wrap and refrigerate for up to 2 days.)*

Makes 4 servings. PER SERVING: about 223 cal, 16 g pro, 13 g total fat (6 g sat. fat), 9 g carb, 1 g fibre, 259 mg chol, 517 mg sodium. % RDI: 15% calcium, 10% iron, 20% vit A, 35% vit C, 21% folate.

Asian Pork Chops with Green Onions

A jar of hoisin sauce in the fridge is an instant source of Asian flavour. Serve the chops with steamed baby bok choy or broccoli alongside noodles or rice.

¼ cup	hoisin sauce	50 mL
2 tbsp	soy sauce	25 mL
2 tbsp	lime juice	25 mL
2	cloves garlic, minced	2
1 tsp	minced gingerroot (or ¼ tsp/1 mL ground ginger)	5 mL
¼ tsp	pepper	1 mL
4	pork loin centre chops, boneless or bone in, trimmed	4
2	green onions, thinly sliced	2

❯ In shallow dish, combine hoisin sauce, soy sauce, lime juice, garlic, ginger and pepper. Slash edges of pork chops to prevent curling. Add to marinade, turning to coat; let stand for 30 minutes. *(Make-ahead: Cover and refrigerate, turning occasionally, for up to 24 hours.)*

❯ Reserving marinade, place chops on foil-lined toaster oven or oven broiler pan or greased grill; spoon marinade over top. Broil or close lid and grill, turning once, until juices run clear when pork is pierced and just a hint of pink remains inside, about 8 minutes. Sprinkle with green onions.

Makes 4 servings. PER SERVING: about 213 cal, 27 g pro, 7 g total fat (2 g sat. fat), 10 g carb, 1 g fibre, 72 mg chol, 837 mg sodium. % RDI: 4% calcium, 11% iron, 1% vit A, 5% vit C, 6% folate.

Tortilla Pizzas

These toppings are just a starting point. Use your imagination to customize these quick and tasty tortilla or pita pizzas.

2	6-inch (15 cm) flour tortillas or pitas	2
3 tbsp	prepared pesto	50 mL
¼ cup	crumbled goat cheese	50 mL
2 tbsp	chopped drained oil-packed sun-dried tomatoes	25 mL
6	Kalamata olives, pitted and halved	6

> Place tortillas on toaster oven broiler pan or rimmed baking sheet; spread each with pesto. Sprinkle with goat cheese, tomatoes and olives.

> Bake in 400°F (200°C) toaster oven or oven until base is crisp and toppings are hot, 8 to 10 minutes.

Makes 2 servings. PER SERVING: about 264 cal, 7 g pro, 17 g total fat (4 g sat. fat), 22 g carb, 3 g fibre, 8 mg chol, 722 mg sodium. % RDI: 8% calcium, 14% iron, 10% vit A, 12% vit C, 19% folate.

VARIATION

Hot and Classic Pizzas
• Replace pesto with pizza sauce; goat cheese with shredded mozzarella cheese; tomatoes with 6 slices pepperoni or 3 slices Genoa salami, halved; and olives with pickled hot pepper rings.

SHOPPING FOR TWO

• Meat, poultry and fish: Unless you love leftovers, say goodbye to family-pack trays. Attendants at the meat and seafood counters can portion one or more servings to suit your needs. Look for 1-lb (500 g) quick-cook roasts.

• Dairy: Look out for half-pounds (250 g) of butter and single servings of yogurt and cottage cheese. The deli counter will slice cheese to order. Buy six- or eight-packs of eggs.

• Produce: Only buy as much as you'll eat. Loose mixed salad or spinach is better than packaged – you get what you need, without a lot of leftovers to throw away at the end of the week. Buy loose vegetables instead of prebagged ones.

• Frozen foods: Resealable bags of individually quick frozen (IQF) fruit and vegetables mean you can take out and use only enough for one meal without any waste.

• Bulk foods: Whether it's a single serving of pasta or a spoonful of herbs or spices you don't usually stock, the bulk food store is a great place to buy exactly how much you need.

• Salad and antipasto bars: When you need only a little of an ingredient for a special recipe, take a look at these offerings.

• When you have extras: Freeze canned tomatoes; chicken, beef or vegetable stock; or tomato juice in airtight containers in amounts that suit your recipes. Freeze unused tomato sauce, tomato paste and chipotle peppers in adobo sauce in ice-cube trays; wrap frozen cubes in plastic wrap and enclose in an airtight container.

CHAPTER 7

Make It Tonight... in the Slow Cooker

Slow Cooker Spanish Pot Roast

In Spanish cooking, ground almonds are often used to thicken sauces. The bonus: the extra mellowness they lend to the dish.

3 lb	boneless beef cross rib pot roast	1.5 kg
¼ tsp	each salt and pepper	1 mL
2 tbsp	vegetable oil (approx)	25 mL
1	onion, thinly sliced	1
2	cloves garlic, minced	2
½ cup	prosciutto, diced (4 oz/125 g)	125 mL
½ tsp	dried marjoram or oregano	2 mL
1 cup	sodium-reduced beef stock	250 mL
½ cup	sherry or sodium-reduced beef stock	125 mL
1	can (28 oz/796 mL) tomatoes, drained	1
1 cup	sliced roasted red peppers	250 mL
2 tbsp	all-purpose flour	25 mL
¼ cup	ground almonds	50 mL
2 tbsp	tomato paste	25 mL
1	sweet green pepper, thinly sliced	1

➤ Sprinkle beef with salt and pepper. In large Dutch oven, heat half of the oil over medium-high heat; brown beef, adding more oil if necessary. Transfer to slow cooker.

➤ Drain fat from pan. Add remaining oil; fry onion, garlic, prosciutto and marjoram over medium heat until onion is softened, about 5 minutes. Add stock and sherry; bring to boil, scraping up brown bits. Pour into slow cooker.

➤ Add tomatoes and red peppers; cover and cook on low for 6 to 8 hours or until beef is tender. Transfer beef to cutting board; tent with foil and let stand for 15 minutes before slicing.

➤ Meanwhile, whisk flour with 3 tbsp (50 mL) water; whisk into slow cooker. Whisk in almonds and tomato paste. Add green pepper; cover and cook on high for 15 minutes or until thickened. Serve with beef.

Makes 8 servings. PER SERVING: about 397 cal, 36 g pro, 23 g total fat (7 g sat. fat), 12 g carb, 2 g fibre, 110 mg chol, 565 mg sodium. % RDI: 6% calcium, 38% iron, 9% vit A, 90% vit C, 12% folate.

VARIATION

Stove Top Spanish Pot Roast

● In large Dutch oven, brown beef as directed. Transfer to plate.

● Fry onion, garlic, prosciutto and marjoram as directed. Add stock and sherry; bring to boil, scraping up brown bits. Add tomatoes and red peppers; return to boil. Return beef to pan; cover and simmer until beef is tender, about 2 hours. Transfer to cutting board; tent with foil and let stand for 15 minutes before slicing.

● Add almonds, tomato paste and green pepper to pan; bring to boil and cook for 10 minutes. Whisk flour with 3 tbsp (50 mL) water; whisk into pan. Bring to boil and cook, stirring, until thickened, about 5 minutes. Serve with beef.

TIP
● The juice drained from the tomatoes is an enriching addition to soups and chilis. Freeze it if you can't use it right away.

Slow Cooker Chunky Beef Chili

Stewing beef is handy but can vary in tenderness. A pot roast, especially a boneless cross rib, is a fine alternative.

2 lb	stewing beef cubes	1 kg
2 tbsp	vegetable oil	25 mL
2	onions, diced	2
2	large carrots, diced	2
2	stalks celery, diced	2
3	cloves garlic, minced	3
1 tbsp	dried oregano	15 mL
1	can (28 oz/796 mL) stewed tomatoes	1
1	can (5½ oz/156 mL) tomato paste	1
2	cans (each 19 oz/540 mL) red kidney beans, drained and rinsed	1
2 tbsp	chili powder	25 mL
½ tsp	salt	2 mL
1	sweet green pepper, diced	1
1 tsp	hot pepper sauce (optional)	5 mL

❯ Cut beef into ½-inch (1 cm) cubes. In large skillet, heat oil over medium-high heat; brown beef, in 4 batches. With slotted spoon, transfer to slow cooker.

❯ Pour off any fat in skillet. Fry onions, carrots, celery, garlic and oregano over medium heat until softened, about 5 minutes. Scrape into slow cooker.

❯ Add tomatoes, tomato paste, beans, chili powder and salt to slow cooker. Cover and cook on low for 6 hours or until beef is tender.

❯ Skim off any fat. Stir in green pepper, and hot pepper sauce (if using). Cover and cook for 30 minutes.

Makes 8 to 12 servings. PER EACH OF 12 SERVINGS: about 252 cal, 23 g pro, 8 g total fat (2 g sat. fat), 23 g carb, 8 g fibre, 37 mg chol, 497 mg sodium. % RDI: 6% calcium, 29% iron, 33% vit A, 37% vit C, 24% folate.

VARIATION

Stove Top Chunky Beef Chili
● Cube and brown beef as directed in Dutch oven. Transfer to plate.

● Drain off fat; in same pan, fry onions, carrots, celery, green pepper, garlic and oregano as directed.

● Add stewed tomatoes, tomato paste, beans, chili powder, salt, hot pepper sauce and beef and any accumulated juices to pan; stir well to combine. Bring to boil.

● Reduce heat, cover and simmer, stirring occasionally, until beef is tender, about 1½ hours.

TECHNIQUE
SEARING

Searing creates a richly flavoured and coloured crust on the outside of meats, poultry and fish. This is technically called the Maillard reaction, based on the combination of sugars and protein.

● Pat meat dry and season.

● Preheat pan; if pan is too cool, the meat will stick and tear. Add required fat and heat. Add meat. Let cook until browned and turns easily.

● You can add liquid, such as stock, wine or water, to pan and stir as you scrape up the brown bits on the bottom (this is called deglazing) and create a lip-smacking sauce or jus.

113

Slow Cooker Fall-off-the-Bone Ribs in Barbecue Sauce

Pork back ribs, often labelled "baby back ribs," are meatier than side ribs, but both are good in this recipe.

3 lb	pork back ribs (2 racks)	1.5 kg
4 tsp	mesquite or Cajun seasoning	20 mL
½ tsp	each salt and pepper	2 mL
2 cups	ketchup	500 mL
½ cup	wine vinegar	125 mL
2 tbsp	granulated sugar	25 mL
2 tbsp	Worcestershire sauce	25 mL

> Trim any fat from ribs. If necessary, remove membrane from underside. Cut into 2-rib portions.

> In small bowl, stir together mesquite seasoning, salt and pepper; rub all over ribs. Arrange on broiler pan; broil until browned, about 5 minutes per side. Transfer to slow cooker.

> In bowl, whisk together ketchup, vinegar, sugar and Worcestershire sauce; add to slow cooker, stirring to coat ribs. Cover and cook on low for 8 to 10 hours or until tender.

Makes 4 to 6 servings. PER EACH OF 6 SERVINGS: about 533 cal, 33 g pro, 32 g total fat (12 g sat. fat), 31 g carb, 2 g fibre, 88 mg chol, 1,452 mg sodium. % RDI: 4% calcium, 16% iron, 14% vit A, 25% vit C, 7% folate.

VARIATION

Shortcut Fall-off-the-Bone Ribs in Barbecue Sauce
● Trim, cut and season ribs; place directly in slow cooker. Pour sauce over ribs; cover and cook on high for 6 hours or until tender.

WHAT SIZE SLOW COOKER?

Slow cookers are available in a variety of shapes and sizes, so choose one that best suits your needs.

● For 4 to 8 servings, choose a 20- to 24-cup (5 to 6 L) slow cooker.

● For 2 to 4 servings, choose a 10- to 16-cup (2.5 to 4 L) slow cooker.

● For smaller amounts, such as dips, sauces and appetizers, choose a 2-cup (500 mL) or 6-cup (1.5 L) slow cooker.

Slow Cooker Beef and Mushroom Stew

When browning meat, it's vital to do so in batches – each no more than what fits without touching in a heated pan. A chef's tip for browning: first heat the pan, then add and heat the oil before adding any meat.

2 lb	stewing beef cubes	1 kg
½ cup	all-purpose flour	125 mL
¾ tsp	salt	4 mL
¼ tsp	pepper	1 mL
2 tbsp	vegetable oil (approx)	25 mL
2 cups	sodium-reduced beef stock	500 mL
1	onion, sliced	1
2	slices bacon, chopped	2
1 tsp	dried thyme	5 mL
4 cups	button mushrooms, halved (12 oz/375 g)	1 L
2	stalks celery, chopped	2
3 cups	cubed peeled potatoes	750 mL
1	pkg (14 g) dried porcini mushrooms	1
1	bay leaf	1
1 cup	frozen peas	250 mL

➤ Trim and cut beef into 1-inch (2.5 cm) cubes; toss with ¼ cup (50 mL) of the flour. Sprinkle with salt and pepper. In large skillet, heat half of the oil over medium-high heat; brown meat, in 4 batches and adding more oil if necessary. Transfer to slow cooker.

➤ Add stock to skillet and bring to boil, scraping up any brown bits; pour into slow cooker.

➤ In same skillet, heat remaining oil over medium heat; fry onion, bacon and thyme for 1 minute. Add button mushrooms; fry until softened and almost no liquid remains, about 8 minutes. Add to slow cooker.

➤ Add celery, potatoes, porcini mushrooms, bay leaf and 1 cup (250 mL) water to slow cooker; stir to combine. Cover and cook on low for 6 hours or until meat and vegetables are tender.

➤ Whisk remaining flour with ¼ cup (50 mL) water; whisk into slow cooker. Add peas. Cover and cook on high for 15 minutes or until thickened. Discard bay leaf.

Makes 8 servings. PER SERVING: about 344 cal, 30 g pro, 14 g total fat (5 g sat. fat), 23 g carb, 3 g fibre, 60 mg chol, 503 mg sodium. % RDI: 3% calcium, 28% iron, 4% vit A, 12% vit C, 22% folate.

VARIATION

Stove Top Beef and Mushroom Stew

● Reduce flour to ¼ cup (50 mL) and use only for browning meat.

● In Dutch oven, brown beef as directed; transfer to plate. Deglaze with stock as directed; set aside.

● Fry onion, bacon, thyme and button mushrooms as directed.

● Stir in celery, potatoes, porcini mushrooms, bay leaf, stock mixture, 1 cup (250 mL) water and beef; bring to boil. Reduce heat, cover and simmer until beef is tender, about 1 hour.

● Add peas; simmer until heated through. Discard bay leaf. (Make-ahead: Let cool for 30 minutes. Refrigerate, uncovered, in airtight container until cold; cover and refrigerate for up to 2 days or freeze for up to 1 month.)

Slow Cooker Short Ribs in Red Wine Sauce

Short ribs are a trendy cut nowadays. The meat on the bone is so rich in flavour, and because short ribs are fairly fatty, they are always moist.

1	pkg (14 g) dried porcini or shiitake mushrooms	1
3 lb	beef simmering short ribs	1.5 kg
1 tbsp	vegetable oil	15 mL
2 cups	button mushrooms	500 mL
2	onions, chopped	2
3	cloves garlic, minced	3
2	carrots, diced	2
1 tbsp	crumbled dried rosemary	15 mL
¾ tsp	salt	4 mL
½ tsp	pepper	2 mL
1	can (28 oz/796 mL) diced tomatoes	1
¾ cup	red wine (or ¾ cup/175 mL beef stock and 1 tbsp/15 mL wine vinegar)	175 mL
2 tbsp	tomato paste	25 mL
¼ cup	all-purpose flour	50 mL
2 tbsp	balsamic or wine vinegar	25 mL
2 tbsp	chopped fresh parsley	25 mL

> In measuring cup, pour boiling water over porcini mushrooms; let stand for 20 minutes. Strain, reserving liquid. Set mushrooms and liquid aside.

> Cut ribs into 2-bone pieces. Broil, turning once, until browned, 5 minutes. Place in slow cooker.

> In skillet, heat oil over medium-high heat; sauté porcini and button mushrooms, onions, garlic, carrots, rosemary, salt and pepper until softened, 5 minutes. Scrape into slow cooker. Add tomatoes.

> Whisk together soaking liquid, wine and tomato paste; pour into slow cooker. Cover and cook on low for 7 to 8 hours or until meat is tender. Skim off fat.

> In small bowl, whisk together flour, vinegar and ⅓ cup (75 mL) water; whisk into slow cooker. Cover and cook on high for 15 minutes or until thickened. Stir in parsley.

Makes 6 to 8 servings. PER EACH OF 8 SERVINGS: about 468 cal, 20 g pro, 36 g total fat (15 g sat. fat), 17 g carb, 3 g fibre, 69 mg chol, 441 mg sodium. % RDI: 6% calcium, 21% iron, 53% vit A, 33% vit C, 14% folate.

VARIATION

Stove Top Short Ribs in Red Wine Sauce
● Follow recipe as directed, using Dutch oven instead of slow cooker; cover and simmer over medium-low heat until ribs are tender, about 2 hours. Skim off fat. Reduce flour to 2 tbsp (25 mL) and water to ¼ cup (50 mL); whisk into pan and simmer until thickened, about 5 minutes. Stir in parsley.

Slow Cooker Scalloped Potatoes

Scalloped potatoes in the slow cooker? You bet. Add the ham if you like, or keep the dish vegetarian.

¼ cup	butter	50 mL
1	small onion, diced	1
¼ cup	all-purpose flour	50 mL
1 tsp	salt	5 mL
½ tsp	pepper	2 mL
½ tsp	dried thyme or marjoram	2 mL
2½ cups	milk	625 mL
1 cup	shredded Gruyère or Swiss cheese	250 mL
1 tbsp	dried parsley	15 mL
6	Yukon Gold potatoes	6
½ cup	chopped cooked ham or turkey (optional)	125 mL

❯ In heavy saucepan, melt butter over medium heat; fry onion, stirring occasionally, until softened, about 5 minutes.

❯ Add flour, salt, pepper and thyme; cook, stirring, for 1 minute. Gradually stir in milk and bring to boil; cook, stirring, until thickened, 5 to 8 minutes. Stir in half each of the cheese and parsley.

❯ Peel and thinly slice potatoes. Add to sauce along with ham (if using); stir to coat. Scrape into slow cooker. Sprinkle with remaining cheese and parsley. Cover and cook on low for 6 hours or until potatoes are tender and sauce is bubbly.

Makes 6 servings. PER SERVING: about 360 cal, 13 g pro, 16 g total fat (10 g sat. fat), 42 g carb, 3 g fibre, 53 mg chol, 587 mg sodium. % RDI: 31% calcium, 15% iron, 18% vit A, 47% vit C, 15% folate.

Slow Cooker Mac and Cheese

This family-pleaser fits everyone's busy schedule.

2 tbsp	butter	25 mL
1	onion, chopped	1
⅓ cup	all-purpose flour	75 mL
3 cups	milk	750 mL
3 cups	shredded old Cheddar cheese	750 mL
2 tsp	Dijon mustard	10 mL
¾ tsp	salt	4 mL
½ tsp	pepper	2 mL
2 cups	macaroni	500 mL
¼ cup	chopped fresh parsley	50 mL

❯ In saucepan, melt butter over medium heat; fry onion, stirring, until softened, 3 minutes.

❯ Add flour; cook, whisking, for 1 minute. Whisk in milk; cook, whisking, until thickened, about 8 minutes. Add Cheddar cheese, mustard, salt and pepper. Scrape into slow cooker.

❯ Meanwhile, in pot of boiling salted water, cook macaroni until tender but firm, 8 minutes. Drain; add to slow cooker, stirring to coat. Cover; cook on low for 3 hours or until bubbly. Stir in parsley.

Makes 4 to 6 servings. PER EACH OF 6 SERVINGS: about 487 cal, 24 g pro, 26 g total fat (16 g sat. fat), 40 g carb, 2 g fibre, 81 mg chol, 854 mg sodium. % RDI: 52% calcium, 13% iron, 26% vit A, 7% vit C, 35% folate.

VARIATION

Baked Crusty-Topped Mac and Cheese
● Boil macaroni and make cheese sauce as directed. Combine in 8-inch (2 L) square glass baking dish. Sprinkle ¼ cup (50 mL) dry bread crumbs over top. Bake in 350°F (180°C) oven until crusty, about 30 minutes.

Slow Cooker Spaghetti Sauce

This classic spaghetti sauce is designed for you to serve a bunch of friends, have leftovers for a quick dinner within three days, or freeze for later. Try switching the ground beef to chicken or lean pork.

1½ lb	lean ground beef	750 g
2	cans (each 28 oz/796 mL) tomatoes	2
1	can (5½ oz/156 mL) tomato paste	1
1½ cups	sliced mushrooms	375 mL
2	carrots, chopped	2
2	stalks celery, chopped	2
1	large onion, chopped	1
1	sweet red or yellow pepper, chopped	1
4	cloves garlic, minced	4
1 tbsp	each dried basil and oregano	15 mL
1 tsp	each dried thyme and salt	5 mL
½ tsp	pepper	2 mL
¼ tsp	cayenne pepper	1 mL
4 tsp	balsamic vinegar	20 mL

❯ In large skillet, sauté beef over medium-high heat, breaking up with fork, until no longer pink, 5 to 8 minutes. Drain off fat.

❯ Place tomatoes in slow cooker; mash until slightly chunky. Stir in tomato paste, beef, mushrooms, carrots, celery, onion, red pepper, garlic, basil, oregano, thyme, salt, pepper and cayenne pepper.

❯ Cover and cook on low for 8 to 10 hours or until thickened and vegetables are tender. Stir in vinegar.

Makes 10 cups (2.5 L), enough for 8 servings. PER SERVING: about 243 cal, 20 g pro, 10 g total fat (4 g sat. fat), 20 g carb, 4 g fibre, 44 mg chol, 706 mg sodium. % RDI: 9% calcium, 31% iron, 68% vit A, 93% vit C, 14% folate.

VARIATION
Stove Top Spaghetti Sauce
● In Dutch oven, brown beef as directed.

● Drain off fat; in same pan, fry mushrooms, carrots, celery, onion, red pepper, garlic, basil, oregano, thyme, salt, pepper and cayenne pepper until onions are softened, about 8 minutes.

● Add tomatoes, tomato paste and beef and any accumulated juices to pan; stir well to combine. Bring to boil.

● Reduce heat, cover and simmer, stirring occasionally, until sauce is thickened, about 1 hour. Stir in vinegar.

Slow Cooker Port and Prune Pork Roast

A pork shoulder blade roast is well marbled and, unlike leaner cuts, stays succulent and moist even after six hours in the slow cooker.

2	sweet potatoes, cut into ¾-inch (2 cm) thick rounds	2
1	pkg (10 oz/300 g) pearl onions, peeled	1
3 lb	boneless pork shoulder blade roast	1.5 kg
½ tsp	pepper	2 mL
¼ tsp	salt	1 mL
1 tbsp	vegetable oil (approx)	15 mL
1½ cups	sodium-reduced chicken stock	375 mL
½ cup	port or sodium-reduced chicken stock (or ½ cup/125 mL dry red wine and 1 tsp/5 mL granulated sugar)	125 mL
1 cup	pitted prunes	250 mL
2	bay leaves	2
½ tsp	each dried sage, thyme and dry mustard	2 mL
⅓ cup	all-purpose flour	75 mL

❯ In slow cooker, mix sweet potatoes with pearl onions.

❯ Trim fat from pork; sprinkle with pepper and salt. In large skillet, heat oil over medium-high heat; brown pork, adding more oil if necessary. Transfer to slow cooker.

❯ Drain fat from skillet. Add stock and port; bring to boil, scraping up brown bits from bottom of pan. Add to slow cooker.

❯ Add prunes, bay leaves, sage, thyme and mustard to slow cooker. Cover and cook on low for 6 hours or until meat is tender. Transfer meat and vegetables to platter; tent with foil and keep warm. Discard bay leaves.

❯ Whisk flour with ⅓ cup (75 mL) water; whisk into slow cooker. Cover and cook on high for 15 minutes or until thickened. Slice meat; serve with sauce and vegetables.

Makes 8 servings. PER SERVING: about 357 cal, 29 g pro, 12 g total fat (4 g sat. fat), 35 g carb, 4 g fibre, 89 mg chol, 308 mg sodium. % RDI: 5% calcium, 20% iron, 114% vit A, 20% vit C, 11% folate.

VARIATION

Stove Top Port and Prune Pork Roast
● In Dutch oven, brown pork as directed. Transfer to plate.

● Drain all but 1 tbsp (15 mL) of fat from pan. Reduce heat to medium and fry pearl onions, sage, thyme and mustard until onions are golden, about 5 minutes. Add stock and port; bring to boil, stirring and scraping up brown bits.

● Return pork to pan. Add sweet potatoes, prunes and bay leaves; cover and simmer until meat is tender, about 2 hours. Transfer meat and vegetables to platter; tent with foil and keep warm. Discard bay leaves.

● Whisk flour with 3 tbsp (50 mL) water; whisk into pan. Bring to boil and cook, stirring, until thickened, about 4 minutes. Serve pork with sauce and vegetables.

TIP
● No time to peel pearl onions? Quarter 4 cooking onions instead.

121

Slow Cooker Greek Lamb Stew with Artichokes

This savoury stew combines classic Greek flavours (oregano, lemon and cinnamon) and ingredients (artichokes, lamb shoulder and feta cheese). It's company fare and, best of all, you can make it ahead of time.

3 lb	boneless lamb shoulder	1.5 kg
1 tbsp	extra-virgin olive oil	15 mL
3	onions, sliced	3
6	cloves garlic, minced	6
1 tbsp	dried oregano	15 mL
1 tbsp	grated lemon rind	15 mL
¼ tsp	salt	1 mL
Pinch	each ground allspice and cinnamon	Pinch
2 tbsp	all-purpose flour	25 mL
1½ cups	beef stock	375 mL
¼ cup	tomato paste	50 mL
1	can (14 oz/398 mL) artichoke hearts, drained and quartered	1
½ cup	crumbled feta cheese	125 mL
2 tbsp	chopped fresh parsley	25 mL

❯ Trim fat from lamb; cut into 1-inch (2.5 cm) cubes. In shallow Dutch oven, heat oil over medium-high heat; brown lamb, in batches. Transfer to plate.

❯ Drain any fat from pan. Add onions, garlic, oregano, lemon rind, salt, allspice and cinnamon; cook over medium heat, stirring occasionally, until onions are softened, about 5 minutes.

❯ Sprinkle with flour; cook, stirring, for 1 minute. Add stock and tomato paste; bring to boil, scraping up any brown bits from bottom of pan.

❯ Transfer to slow cooker; add lamb and any accumulated juices and stir to combine. Cover and cook on low for 6 to 8 hours or on high for 4 to 6 hours or until lamb is tender. Stir in artichokes; cook for 15 minutes or until heated through. Serve sprinkled with feta cheese and parsley.

Makes 6 to 8 servings. PER EACH OF 8 SERVINGS: about 242 cal, 25 g pro, 11 g total fat (4 g sat. fat), 11 g carb, 3 g fibre, 77 mg chol, 535 mg sodium. % RDI: 8% calcium, 21% iron, 4% vit A, 18% vit C, 21% folate.

VARIATION

Stove Top Greek Lamb Stew with Artichokes

● Follow first 3 paragraphs, increasing stock to 2 cups (500 mL).

● Return lamb and any accumulated juices to pan; cover and simmer until lamb is tender, about 45 minutes. Add artichokes and heat through, about 15 minutes. *(Make-ahead: Let cool for 30 minutes. Transfer to airtight container; refrigerate, uncovered, until cold. Cover and refrigerate for up to 2 days or freeze for up to 2 weeks.)* Serve sprinkled with feta cheese and parsley.

Slow Cooker Sausage and Seafood Ragout

A good substitute for white wine is an equal amount of reduced-sodium chicken stock. Add 1 tbsp (15 mL) wine vinegar to give it a nice tart winelike edge.

1 tbsp	extra-virgin olive oil	15 mL
1 lb	chorizo or mild Italian sausages, cut into chunks	500 g
1	onion, diced	1
2	cloves garlic, minced	2
½ cup	diced celery	125 mL
½ tsp	dried thyme	2 mL
1	small eggplant, cut into 1-inch (2.5 cm) cubes	1
1	can (28 oz/796 mL) diced tomatoes	1
¾ cup	dry white wine	175 mL
¼ cup	tomato paste	50 mL
1 tbsp	paprika	15 mL
2 lb	mussels	1 kg
12 oz	catfish or grouper fillets	375 g
2 tbsp	chopped fresh parsley	25 mL

❯ In large skillet, heat oil over medium-high heat; brown sausages, in batches. Transfer to slow cooker.

❯ Drain fat from skillet. Add onion, garlic, celery and thyme; fry, stirring often, until softened, about 5 minutes. Add to slow cooker. Add eggplant, tomatoes, wine, tomato paste and paprika to slow cooker. Cover and cook on low for 6 hours or until eggplant is tender.

❯ Meanwhile, scrub mussels; trim off any beards. Discard any that do not close when tapped. Cut catfish into 2-inch (5 cm) pieces. Add mussels and fish to slow cooker, pushing into liquid. Cover and cook on high until mussels open, about 20 minutes. Discard any that do not open. Sprinkle with parsley.

Makes 8 to 10 servings. PER EACH OF 10 SERVINGS: about 313 cal, 22 g pro, 20 g total fat (7 g sat. fat), 11 g carb, 2 g fibre, 63 mg chol, 781 mg sodium. % RDI: 5% calcium, 23% iron, 11% vit A, 27% vit C, 11% folate.

VARIATION
Stove Top Sausage and Seafood Ragout
● In large shallow Dutch oven, brown sausages as directed. Transfer to plate.

● Drain fat from pan; fry onion, garlic, celery and thyme as directed. Add wine; bring to boil, stirring and scraping up brown bits. Add eggplant, tomatoes, tomato paste and paprika; bring to boil. Return sausage to pan; cover and simmer, stirring occasionally, until eggplant is tender, about 40 minutes.

● Nestle mussels and fish into liquid; cover and cook, gently stirring once, until mussels open, about 10 minutes. Discard any that do not open. Sprinkle with parsley.

TIP
● Cultivated mussels are so clean that all they usually need is a good rinse.

Slow Cooker Squash and Chickpea Curry

Cashew butter – or good old peanut butter – enriches this aromatic dish.

2 cups	cubed peeled butternut squash	500 mL
2 cups	diced peeled potato	500 mL
1	can (19 oz/540 mL) chickpeas, drained and rinsed	1
1 tbsp	vegetable oil	15 mL
1	onion, diced	1
2	cloves garlic, minced	2
1 tbsp	minced gingerroot	15 mL
3 tbsp	mild curry paste	50 mL
1	can (400 mL) light coconut milk	1
1 cup	vegetable stock	250 mL
¼ cup	natural cashew butter or peanut butter	50 mL
¼ tsp	salt	1 mL
2 cups	packed shredded Swiss chard	500 mL
1 cup	frozen green peas	250 mL
2 tbsp	chopped fresh coriander	25 mL

➤ In slow cooker, combine squash, potato and chickpeas.

➤ In large skillet, heat oil over medium heat; fry onion, garlic and ginger, stirring occasionally, until onion is light golden, about 7 minutes. Add curry paste; cook, stirring, until fragrant, about 1 minute. Add to slow cooker.

➤ Add coconut milk and stock to slow cooker; stir in cashew butter and salt. Cover and cook on low for about 4 hours or until vegetables are tender.

➤ Stir in Swiss chard and peas. Cover and cook on high for 15 minutes or until Swiss chard wilts. Sprinkle with coriander.

Makes 6 to 8 servings. PER EACH OF 8 SERVINGS: about 217 cal, 6 g pro, 8 g total fat (3 g sat. fat), 32 g carb, 5 g fibre, 0 mg chol, 543 mg sodium. % RDI: 4% calcium, 11% iron, 50% vit A, 23% vit C, 25% folate.

VARIATION

Stove Top Squash and Chickpea Curry

● In Dutch oven, fry onion, garlic and ginger as directed. Add curry paste; cook, stirring, until fragrant, about 1 minute.

● Add squash, potato and chickpeas; stir to coat. Add coconut milk, stock, cashew butter and salt; bring to boil. Cover and simmer, stirring twice, until vegetables are tender, about 30 minutes.

● Gently stir in Swiss chard and peas; cook, stirring, until Swiss chard wilts, about 5 minutes. Sprinkle with coriander.

Slow Cooker Chicken with Coriander, Lemon and Figs

Figs (or, if you like, dried apricots or prunes) add subtle sweetness to this party dish.

1 tbsp	vegetable oil	15 mL
3 lb	chicken thighs or thighs and drumsticks	1.5 kg
3	cloves garlic, minced	3
1	onion, chopped	1
1 tsp	ground coriander	5 mL
1 tsp	each salt and pepper	5 mL
2 cups	sodium-reduced chicken stock	500 mL
16	dried figs	16
2 tsp	grated lemon rind	10 mL
3 tbsp	lemon juice	50 mL
⅓ cup	chopped fresh coriander	75 mL
2 tbsp	cornstarch	25 mL
Half	lemon, thinly sliced	Half

❯ In shallow Dutch oven, heat oil over medium-high heat; brown chicken. Transfer to slow cooker. Drain fat from pan.

❯ Add garlic, onion, ground coriander, salt and pepper to pan; fry over medium heat until softened, about 3 minutes. Add stock and bring to boil, stirring and scraping up brown bits; pour into slow cooker. Trim stems from figs; add figs to slow cooker. Cover and cook on low for 5 to 6 hours or until chicken is tender. Remove chicken skin, if desired. Transfer to deep platter; keep warm.

❯ Skim fat from liquid. Stir in lemon rind and juice, and half of the fresh coriander. In bowl, whisk cornstarch with 2 tbsp (25 mL) water; whisk into slow cooker. Cover and cook on high for 20 minutes or until thickened; pour over chicken. Sprinkle with remaining fresh coriander. Garnish with lemon.

Makes 8 servings. PER SERVING: about 190 cal, 17 g pro, 6 g total fat (1 g sat. fat), 17 g carb, 3 g fibre, 58 mg chol, 358 mg sodium. % RDI: 4% calcium, 9% iron, 2% vit A, 13% vit C, 4% folate.

VARIATION

Oven-Braised Chicken with Coriander, Lemon and Figs

● Use 8 chicken legs instead of thighs. Decrease salt and pepper to ½ tsp (2 mL), lemon rind to 1 tsp (5 mL) and cornstarch to 1 tbsp (15 mL). Omit ground coriander.

● Remove skin from chicken. Cut drumsticks from thighs at joint. Sprinkle with ¼ tsp (1 mL) each of the salt and pepper. Brown chicken as directed; transfer to plate. Drain fat from pan. Add garlic, onion, and remaining salt and pepper; fry as directed. Add stock and lemon rind and juice; bring to boil, stirring and scraping up brown bits. Return chicken and any accumulated juices to pan.

● Add figs and half of the fresh coriander; bring to simmer. Cover and braise in 325°F (160°C) oven until juices run clear when chicken is pierced, 45 to 60 minutes. Transfer chicken to platter.

● Whisk cornstarch with 1 tbsp (15 mL) water. Skim fat from pan juices; bring juices to boil. Whisk in cornstarch mixture; boil, whisking, until thickened, about 1 minute. Pour over chicken. Sprinkle with remaining coriander. Garnish with lemon.

Slow Cooker Curried Chicken

Bone-in thighs are best for this aromatic dish because they taste better. In the Test Kitchen, we've found that chicken has a better texture if the skin stays on in the slow cooker. However, the flabby skin itself is not appealing, so we recommend removing it before serving. Serve with basmati rice and wafer-thin pappadams.

1 tbsp	vegetable oil	15 mL
12	chicken thighs	12
4 cups	thinly sliced onions	1 L
½ cup	each orange juice and sodium-reduced chicken stock	125 mL
2 tbsp	mild curry paste	25 mL
3	cloves garlic, minced	3
1 tbsp	grated gingerroot	15 mL
3 tbsp	all-purpose flour	50 mL
TOPPING:		
⅔ cup	thinly sliced red onion	150 mL
½ tsp	salt	2 mL
2 tbsp	lime or lemon juice	25 mL
¾ cup	plain yogurt	175 mL
2 tbsp	chopped fresh coriander	25 mL

❯ In Dutch oven, heat oil over medium-high heat; brown chicken. Transfer to slow cooker. Drain fat from pan.

❯ Fry onions, stirring occasionally, until almost softened, about 10 minutes; scrape over chicken.

❯ Whisk together orange juice, stock, curry paste, garlic and ginger; pour into slow cooker. Cover and cook on low for 4 to 6 hours or until juices run clear when chicken is pierced.

❯ Scrape onions off chicken. Remove skin. With slotted spoon, transfer chicken to platter; cover and keep warm. Whisk flour with ¼ cup (50 mL) water; whisk into slow cooker. Cover and cook on high until thickened, about 15 minutes. Pour over chicken.

❯ TOPPING: Meanwhile, sprinkle onion with salt; let stand for 15 minutes. Rinse in cold water; pat dry. In small bowl, toss onion with lime juice. Top each serving with yogurt then red onion mixture. Sprinkle with coriander.

Makes 6 servings. PER SERVING: about 276 cal, 26 g pro, 12 g total fat (2 g sat. fat), 17 g carb, 2 g fibre, 98 mg chol, 321 mg sodium. % RDI: 8% calcium, 12% iron, 3% vit A, 25% vit C, 17% folate.

VARIATIONS

Small-Batch Curried Chicken
● Use 10-cup (2.5 L) slow cooker. Halve recipe; cook for 4 hours or until juices run clear when chicken is pierced. **Makes 2 to 4 servings.**

Stove Top Curried Chicken
● Use skinless chicken thighs. Fry onions as directed; transfer to bowl. Brown chicken; top with onions. Add stock mixture; cover and simmer until juices run clear when chicken is pierced, about 45 minutes.

● Transfer chicken to platter; keep warm. Reduce flour to 1 tbsp (15 mL) and whisk with 2 tbsp (25 mL) water; whisk into pan and bring to boil. Reduce heat and simmer until thickened, about 2 minutes. Pour over chicken. Prepare topping as directed.

Slow Cooker No-Fuss Goulash

There's enough time while the goulash is thickening to cook egg noodles, the traditional partner for this saucy dish. We recommend sweet Hungarian paprika.

2	onions, sliced	2
2	cloves garlic, minced	2
2 lb	stewing beef cubes	1 kg
½ cup	chili sauce	125 mL
2 tbsp	packed brown sugar	25 mL
2 tbsp	Worcestershire sauce	25 mL
1 tbsp	sweet paprika	15 mL
1 tsp	dried marjoram	5 mL
½ tsp	each dry mustard and salt	2 mL
¼ tsp	pepper	1 mL
3 tbsp	all-purpose flour	50 mL

❯ Place onions and garlic in slow cooker. Trim and cut beef into 1-inch (2.5 cm) cubes; place on onions.

❯ Combine 1 cup (250 mL) water, chili sauce, brown sugar, Worcestershire sauce, paprika, marjoram, mustard, salt and pepper; pour into slow cooker. Cover and cook on low for 8 to 10 hours or until meat is tender.

❯ Whisk flour with ¼ cup (50 mL) water; whisk into slow cooker. Cover and cook on high for 10 to 15 minutes or until thickened.

Makes 4 servings. PER SERVING: about 480 cal, 54 g pro, 17 g total fat (6 g sat. fat), 27 g carb, 3 g fibre, 111 mg chol, 975 mg sodium. % RDI: 5% calcium, 44% iron, 13% vit A, 15% vit C, 15% folate.

FROM STOVE TOP OR OVEN TO SLOW COOKER

It's easy to adapt your favourite braising recipes for the slow cooker if you keep these basics in mind.

● Because root vegetables often take longer to cook than meat, cut them into pieces no larger than 1 inch (2.5 cm) and place them under meat or poultry, where it is hotter.

● Liquid doesn't evaporate from the slow cooker as in oven or stove-top braising. Most slow-cooker recipes require about half the liquid. Stir in thickening agents near the end.

● The flavour of dried herbs and spices dilutes in the slow cooker. Try increasing them by half or sprinkling with more at the end.

● Green peppers turn bitter when cooked for a long time, so add them near the end.

129

Slow Cooker Chicken Stock

The slow cooker makes fabulous stock – effortlessly.

2 lb	chicken backs, necks and wing tips	1 kg
2	onions (unpeeled), chopped	2
2	large stalks celery (with leaves), chopped	2
1	carrot, chopped	1
1	leek (optional), chopped	1
6	sprigs fresh parsley	6
2	sprigs fresh thyme	2
2	bay leaves	2
½ tsp	whole peppercorns	2 mL

> Place chicken in slow cooker. Add onions, celery, carrot, leek (if using), parsley, thyme, bay leaves and peppercorns. Pour in 8 cups (2 L) water. Cover and cook on low for 12 hours.

> Discard chicken. Strain stock through cheesecloth-lined sieve into large bowl, pressing vegetables to extract liquid. Refrigerate until fat congeals on surface, about 8 hours. Lift off fat and discard. *(Make-ahead: Cover and refrigerate for up to 3 days or freeze for up to 1 month.)*

Makes 8 cups (2 L). PER 1 CUP (250 mL): about 39 cal, 5 g pro, 1 g total fat (trace sat. fat), 1 g carb, 0 g fibre, 1 mg chol, 32 mg sodium. % RDI: 1% calcium, 4% iron, 2% folate.

VARIATION
Stove Top Chicken Stock
• In stockpot, combine chicken, onions, celery, carrot, leek (if using), parsley, thyme, bay leaves and peppercorns. Pour in 14 cups (3.5 L) water; bring to boil. Reduce heat and simmer, skimming occasionally, for about 4 hours. Continue as directed after cooking.

Slow Cooker Smoked Turkey and Noodle Soup

If you can find only a large turkey leg, use 2 cups (500 mL) meat for this soup and the rest in pastas, salads or sandwiches. Smoked turkey thighs are also a good idea for adding smokiness to the soup.

1	smoked turkey leg (about 1 lb/500 g)	1
1½ cups	each chopped carrots and celery	375 mL
1 cup	sliced mushrooms	250 mL
1	onion, diced	1
2	sprigs fresh parsley	2
1	bay leaf	1
½ tsp	each dried thyme and pepper	2 mL
3 cups	sodium-reduced chicken stock	750 mL
1	sweet red pepper, diced	1
½ cup	frozen peas	125 mL
2 cups	small pasta, cooked	500 mL

> Remove skin and meat from turkey leg. Reserve bone; discard skin. Cut meat into bite-size pieces; set aside in refrigerator.

> In slow cooker, combine carrots, celery, mushrooms, onion, parsley, bay leaf, thyme and pepper. Add turkey bone, stock and 3 cups (750 mL) water. Cover and cook on low for 6 hours or until vegetables are tender.

> Add red pepper, peas and turkey meat. Cover and cook on high until vegetables are tender-crisp, about 15 minutes. Discard turkey bone, bay leaf and parsley. Stir in pasta.

Makes 8 to 10 servings. PER EACH OF 10 SERVINGS: about 108 cal, 10 g pro, 2 g total fat (1 g sat. fat), 13 g carb, 2 g fibre, 23 mg chol, 266 mg sodium. % RDI: 3% calcium, 10% iron, 36% vit A, 37% vit C, 17% folate.

CHAPTER 8

Make It Tonight...
and Freeze for Later

Saucy Barbecue Meatballs

Meatballs are basic – some might even call them humble. But do they have potential when it comes to simmer them in sauce. Below is a fine barbecue sauce, but a favourite pasta sauce, curry sauce or sweet-and-sour sauce – or even store-bought barbecue sauce – give you lots of flavour options.

⅔ cup	fresh bread crumbs	150 mL
1	egg	1
1	clove garlic, minced	1
¼ cup	chopped fresh parsley	50 mL
2 tsp	Dijon mustard	10 mL
1 tsp	Worcestershire sauce	5 mL
½ tsp	each salt and pepper	2 mL
1 lb	lean ground beef	500 g
SAUCE:		
1 tbsp	vegetable oil	15 mL
1	onion, finely chopped	1
1	clove garlic, minced	1
1	can (28 oz/796 mL) ground tomatoes	1
¼ cup	packed brown sugar	50 mL
¼ cup	cider vinegar	50 mL
1 tbsp	Dijon mustard	15 mL
1 tbsp	Worcestershire sauce	15 mL
Dash	hot pepper sauce	Dash

❯ In bowl, combine bread crumbs with ½ cup (125 mL) water; let stand until absorbed, about 5 minutes. Beat in egg, garlic, parsley, mustard, Worcestershire sauce, salt and pepper. Mix in beef; roll by rounded tablespoonfuls (15 mL) into balls.

❯ Place, 1 inch (2.5 cm) apart, on foil-lined rimmed baking sheet; bake in 450°F (230°C) oven until no longer pink inside, about 20 minutes.

❯ SAUCE: Meanwhile, in large skillet, heat oil over medium heat; fry onion and garlic, stirring often, for 3 minutes. Add tomatoes, brown sugar, vinegar, mustard, Worcestershire sauce and hot pepper sauce; simmer, stirring occasionally, until slightly thickened, about 25 minutes.

❯ Let cool for 30 minutes. Refrigerate, uncovered, in shallow container until cold. Cover and freeze for up to 1 month.

❯ Let meatballs cool on sheet on rack. Refrigerate until chilled. Transfer to freezer bags; freeze in single layer until solid. Freeze for up to 1 month. Thaw meatballs and sauce in refrigerator.

❯ In large skillet or saucepan, combine meatballs and sauce; simmer, turning meatballs occasionally, until sauce is thickened, about 20 minutes.

Makes 4 servings. PER SERVING: about 430 cal, 28 g pro, 18 g total fat (6 g sat. fat), 38 g carb, 5 g fibre, 110 mg chol, 605 mg sodium. % RDI: 12% calcium, 44% iron, 18% vit A, 38% vit C, 22% folate.

TONIGHT'S DINNER
Follow first 3 paragraphs as directed. Cook as directed in last paragraph.

Top and Bottom Crust Pizza

This double-crust pizza freezes well, so you don't have to wait for the delivery guy when you want a slice. You can wrap and freeze it whole or cut it into wedges and wrap each individually.

1 tbsp	vegetable oil	15 mL
1	onion, chopped	1
2	cloves garlic, minced	2
1	sweet green pepper, chopped	1
¼ tsp	each salt and pepper	1 mL
1 lb	pizza dough	500 g
2	eggs	2
1 cup	shredded mozzarella cheese	250 mL
1 cup	shredded Cheddar cheese	250 mL
6 oz	salami, ham or smoked turkey, diced	175 g
2 tbsp	minced fresh parsley	25 mL
1	egg yolk	1

❯ In skillet, heat oil over medium heat; fry onion, garlic, green pepper, salt and pepper until softened, about 4 minutes. Let cool.

❯ Meanwhile, on floured surface, roll out half of the dough into 10-inch (25 cm) circle. Place on greased pizza pan or rimless baking sheet. Set aside.

❯ In bowl, whisk eggs; stir in mozzarella and Cheddar cheeses, salami, parsley and onion mixture. Spread over dough on pan, leaving 1-inch (2.5 cm) border around edge.

❯ Roll out remaining dough into 10-inch (25 cm) circle. In bowl, whisk egg yolk with 1 tsp (5 mL) water; lightly brush some over border on bottom crust. Place top crust over filling; with fork, press edge to seal. Brush with remaining egg yolk mixture; cut 3 slits in top crust.

❯ Bake in 375°F (190°C) oven until golden, about 45 minutes.

❯ Let baked pizza cool for 30 minutes. Refrigerate until cold. Wrap whole pizza or individual wedges and overwrap with heavy-duty foil; freeze for up to 1 month. Thaw in refrigerator. Place on greased baking sheet; bake in 400°F (200°C) oven until crisp and hot, about 12 minutes.

Makes 6 to 8 servings. PER EACH OF 8 SERVINGS: about 353 cal, 16 g pro, 18 g total fat (8 g sat. fat), 31 g carb, 1 g fibre, 116 mg chol, 733 mg sodium. % RDI: 20% calcium, 16% iron, 12% vit A, 22% vit C, 16% folate.

TONIGHT'S DINNER
Follow first 5 paragraphs. Serve immediately.

Mini-Lasagnas

Because these individual lasagnas use light cheeses, they are lower in calories and fat than many store-bought versions. If you want to freeze one big pan rather than four individual ones, follow the instructions for Tonight's Dinner (below), increasing thawing time and upping baking time to 45 minutes.

12 oz	lean ground beef	375 g
1 tsp	each fennel seeds and dried oregano	5 mL
2 cups	sliced mushrooms	500 mL
1	onion, chopped	1
6	cloves garlic, minced	6
¾ tsp	each salt and pepper	4 mL
½ tsp	hot pepper flakes	2 mL
1	can (5½ oz/156 mL) tomato paste	1
1	can (19 oz/540 mL) tomatoes	1
6	lasagna noodles	6
2 cups	light ricotta cheese	500 mL
1	egg, lightly beaten	1
Pinch	nutmeg	Pinch
1 cup	shredded part-skim mozzarella cheese	250 mL
2 tbsp	grated Parmesan cheese	25 mL
1 tbsp	chopped fresh parsley	15 mL

❯ In large skillet, sauté ground beef over medium-high heat until no longer pink, about 8 minutes; drain off fat. Crush fennel seeds and oregano. Add to pan along with mushrooms, onion, garlic, half each of the salt and pepper and the hot pepper flakes; sauté until onion is softened, about 5 minutes.

❯ Add tomato paste and tomatoes, breaking up with potato masher and scraping up any brown bits. Bring to boil; reduce heat and simmer until sauce is thick enough to mound on spoon, about 15 minutes.

❯ Meanwhile, in large pot of boiling salted water, cook lasagna noodles until tender but firm, about 7 minutes; drain and lay on damp tea towel. Using scissors, cut each in half crosswise.

❯ In small bowl, combine ricotta cheese, egg, nutmeg and remaining salt and pepper.

❯ Spread 1 tbsp (15 mL) sauce in each of 4 metal or foil 5¾- x 3¼-inch (625 mL) loaf pans. Lay 1 noodle half in each pan. Top each with scant ¼ cup (50 mL) of the sauce. Spread half of the ricotta cheese mixture over sauce; sprinkle with half of the mozzarella. Cover with second noodle half. Spread each with scant ¼ cup (50 mL) of the sauce, then remaining ricotta. Top with remaining noodles, sauce and mozzarella. Sprinkle with Parmesan and parsley. Refrigerate until cold. Cover with foil, overwrap with heavy-duty foil and freeze for up to 1 month. Thaw in refrigerator; remove heavy-duty foil.

❯ Bake in 400°F (200°C) oven or toaster oven until cheese is bubbly and knife inserted in centre for 5 seconds feels hot, about 30 minutes. Uncover and broil until golden, about 3 minutes.

Makes 4 servings. PER SERVING: about 686 cal, 50 g pro, 30 g total fat (15 g sat. fat), 55 g carb, 6 g fibre, 150 mg chol, 1,191 mg sodium. % RDI: 63% calcium, 44% iron, 39% vit A, 70% vit C, 44% folate.

TONIGHT'S DINNER

Follow first 4 paragraphs. Spread 1 cup (250 mL) of the sauce in 8-inch (2 L) square glass baking dish. Top with 4 noodle halves, then 1 cup (250 mL) of the sauce, 1 cup (250 mL) of the ricotta mixture and ½ cup (125 mL) of the mozzarella. Repeat with noodles and sauce. Layer remaining ricotta mixture, noodles, sauce and mozzarella over top. Sprinkle with Parmesan and parsley. Bake as directed in last paragraph.

Vegetarian Tomato Sauce

This quick-cooking sauce makes 4 cups (1 L), which is perfect for 1 lb (500 g) of spaghetti. Double or triple it and make a freezerful.

2 tbsp	vegetable oil	25 mL
1	small onion, chopped	1
1	each carrot and stalk celery, diced	1
1	sweet green pepper, diced	1
¾ tsp	each salt and dried basil	4 mL
Pinch	hot pepper flakes	Pinch
¼ cup	tomato paste	50 mL
1	can (28 oz/796 mL) diced tomatoes	1

❯ In saucepan, heat oil over medium heat; fry onion, carrot, celery, green pepper, salt, basil and hot pepper flakes, stirring occasionally, until softened, about 8 minutes.

❯ Add tomato paste and tomatoes; bring to boil. Reduce heat and simmer, uncovered, until thick enough to mound on spoon, about 30 minutes.

❯ Let cool for 30 minutes. Refrigerate, uncovered, in airtight container until cold. Cover and refrigerate for up to 2 days or freeze for up to 2 months. Thaw in refrigerator. Reheat to serve with pasta (see Tonight's Dinner, below).

Makes 4 cups (1 L). PER ⅔ CUP (150 mL): about 91 cal, 2 g pro, 5 g total fat (trace sat. fat), 12 g carb, 2 g fibre, 0 mg chol, 506 mg sodium. % RDI: 5% calcium, 9% iron, 42% vit A, 63% vit C, 8% folate.

TONIGHT'S DINNER

Follow first 2 paragraphs. In large pot of boiling salted water, cook 1 lb (500 g) spaghetti until tender but firm, about 8 minutes. Drain and return to pot; add sauce and toss to coat. **Makes 4 or 5 servings.**

FREEZE!

CASSEROLES

● Line baking dishes with heavy-duty foil before filling. Let casserole cool and chill completely before freezing. Once frozen, lift block out using foil as handles.

● Rewrap block tightly in plastic wrap or foil then overwrap in heavy-duty foil or place in freezer bag, pressing out air and sealing.

● Label and date the package for easy identification, and include heating directions.

● To use, unwrap and return frozen block to same baking dish. Cover and thaw in refrigerator for up to 48 hours, depending on density of food.

STEWS, CHILIS AND CURRIES

● Let cool for 30 minutes.

● Scoop into shallow airtight freezer containers and refrigerate, uncovered, until cold. Seal, label and date the container, then freeze. Include the reheating information, especially if someone else is going to reheat.

● Thaw in the refrigerator or microwave.

Hint of Jamaica Pork Stew

This saucy Jamaican-inspired dish is excellent with plain rice or Peas, Pepper and Rice (recipe, page 38). You can buy cubed pork shoulder in many grocery stores. Or buy pork shoulders when they're on special and trim, cube and freeze them in handy 1-lb (500 g) portions – perfect for this recipe.

3	green onions	3
¼ cup	all-purpose flour	50 mL
1 tsp	dried thyme	5 mL
½ tsp	ground allspice	2 mL
¼ tsp	cayenne pepper	1 mL
1 lb	pork shoulder, trimmed and cubed, or stewing cubes	500 g
3 tbsp	vegetable oil	50 mL
6	cloves garlic, minced	6
1 tbsp	minced gingerroot	15 mL
2 cups	chicken stock	500 mL
2 tbsp	soy sauce	25 mL
1 tbsp	packed brown sugar	15 mL

❯ Chop green onions, keeping white and green parts separate; set aside.

❯ In plastic bag, combine flour, thyme, allspice and cayenne. Add pork and shake to coat, reserving remaining flour mixture.

❯ In Dutch oven, heat 2 tbsp (25 mL) of the oil over medium heat; brown pork, in 2 batches, about 5 minutes. Remove to plate. Add remaining oil to pan; fry white parts of green onions, garlic and ginger until fragrant, about 2 minutes. Add reserved flour mixture; stir for 1 minute. Add stock and 1 cup (250 mL) water; bring to boil, scraping up brown bits.

❯ Return pork and any accumulated juices to pan; stir in soy sauce and brown sugar. Reduce heat, cover and simmer, stirring occasionally, until pork is tender, about 45 minutes. Add green parts of green onions; simmer for 5 minutes.

❯ Let cool for 30 minutes. Refrigerate, uncovered, until cold. Cover and refrigerate in airtight container for up to 2 days or freeze for up to 1 month. Thaw in refrigerator and reheat to serve.

Makes 4 servings. PER SERVING: about 337 cal, 27 g pro, 19 g total fat (4 g sat. fat), 14 g carb, 1 g fibre, 76 mg chol, 995 mg sodium. % RDI: 4% calcium, 20% iron, 1% vit A, 5% vit C, 10% folate.

TONIGHT'S DINNER

Follow first 4 paragraphs and serve immediately.

Pork Tenderloin with Lime-Beer Marinade

Marinated pork tenderloin is a handy item to keep in the freezer. With this recipe, you can grill one or both tenderloins, depending on the number of people you're serving.

½ cup	beer or nonalcoholic beer	125 mL
⅓ cup	lime juice	75 mL
2	cloves garlic, minced	2
2 tbsp	minced fresh parsley	25 mL
1 tsp	chili powder	5 mL
½ tsp	ground cumin	2 mL
¼ tsp	each ground coriander, salt and pepper	1 mL
2	pork tenderloins (about 12 oz/375 g each)	2

> In large bowl, whisk together beer, lime juice, garlic, parsley, chili powder, cumin, coriander, salt and pepper. Add pork; turn to coat.

> Transfer each tenderloin to large resealable plastic freezer bag; pour marinade over pork. Press out air and seal bags. Freeze for up to 1 month. Thaw in refrigerator.

> Place pork on greased grill over medium-high heat; brush with any remaining marinade. Close lid and grill, turning occasionally, until juices run clear when pork is pierced and just a hint of pink remains inside, about 18 minutes.

> Transfer to cutting board; tent with foil and let stand for 5 minutes before slicing.

Makes 4 to 6 servings. PER EACH OF 6 SERVINGS: about 157 cal, 28 g pro, 3 g total fat (1 g sat. fat), 2 g carb, trace fibre, 61 mg chol, 154 mg sodium. % RDI: 1% calcium, 12% iron, 2% vit A, 5% vit C, 4% folate.

TONIGHT'S DINNER
Follow first paragraph. Cover and marinate in refrigerator for 4 hours. Grill and serve as directed in last 2 paragraphs.

EASY LEFTOVER SOLUTIONS

• <u>Hot barbecue sandwiches</u>: Shred beef or pork and heat in barbecue sauce to stack on a bun.

• <u>Meaty Caesar</u>: Top Caesar salad with sliced cooked chicken or ham.

• <u>Panini</u>: Layer cheese, sliced cooked meat or poultry, mustard and sun-dried tomatoes in panini buns then heat.

• <u>Ham, turkey or chicken sandwich filling</u>: Pulse cooked ham, turkey or chicken in food processor until chunky; combine with light mayonnaise, mustard, minced celery, green onion or finely diced roasted red pepper or sun-dried tomatoes.

• <u>Pasta salad</u>: Combine cooked pasta, chopped vegetables, meat or poultry, cheese and favourite salad dressing.

• <u>Ham and eggs</u>: Add cubed ham to scrambled eggs.

• <u>Meat or poultry and salad wraps</u>: Try sliced cooked meat or poultry, torn lettuce, halved cherry tomatoes, grated carrot, sliced radishes, croutons and a drizzle of dressing.

• <u>Subs</u>: Use thinly sliced cooked meat or poultry, torn lettuce, sliced tomatoes, peppers, onions, cheese and mayonnaise.

Chicken and Black Bean Burritos

These burritos make a great last-minute supper. You can pack and freeze them all in one big dish or wrap them separately for individual portions.

1 tbsp	vegetable oil	15 mL
1	onion, chopped	1
2	cloves garlic, minced	2
¼ tsp	each salt and pepper	1 mL
4	boneless skinless chicken breasts, cubed	4
1	jalapeño pepper, seeded and minced	1
1	sweet red pepper, chopped	1
1	can (19 oz/540 mL) black beans, drained and rinsed	1
1 cup	salsa	250 mL
8	large whole wheat tortillas	8
2½ cups	shredded Cheddar cheese	625 mL
½ cup	light sour cream	125 mL

❯ In skillet, heat oil over medium-high heat; fry onion, garlic, salt and pepper until onion is softened, about 3 minutes. Add chicken, jalapeño, red pepper, beans and salsa; cook, stirring, until chicken is no longer pink inside, about 10 minutes. Let cool.

❯ Spoon about ¾ cup (175 mL) of the filling down centre of each tortilla; sprinkle each with ¼ cup (50 mL) of the cheese. Fold in bottom edge, then sides; roll up. Place, seam side down, in 13- x 9-inch (3 L) glass baking dish. Sprinkle remaining cheese over top.

❯ Let cool for 30 minutes. Refrigerate until cold. Cover and overwrap with heavy-duty foil (or wrap individually in heavy-duty foil) and freeze for up to 1 month.

❯ Bake from frozen, loosely covered with foil, in 400°F (200°C) oven until golden and hot, and cheese is melted, about 25 minutes. Serve with sour cream.

Makes 8 servings. PER SERVING: about 436 cal, 34 g pro, 16 g total fat (9 g sat. fat), 48 g carb, 8 g fibre, 78 mg chol, 938 mg sodium. % RDI: 31% calcium, 21% iron, 19% vit A, 57% vit C, 27% folate.

TONIGHT'S DINNER
Follow first 2 paragraphs. Bake in 400°F (200°C) oven until golden and hot, and cheese is melted, about 15 minutes. Serve with sour cream.

Pea Soup with Ham

This chunky yet smooth soup simmers away when you're relaxing or puttering around the house. If you cook a bone-in ham, save the bone to use in this soup instead of the smoked hock. Another substitute for the hock is smoked turkey leg or thigh.

1	smoked ham hock (about 1 lb/500 g)	1
1 tbsp	vegetable oil	15 mL
1	large onion, finely chopped	1
2	each carrots and stalks celery, finely chopped	2
2	cloves garlic, minced	2
2	bay leaves	2
½ tsp	each salt and pepper	2 mL
4 cups	sodium-reduced chicken stock	1 L
2 cups	dry green or yellow split peas	500 mL
3	green onions, thinly sliced	3

❯ Using paring knife, pare off and discard skin from ham hock. Trim off and discard fat. Set aside.

❯ In Dutch oven, heat oil over medium-low heat; fry onion, carrots, celery, garlic, bay leaves, salt, pepper and ham hock, stirring occasionally, until vegetables are softened, about 5 minutes.

❯ Add stock, peas and 2 cups (500 mL) water; bring to boil over medium-high heat, skimming off any foam. Cover and simmer over medium-low heat until peas break down and meat is tender enough to fall off hock, about 1¾ hours.

❯ Remove ham hock; pull off and shred meat. Set meat aside. Discard ham bone and bay leaves. In blender, purée half of the soup; return to pot along with meat.

TIP
● After removing the ham hock, you can also use an immersion blender to blend soup to a half-chunky stage while still in the pot.

❯ Let cool for 30 minutes. Transfer to airtight container and refrigerate, uncovered, until cold. Cover and refrigerate for up to 2 days or freeze for up to 1 month. Thaw in refrigerator. Reheat.

❯ Ladle into bowls; garnish with green onions.

Makes 8 servings. PER SERVING: about 232 cal, 16 g pro, 3 g total fat (trace sat. fat), 36 g carb, 5 g fibre, 6 mg chol, 594 mg sodium. % RDI: 4% calcium, 17% iron, 46% vit A, 8% vit C, 49% folate.

TONIGHT'S DINNER
Follow first 4 paragraphs. Garnish with green onions and serve immediately.

SOUP TOPPERS
Dress up a simple bowl of soup with a sprinkle or drizzle of drama. These give homemade flair to high-quality store-bought soups, too.
● Diced avocado, tomato or roasted red pepper
● Chopped sweet red or green pepper
● Chopped fresh herbs
● Sliced green onions or chives
● Crushed tortilla or other chips
● Popcorn
● Croutons
● Shredded cheese
● Crumbled feta cheese
● Yogurt
● Sour cream
● Pesto
● Balsamic vinegar
● Salsa
● Paprika
● Hot pepper flakes

140

Spaghetti Bake

This recipe is as good as a lasagna but a lot easier. When you're freezing a pasta dish, undercook the noodles slightly so that they won't end up mushy, and use plenty of sauce since some will be absorbed by the thawing noodles. If you're feeding a crowd, make the whole recipe in a 13- x 9-inch (3 L) glass baking dish.

2 lb	mild Italian sausage, casings removed	1 kg
2	onions, chopped	2
6	cloves garlic, minced	6
1 tbsp	dried basil	15 mL
4 cups	sliced mushrooms	1 L
2	cans (each 28 oz/796 mL) tomatoes, chopped	2
1	can (5½ oz/156 mL) tomato paste	1
½ tsp	pepper	2 mL
6 cups	chopped fresh spinach	1.5 L
12 oz	spaghetti	375 g
TOPPING:		
2 tbsp	butter	25 mL
⅓ cup	all-purpose flour	75 mL
3 cups	milk	750 mL
¾ cup	shredded mozzarella cheese	175 mL
¼ tsp	each salt and pepper	1 mL
½ cup	grated Parmesan cheese	125 mL

➤ In Dutch oven, sauté sausage over medium-high heat, breaking up with fork, until no longer pink, 5 minutes. Drain off fat. Add onions, garlic and basil; fry, stirring, for 5 minutes. Add mushrooms; cook until liquid is evaporated, 5 minutes.

➤ Add tomatoes, tomato paste and pepper; bring to boil. Reduce heat and simmer until most of the liquid is evaporated, 15 minutes. Add spinach.

➤ TOPPING: Meanwhile, in saucepan, melt butter over medium heat; whisk in flour and cook, whisking, for 1 minute. Whisk in milk; cook, whisking constantly, until thickened, 12 to 15 minutes. Add mozzarella, salt and pepper.

➤ Meanwhile, in large pot of boiling salted water, cook spaghetti until tender but firm, about 5 minutes. Drain and add to meat sauce; toss to coat. Spread in 2 greased 8-inch (2 L) square glass baking dishes; pour topping over spaghetti mixture. Sprinkle with Parmesan.

➤ Let cool for 30 minutes. Cover and refrigerate for up to 2 days or overwrap with heavy-duty foil and freeze for up to 1 month. Thaw in refrigerator for 48 hours.

➤ Bake in 375°F (190°C) oven until bubbly and golden, 50 to 60 minutes.

Makes 8 servings. PER SERVING: about 614 cal, 35 g pro, 27 g total fat (12 g sat. fat), 61 g carb, 7 g fibre, 77 mg chol, 1,501 mg sodium. % RDI: 38% calcium, 46% iron, 61% vit A, 62% vit C, 70% folate.

TONIGHT'S DINNER
Follow first 4 paragraphs. Bake as directed in last paragraph, decreasing baking time to 30 to 40 minutes.

TIPS
● When making casseroles such as Spaghetti Bake, make extra and fill pans that suit your family members' schedules. Chill, wrap in heavy-duty foil and freeze. Thaw in refrigerator. Reheat in toaster oven or oven.

● Trade cooking chores with a friend – plan to each make double batches of a favourite recipe, then share your wares. You'll both end up with two meals ready for busy nights.

Chicken with Mango Chutney and Brie

Just because it's from your freezer doesn't mean it has to be an everyday meal. This chicken is fancy enough to make you feel like you're dining out.

4	boneless skinless chicken breasts (about 1¼ lb/625 g)	4
¼ cup	Dijon mustard	50 mL
2	cloves garlic, minced	2
¼ tsp	each dried thyme, salt and pepper	1 mL
⅔ cup	dry bread crumbs	150 mL
2 tbsp	vegetable oil (approx)	25 mL
¼ cup	mango chutney, warmed	50 mL
4 oz	Brie cheese, sliced	125 g

> Place chicken between waxed paper; pound to scant ½-inch (1 cm) thickness.

> In small bowl, combine mustard, garlic, thyme, salt and pepper; brush over both sides of chicken. In shallow dish, press chicken into bread crumbs, turning to coat.

> In large skillet, heat oil over medium heat; fry chicken, adding more oil if necessary, until golden and no longer pink inside, 4 minutes per side.

> Transfer chicken to four 8- x 5-inch (20 x 12 cm) baking dishes or foil pans, or 13- x 9-inch (3 L) glass baking dish. Drizzle with mango chutney; top with Brie. Cover and refrigerate for up to 24 hours or overwrap with heavy-duty foil and freeze for up to 1 month. Thaw in refrigerator and remove heavy-duty foil.

> Bake in 400°F (200°C) oven until hot and cheese is bubbly, about 18 minutes.

Makes 4 servings. PER SERVING: about 416 cal, 39 g pro, 19 g total fat (6 g sat. fat), 22 g carb, 1 g fibre, 106 mg chol, 929 mg sodium. % RDI: 11% calcium, 15% iron, 7% vit A, 3% vit C, 11% folate.

TONIGHT'S DINNER
Follow first 3 paragraphs. Use 13- x 9-inch (3 L) glass baking dish. Drizzle with mango chutney; top with Brie. Cover with foil; bake in 400°F (200°C) oven until hot, about 15 minutes.

THE WELL-STOCKED KITCHEN
ESSENTIAL FRIDGE AND FREEZER STAPLES

- Dairy: milk, butter, plain yogurt (regular and/or Balkan-style), large eggs, Parmesan cheese (a fresh wedge is tastiest), old Cheddar cheese, mozzarella cheese and other favourites

- Fruit: fresh (oranges, lemons, apples and anything else you like) and frozen (blueberries, strawberries, raspberries and/or a mixed-berry blend)

- Vegetables: fresh (carrots and celery) and frozen (peas, corn, edamame or your favourites)

- Light mayonnaise

- Pasta: frozen tortellini and gnocchi

Burnished Hoisin Chicken

When you're freezing the chicken in the marinade, you can divide it into individual servings so you only have to thaw as many portions as you need at one time.

½ cup	hoisin sauce	125 mL
2 tbsp	soy sauce	25 mL
2 tbsp	rice vinegar	25 mL
2	cloves garlic, minced	2
1 tbsp	minced gingerroot (or 1 tsp/5 mL ground ginger)	15 mL
¼ tsp	each salt and pepper	1 mL
2 lb	chicken pieces	1 kg
1 tbsp	sesame seeds, toasted	15 mL

➤ In large bowl, whisk together hoisin sauce, soy sauce, rice vinegar, garlic, ginger, salt and pepper. Add chicken; turn to coat. Cover and marinate in refrigerator for 4 hours.

➤ Divide chicken between 2 large resealable plastic freezer bags; pour marinade over chicken. Press out air and seal bags. Freeze for up to 1 month. Thaw in refrigerator.

➤ Heat 1 burner of 2-burner barbecue, or 2 outside burners of 3-burner barbecue, to medium. Brush grill over unlit burner with oil. Place chicken, bone side down, on greased grill. Close lid and grill until bottom is marked, about 25 minutes. Turn and grill until juices run clear when chicken is pierced, about 20 minutes. Move any pieces that need more crisping or colouring over direct medium heat. Close lid and grill until golden brown, about 5 minutes. (Or place chicken, bone side down, in large roasting pan; brush with any remaining marinade. Roast in 425°F/220°C oven until golden, crisp and juices run clear when chicken is pierced, about 30 minutes.) Sprinkle with sesame seeds.

Makes 4 servings. PER SERVING (WITH SKIN): about 366 cal, 32 g pro, 19 g total fat (5 g sat. fat), 17 g carb, 1 g fibre, 111 mg chol, 1,272 mg sodium. % RDI: 2% calcium, 12% iron, 5% vit A, 2% vit C, 8% folate.

TONIGHT'S DINNER
Follow first paragraph. Cook and garnish as directed in last paragraph.

TIP
● Toast sesame seeds in a small dry skillet over medium heat. Swirl the pan often to brown the seeds evenly.

Chicken Fingers with Honey Mustard Sauce

Finely grated Parmigiano-Reggiano, the authentic Parmesan cheese, helps form a crisp and golden coating on chicken. Panko bread crumbs are available at many grocery stores and Asian markets. When freezing the chicken fingers, hold off on making the sauce until just before serving.

4	boneless skinless chicken breasts	4
2	eggs	2
1 cup	finely grated Parmigiano-Reggiano or Parmesan cheese	250 mL
1 cup	panko (Japanese bread crumbs) or fresh bread crumbs	250 mL
4 tsp	chopped fresh oregano (or 2 tsp/10 mL dried)	20 mL
1 tsp	salt	5 mL
½ tsp	each pepper and paprika	2 mL
¼ cup	butter, melted	50 mL
HONEY MUSTARD SAUCE:		
⅓ cup	light mayonnaise	75 mL
2 tbsp	Dijon mustard	25 mL
1 tbsp	liquid honey	15 mL

❯ HONEY MUSTARD SAUCE: In small bowl, stir together mayonnaise, mustard and honey. *(Make-ahead: Cover and refrigerate for up to 3 days.)*

❯ Between sheets of plastic wrap, pound chicken with flat side of meat pounder or with rolling pin until ½ inch (1 cm) thick. Cut lengthwise on diagonal into 4- x 1½-inch (10 x 4 cm) strips. In bowl, whisk eggs. In shallow bowl, combine cheese, bread crumbs, oregano, salt, pepper and paprika.

❯ One at a time, dip chicken strips into eggs, letting any excess drip back into bowl. Coat generously with cheese mixture, pressing to adhere.

❯ Refrigerate, layered between waxed paper, in airtight container for up to 24 hours or freeze for up to 2 weeks. Bake from frozen.

❯ Arrange on greased baking sheets; drizzle with butter. Bake in 425°F (220°C) oven until golden, crispy and no longer pink inside, about 20 minutes. Serve with dipping sauce.

Makes 4 servings. PER SERVING: about 556 cal, 53 g pro, 32 g total fat (14 g sat. fat), 14 g carb, 1 g fibre, 251 mg chol, 1,455 mg sodium. % RDI: 31% calcium, 16% iron, 20% vit A, 3% vit C, 15% folate.

TONIGHT'S DINNER
Follow first 3 paragraphs. Bake as directed in last paragraph, decreasing baking time to 15 minutes.

TIP
● Fresh bread crumbs give an almost-as-crispy coating. To make them, whiz a slice or two of crusty bread in the food processor. Make extra and store in the freezer for another round of chicken fingers.

Big-Batch Bean and Lentil Soup

This substantial three-bean soup takes away the cold-weather chill. It's also great to come home to if you make the slow-cooker version. Though the recipe calls for three different kinds of beans, you can use all one kind – whatever type your family likes.

2 tsp	vegetable oil	10 mL
2	onions, chopped	2
2	cloves garlic, minced	2
1 tbsp	chili powder	15 mL
1	can (28 oz/796 mL) tomatoes	1
6 cups	vegetable or chicken stock	1.5 L
2 cups	water	500 mL
¾ cup	red lentils	175 mL
1	each can (19 oz/540 mL) chickpeas, red kidney beans and black beans, drained and rinsed	1
1 tbsp	chopped fresh coriander	15 mL
1 tsp	lemon juice	5 mL
½ tsp	salt	2 mL
¼ tsp	pepper	1 mL

❯ In large saucepan or Dutch oven, heat oil over medium heat; fry onions, garlic and chili powder, stirring occasionally, until softened, about 5 minutes.

❯ Add tomatoes, mashing with potato masher. Add stock, water and lentils; bring to boil. Reduce heat to medium-low; simmer until lentils are softened, about 20 minutes.

❯ Add chickpeas, red kidney beans and black beans; cook until heated through, about 15 minutes.

❯ Let cool for 30 minutes. Refrigerate in shallow airtight containers for up to 2 days or freeze for up to 2 weeks. Reheat.

❯ Stir in coriander, lemon juice, salt and pepper.

Makes ten 1½-cup (375 mL) servings, or 16 cups (4 L). PER SERVING: about 246 cal, 14 g pro, 4 g total fat (trace sat. fat), 41 g carb, 10 g fibre, 0 mg chol, 922 mg sodium. % RDI: 6% calcium, 26% iron, 5% vit A, 18% vit C, 80% folate.

TONIGHT'S DINNER

Follow first 3 paragraphs. Stir in coriander, lemon juice, salt and pepper. Serve immediately.

VARIATION

Slow Cooker Big-Batch Bean and Lentil Soup

● Omit oil. To 16-cup (4 L) slow cooker, add onions, garlic, chili powder, tomatoes, stock, water and lentils. Cook on low for 8 hours. Add chickpeas, red kidney beans and black beans; cook on high for 30 minutes or until heated through. Stir in coriander, lemon juice, salt and pepper.

CHAPTER 9

Make It Tonight...
on the Barbecue

Rib Eye Steaks

Rib eyes are one of the top butcher-recommended steaks. Garlic and a touch of heat via the hot pepper flakes are all a good steak needs.

2	rib eye grilling steaks, each 1 inch (2.5 cm) thick (about 1 lb/500 g)	2
MARINADE:		
¼ cup	extra-virgin olive oil	50 mL
3	cloves garlic, minced	3
½ tsp	each salt and pepper	2 mL
¼ tsp	hot pepper flakes	1 mL

❯ **MARINADE:** In glass baking dish, combine oil, garlic, salt, pepper and hot pepper flakes. Add steaks; turn and rub marinade all over. Cover and refrigerate for 4 hours. *(Make-ahead: Refrigerate for up to 24 hours.)*

❯ Place steaks on greased grill over medium-high heat; brush with remaining marinade. Close lid and grill, turning once, until medium-rare, about 10 minutes. Transfer to cutting board; tent with foil and let stand for 5 minutes. Cut each in half to serve.

Makes 4 servings. PER SERVING: about 319 cal, 24 g pro, 24 g total fat (6 g sat. fat), 1 g carb, trace fibre, 57 mg chol, 337 mg sodium. % RDI: 1% calcium, 14% iron, 1% vit A, 2% vit C, 3% folate.

BBQ GOLDEN RULES

THE CLEAN PLATE RULE

Place cooked meat, poultry or seafood on a clean plate – not the one you used to carry the raw food to the barbecue.

THE MARINADE RULE

Throw away marinade left over from flavouring and tenderizing raw meat, poultry or seafood. Never brush it over cooked food.

THE BRUSH RULE

When brushing a glaze or sauce over cooked food just before taking it off the grill, be sure to use a clean brush.

Ginger Beef Kabobs

You can buy grilling steaks and marinating steaks. The grilling ones are the most tender and marbled, so when we marinate or rub them with seasoning, it's strictly for flavour. Marinating steaks need – you guessed it – marinating to improve tenderness.

3	cloves garlic, minced	3
2 tbsp	grated gingerroot (or 1 tsp/5 mL ground ginger)	25 mL
2 tbsp	soy sauce	25 mL
2 tsp	rice vinegar or cider vinegar	10 mL
2 tsp	sesame oil	10 mL
½ tsp	granulated sugar	2 mL
1	top sirloin grilling steak or sirloin tip marinating steak, 1 inch (2.5 cm) thick (1 lb/500 g)	1
10	green onions, white part only	10

❯ In large bowl, whisk together garlic, ginger, soy sauce, vinegar, sesame oil and sugar. Trim fat from steak; cut into 1-inch (2.5 cm) cubes. Add to marinade and turn to coat; let stand for 10 minutes. *(Make-ahead: Cover and refrigerate for up to 8 hours.)*

❯ Meanwhile, cut onions into 2-inch (5 cm) lengths. Alternately thread onions and beef onto metal or soaked wooden skewers; brush with remaining marinade. Place on greased grill over medium-high heat; close lid and grill, turning 3 times, until browned but still pink inside, about 10 minutes.

Makes 4 servings. PER SERVING: about 179 cal, 22 g pro, 7 g total fat (2 g sat. fat), 6 g carb, 1 g fibre, 51 mg chol, 563 mg sodium. % RDI: 4% calcium, 21% iron, 1% vit A, 8% vit C, 11% folate.

Tangy Snow Peas

1 tbsp	white vinegar	15 mL
1 tsp	granulated sugar	5 mL
1 tsp	sesame oil	5 mL
1	clove garlic, minced	1
¼ tsp	hot pepper sauce	1 mL
2 cups	steamed snow peas	500 mL

❯ In bowl, whisk together vinegar, sugar, sesame oil, garlic and hot pepper sauce. Add snow peas; toss to coat.

Makes 4 servings. PER SERVING: about 49 cal, 3 g pro, 1 g total fat (trace sat. fat), 7 g carb, 2 g fibre, 0 mg chol, 5 mg sodium. % RDI: 3% calcium, 11% iron, 1% vit A, 65% vit C, 10% folate.

Best-Ever Burgers

This basic beef patty formula is the foundation for many burgers to come. With a slice of cheese melted over the top and crowned with a curl of crisp bacon, it's a banquet burger. Add herbs or a dollop of pesto or finish with a barbecue sauce glaze and you have a whole new burger. Or switch the beef for lean ground pork, lamb, chicken or turkey – the formula works just as well.

1	egg	1
2 tbsp	water	25 mL
¼ cup	dry bread crumbs	50 mL
1	small onion, grated	1
1 tbsp	Dijon mustard	15 mL
1	clove garlic, minced	1
½ tsp	each salt and pepper	2 mL
1 lb	lean ground beef	500 g

➤ In large bowl, beat egg with water; stir in bread crumbs, onion, mustard, garlic, salt and pepper. Add beef; mix just until combined. Shape into four ¾-inch (2 cm) thick patties. *(Make-ahead: Layer between waxed paper in airtight container and refrigerate for up to 24 hours or freeze for up to 1 month. Thaw in refrigerator.)*

➤ Place on greased grill over medium heat; close lid and grill, turning once, until digital thermometer inserted sideways into centre reads 160°F (71°C), about 15 minutes.

Makes 4 servings. PER SERVING: about 280 cal, 25 g pro, 15 g total fat (6 g sat. fat), 7 g carb, 1 g fibre, 110 mg chol, 468 mg sodium. % RDI: 4% calcium, 19% iron, 2% vit A, 2% vit C, 10% folate.

IT'S BETTER WITH BUTTERS

A thin slice of one of these deliciously seasoned butters melting over a roasted fish fillet, burger, pork chop or flank steak pays big flavour dividends. Try a dab on a bowl full of vegetables – brussels sprouts, broccoli and corn are especially divine. Or spread them on bread or melt over a baked potato.

● In bowl, soften ¼ cup (50 mL) butter at room temperature, then mash in these seasonings.

● Mixed Peppercorn: 2 tsp (10 mL) coarsely ground mixed peppercorns. Doll up with 1 tsp (5 mL) chopped fresh thyme or generous pinch dried thyme, if desired.

● Horseradish Mustard: 2 tbsp (25 mL) minced fresh parsley; 1 tbsp (15 mL) prepared horseradish; 2 tsp (10 mL) grainy Dijon mustard; and generous pinch pepper.

● Mixed Herb: 2 tbsp (25 mL) minced fresh chives or green part of green onion; 2 tsp (10 mL) each Dijon mustard and minced fresh tarragon; and generous pinch pepper.

● Ginger Green Onion: 2 tbsp (25 mL) minced green onion; 1 tsp (5 mL) grated gingerroot or ½ tsp (2 mL) ground ginger; ½ tsp (2 mL) Worcestershire sauce; and generous pinch pepper.

● Lemon Dill: 1 tbsp (15 mL) minced fresh dill; 2 tsp (10 mL) grated lemon rind; 1 tsp (5 mL) lemon juice; and generous pinch pepper.

Grilled Liver with Mushrooms and Onions

Calves' liver is mild, fork-tender and pricey. If using less-expensive beef liver, soak in milk in the fridge for up to 4 hours before using. Drain, pat dry and cook.

3 cups	sliced mushrooms (8 oz/250 g)	750 mL
1	onion, sliced	1
3 tbsp	balsamic vinegar	50 mL
1 tbsp	butter, melted	15 mL
½ tsp	crumbled dried sage	2 mL
½ tsp	each salt and pepper	2 mL
1 tsp	Dijon mustard	5 mL
1 lb	thinly sliced calves' or beef liver	500 g
1 tbsp	vegetable oil	15 mL
2 tbsp	minced fresh parsley	25 mL

❯ Cut 16-inch (40 cm) length of heavy-duty foil; arrange mushrooms and onion on one half. Drizzle with 1 tbsp (15 mL) of the vinegar and butter; sprinkle with sage and half each of the salt and pepper. Fold foil over vegetables; fold in sides and seal. Place on grill over medium heat; close lid and cook, turning once, until tender, 10 minutes.

❯ Meanwhile, in small bowl, whisk remaining vinegar with mustard; set aside. Pat liver dry; brush with oil and sprinkle with remaining salt and pepper. Add to greased grill; close lid and grill for 2 minutes. Turn and brush with half of the vinegar mixture; close lid and grill for 2 minutes. Turn and brush with remaining vinegar mixture; close lid and grill until glazed, browned on both sides and still slightly pink inside, 1 minute. Serve with mushrooms and onions. Sprinkle with parsley.

Makes 4 servings. PER SERVING: about 252 cal, 24 g pro, 11 g total fat (4 g sat. fat), 14 g carb, 1 g fibre, 410 mg chol, 418 mg sodium. % RDI: 2% calcium, 62% iron, 897% vit A, 40% vit C, 89% folate.

Beef Koftas with Minted Yogurt

A change of shape, seasonings and condiments and you have a brand-new take on the humble burger.

1 cup	lightly packed fresh parsley leaves	250 mL
3	green onions, coarsely chopped	3
2 tsp	dried mint	10 mL
½ tsp	each ground cumin, paprika and salt	2 mL
¼ tsp	pepper	1 mL
1	egg	1
1 lb	lean ground beef	500 g
½ cup	plain yogurt	125 mL
2 tbsp	minced fresh parsley	25 mL
4	whole wheat pitas	4

❯ In food processor, purée together parsley leaves, green onions, half of the mint, the cumin, paprika, salt and pepper. Transfer to large bowl; beat in egg. Add beef and 2 tbsp (25 mL) water; mix well.

❯ Shape beef mixture by heaping 2 tbsp (25 mL) into small sausage shapes; thread each lengthwise onto metal or soaked wooden skewer.

❯ Place skewers on greased grill over medium heat; close lid and grill, turning once, until no longer pink inside and digital thermometer inserted into several koftas registers 160°F (71°C), 12 minutes. (Or broil, turning once, for 7 minutes.)

❯ Meanwhile, combine yogurt with remaining mint and minced parsley. Grill or broil pitas, turning once, until hot and lightly crisped, about 4 minutes; cut each into quarters. Serve koftas with pita quarters and yogurt.

Makes 4 servings. PER SERVING: about 393 cal, 31 g pro, 14 g total fat (5 g sat. fat), 37 g carb, 5 g fibre, 109 mg chol, 712 mg sodium. % RDI: 10% calcium, 41% iron, 14% vit A, 42% vit C, 36% folate.

Grilled Sausage Spiedini

Spiedini are Italian brochettes threaded with chunks of baguette and other tasty things, such as sausage and onion. Serve with mustard and grilled peppers drizzled lightly with balsamic vinegar.

4	Italian sausages (about 1 lb/500 g)	4
2 tbsp	extra-virgin olive oil	25 mL
1	clove garlic, minced	1
Pinch	each salt and pepper	Pinch
1	baguette (8 inches/20 cm), cut into 1-inch (2.5 cm) cubes	1
Half	red onion, cut into 1-inch (2.5 cm) cubes	Half

❯ Prick sausages with fork. Place on microwaveable plate; cover and microwave at high until no longer pink, about 5 minutes. *(Make-ahead: Refrigerate until cold; wrap and refrigerate for up to 24 hours.)* Cut into 1½-inch (4 cm) pieces.

❯ Meanwhile, in bowl, whisk together oil, garlic, salt and pepper. Alternately thread sausage, bread cubes and onion onto metal or soaked wooden skewers; brush bread with oil mixture.

❯ Place skewers on greased grill over medium heat; close lid and grill, turning 3 times, until crisped, browned and onion is tender, about 10 minutes.

Makes 4 servings. PER SERVING: about 354 cal, 19 g pro, 23 g total fat (7 g sat. fat), 17 g carb, 1 g fibre, 48 mg chol, 854 mg sodium. % RDI: 4% calcium, 14% iron, 5% vit C, 11% folate.

Ginger Pork Sandwiches

Start with one pork tenderloin and finish with a casual supper for four.

2 tbsp	sesame oil	25 mL
½ tsp	ground ginger	2 mL
½ tsp	each salt and pepper	2 mL
1	pork tenderloin (12 oz/375 g)	1
½ cup	light mayonnaise	125 mL
2	green onions, thinly sliced	2
1 tsp	rice vinegar	5 mL
4	kaiser rolls, halved	4
8	lettuce leaves	8
8	thin slices tomato	8

❯ In shallow dish, combine oil, ginger and half each of the salt and pepper; add pork and roll to coat all over. Place on greased grill over medium-high heat; close lid and grill, turning once, until juices run clear when pork is pierced and just a hint of pink remains inside, about 18 minutes. Transfer to cutting board and tent with foil; let stand for 5 minutes before slicing.

❯ Meanwhile, in bowl, mix together mayonnaise, green onions, vinegar and remaining salt and pepper; spread on cut sides of rolls. Sandwich pork, lettuce and tomato in rolls.

Makes 4 servings. PER SERVING: about 457 cal, 27 g pro, 21 g total fat (4 g sat. fat), 38 g carb, 2 g fibre, 55 mg chol, 888 mg sodium. % RDI: 8% calcium, 26% iron, 6% vit A, 18% vit C, 38% folate.

Lemon Dill Salmon Skewers

A grilled lemon wedge adds a classy restaurant touch to salmon. Just brush thick wedges with oil and grill alongside the salmon. The hot juice literally bursts out of them!

4	centre-cut salmon fillets (about 6 oz/175 g each), skinned	4
3 tbsp	chopped fresh dill	50 mL
2 tbsp	extra-virgin olive oil	25 mL
½ tsp	grated lemon rind	2 mL
2 tbsp	lemon juice	25 mL
½ tsp	salt	2 mL
¼ tsp	pepper	1 mL
Dash	hot pepper sauce	Dash
1	lemon, cut into 8 wedges	1

❯ Cut salmon into 1½-inch (4 cm) cubes to make 24 pieces.

❯ In large glass bowl, mix together dill, oil, lemon rind and juice, salt, pepper and hot pepper sauce. Add salmon cubes and toss to coat; let stand for 10 minutes.

❯ Beginning and ending with lemon wedge, thread salmon loosely onto 4 metal or soaked wooden skewers, reserving marinade. Place on greased grill over medium heat; brush with remaining marinade. Close lid and grill, turning twice, until fish flakes easily when tested, about 10 minutes.

Makes 4 servings. PER SERVING: about 338 cal, 29 g pro, 23 g total fat (4 g sat. fat), 2 g carb, trace fibre, 84 mg chol, 368 mg sodium. % RDI: 2% calcium, 4% iron, 2% vit A, 23% vit C, 21% folate.

Two-Bean Packet

8 oz	each green and yellow beans, trimmed	250 g
1 tbsp	butter or extra-virgin olive oil	15 mL
Pinch	each salt and pepper	Pinch

❯ Arrange green and yellow beans on large piece of heavy-duty foil. Dot with butter; sprinkle with salt and pepper. Fold up sides and seal to form packet. Place on grill over medium heat; close lid and cook until tender-crisp, about 20 minutes.

Makes 4 servings. PER SERVING: about 106 cal, 5 g pro, 3 g total fat (2 g sat. fat), 15 g carb, 6 g fibre, 9 mg chol, 32 mg sodium. % RDI: 4% calcium, 10% iron, 6% vit A, 8% vit C, 24% folate.

TIP
• **Make life easier at the grocery store by using 1 lb (500 g) of all one colour bean – choose whatever looks freshest.**

Grilled Pork Chops and Apple Rings

There is no better way to cook pork chops than on a grill or grill pan. The fat crisps and, as long as you don't grill it past the hint-of-pink-inside stage, the meat is totally toothsome.

4	pork loin centre chops (1¼ lb/625 g)	4
½ tsp	salt	2 mL
¼ tsp	each ground cumin, ginger and cinnamon	1 mL
Pinch	cayenne pepper	Pinch
2	Golden Delicious apples	2
2 tsp	maple syrup or liquid honey	10 mL

> Trim fat from pork chops; slash edges at ½-inch (1 cm) intervals. In small bowl, combine salt, cumin, ginger, cinnamon and cayenne pepper; rub on both sides of chops.

> Place on greased grill or in grill pan over medium-high heat; close lid for barbecue and grill, turning once, until juices run clear when pork is pierced and just a hint of pink remains inside, 8 to 10 minutes.

> Meanwhile, cut apples into ½-inch (1 cm) thick rings. Add to grill with pork chops; grill, turning once, until grill-marked and tender, about 4 minutes. Brush with maple syrup. Arrange apples and pork chops on platter.

Makes 4 servings. PER SERVING: about 198 cal, 21 g pro, 7 g total fat (3 g sat. fat), 13 g carb, 2 g fibre, 58 mg chol, 336 mg sodium. % RDI: 3% calcium, 8% iron, 7% vit C, 2% folate.

Corn and Zucchini Sauté

1 tbsp	vegetable oil	15 mL
3	green onions, sliced	3
1	zucchini, halved lengthwise and sliced	1
½ tsp	dried oregano	2 mL
¼ tsp	each salt and pepper	1 mL
2 cups	frozen corn kernels	500 mL

> In large skillet, heat oil over medium heat; fry green onions until softened, about 3 minutes.

> Add zucchini, oregano, salt and pepper. Fry, stirring occasionally, until zucchini is tender-crisp, about 3 minutes. Stir in corn; fry until hot, about 3 minutes.

Makes 4 servings. PER SERVING: about 104 cal, 3 g pro, 4 g total fat (trace sat. fat), 18 g carb, 2 g fibre, 0 mg chol, 150 mg sodium. % RDI: 2% calcium, 5% iron, 3% vit A, 10% vit C, 16% folate.

Barbecued Chicken Pizzas

You need already-grilled chicken for these personal pizzas, but it's a snap to prepare. Brush 3 boneless skinless chicken breasts lightly with vegetable oil and sprinkle with salt and pepper. Place on greased grill over medium-high heat; close lid and grill until no longer pink inside, about 12 minutes.

3	grilled boneless skinless chicken breasts	3
1 lb	pizza dough	500 g
⅓ cup	barbecue sauce	75 mL
2 cups	shredded Monterey Jack cheese	500 mL
1	sweet green pepper, cut into rings	1
½ tsp	hot pepper flakes	2 mL
½ tsp	dried oregano	2 mL

> Cut chicken crosswise into slices; set aside.

> On lightly floured surface, divide dough into quarters; shape each into disc. Roll out each into 8-inch (20 cm) oval. Place on greased grill over medium heat; close lid and grill, turning once, until crisp, about 7 minutes. Remove from grill.

> Brush with half of the barbecue sauce. Sprinkle evenly with half of the cheese. Arrange chicken over top; drizzle with remaining barbecue sauce. Add green pepper; sprinkle with remaining cheese, hot pepper flakes and oregano.

> Return to grill; close lid and grill until cheese is melted and bubbly and crust is golden, about 10 minutes.

Makes 4 servings. PER SERVING: about 649 cal, 46 g pro, 24 g total fat (13 g sat. fat), 60 g carb, 3 g fibre, 114 mg chol, 1,070 mg sodium. % RDI: 43% calcium, 27% iron, 19% vit A, 38% vit C, 25% folate.

TIP
• You can vary the toppings to include a mix of sliced peppers and thinly sliced red onion, jalapeño pepper and Cheddar cheese.

VARIATION
Baked Chicken Pizzas
• Instead of grilling, bake pizzas on bottom rack of 500°F (260°C) oven for 12 minutes.

NEVER ORDER PIZZA AGAIN

Believe it or not, it takes less time to make a pizza from scratch than it does to wait for the delivery guy or gal. Here's how.

• Stock Up. Freeze prepared pizza bases, pita breads or tortillas and stockpile jars of pizza or pasta sauce. Keep some stretchy cheese, such as mozzarella or provolone – already shredded if you like – on hand in the fridge. When you shop, fill your cart with favourite toppings: pepperoni; smoked or cured sausage; ham or smoked turkey; olives; onions; peppers (raw or roasted); mushrooms; pesto; anchovies; or sliced pineapple. Don't forget leftover or ready-made grilled or roasted vegetables – yum!

• Measure Out. For each 12-inch (30 cm) pizza (enough for 2 adults), you need about: ¾ cup (175 mL) pizza or pasta sauce, 2 cups (500 mL) shredded cheese and 2 cups (500 mL) toppings.

• Build. Place base on pizza pan or baking sheet; spread with sauce. Sprinkle with half of the cheese, all of the toppings, then the rest of the cheese.

• Bake. On bottom rack of 500°F (260°C) oven until base is crisp and cheese is bubbly, about 12 minutes.

Lamb Burgers with Grilled Vegetables

Top with Balkan-style yogurt or hummus – homemade (recipe, page 29) or store-bought – and tuck into pitas or hamburger buns. You can use 16 slices from smaller eggplants and top the burgers with multiple slices, as we have in our photo.

1	egg	1
1 tbsp	ketchup	15 mL
1 cup	minced red onion	250 mL
¼ cup	fresh bread crumbs	50 mL
¼ cup	each chopped fresh dill and parsley	50 mL
4	cloves garlic, minced	4
1 tbsp	pine nuts (optional)	15 mL
½ tsp	each salt and pepper	2 mL
¼ tsp	each paprika and cayenne pepper	1 mL
1 lb	lean ground lamb or beef	500 g
	Pickled peppers (optional)	
GRILLED VEGETABLES:		
4	each thick slices eggplant and tomato	4
2 tbsp	extra-virgin olive oil	25 mL
¼ tsp	each salt and pepper	1 mL

❯ In large bowl, beat egg with ketchup; stir in onion, bread crumbs, dill, parsley, garlic, pine nuts (if using), salt, pepper, paprika and cayenne. Add lamb; mix just until combined. Shape into four ¾-inch (2 cm) thick patties. (*Make-ahead: Layer between waxed paper in airtight container and refrigerate for up to 24 hours or freeze for up to 1 month. Thaw in refrigerator.*)

❯ Place on greased grill over medium heat; close lid and grill, turning once, until digital thermometer inserted sideways into centre reads 160°F (71°C), about 15 minutes.

❯ GRILLED VEGETABLES: Meanwhile, brush eggplant and tomato with oil; sprinkle with salt and pepper. Grill, turning once, until tender, about 5 minutes for eggplant and 1 minute for tomato. Serve on burgers. Top with pickled peppers (if using).

Makes 4 servings. PER SERVING: about 336 cal, 24 g pro, 21 g total fat (7 g sat. fat), 13 g carb, 3 g fibre, 126 mg chol, 567 mg sodium. % RDI: 4% calcium, 21% iron, 9% vit A, 27% vit C, 19% folate.

Chicken Pita Skewers

Small chunks of chicken or meat need less marinating time than whole breasts or thighs.

2 tbsp	lemon juice	25 mL
2 tbsp	extra-virgin olive oil	25 mL
2	cloves garlic, minced	2
¼ tsp	each ground allspice, salt and pepper	1 mL
2	large boneless skinless chicken breasts (1 lb/500 g total)	2
4	Greek-style (pocketless) pitas	4
1 cup	shredded romaine lettuce	250 mL
1	small tomato, diced	1

GARLIC MAYONNAISE:

½ cup	light mayonnaise	125 mL
1	clove garlic, minced	1
2 tbsp	lemon juice	25 mL
1 tbsp	minced fresh parsley	15 mL
Dash	hot pepper sauce	Dash

> In large bowl, combine lemon juice, oil, garlic, allspice, salt and pepper. Cut chicken into 1½-inch (4 cm) cubes; add to bowl and toss to coat. Cover and refrigerate for 1 hour. *(Make-ahead: Refrigerate for up to 4 hours.)*

> GARLIC MAYONNAISE: Meanwhile, in bowl, whisk together mayonnaise, garlic, lemon juice, parsley and hot pepper sauce. *(Make-ahead: Cover and refrigerate for up to 24 hours.)*

> Thread chicken onto metal or soaked wooden skewers. Place on greased grill over medium-high heat; brush with any remaining marinade. Close lid and grill, turning once, until no longer pink inside, about 12 minutes.

> Toast pitas on grill, turning once, until light golden, 3 minutes. Spread Garlic Mayonnaise over half of each pita. Push chicken off skewers onto pitas. Top with lettuce and tomato; fold pita over. Wrap end in waxed paper to secure.

Makes 4 servings. PER SERVING: about 455 cal, 32 g pro, 18 g total fat (3 g sat. fat), 39 g carb, 2 g fibre, 76 mg chol, 749 mg sodium. % RDI: 7% calcium, 18% iron, 6% vit A, 22% vit C, 31% folate.

STANDBY MARINADES
Marinate chewier cuts of beef; lean pork; chicken thighs or legs; or tofu in these marinades. There's enough of each for about 1½ lb (750 g). Always marinate in the refrigerator and only for up to 24 hours – no longer.

RED WINE MARINADE
• Combine ¼ cup (50 mL) red wine; 2 tbsp (25 mL) olive oil; 1 tbsp (15 mL) each herbes de Provence and wine vinegar; 2 cloves garlic, minced; 1 shallot or small onion, finely diced; and ¼ tsp (1 mL) each salt and pepper. **Makes about ½ cup (125 mL).**

SUBSTITUTION
No red wine? Use white wine, or 3 tbsp (50 mL) stock and 1 tbsp (15 mL) wine vinegar.

TASTE OF THAILAND MARINADE
• Combine ¼ cup (50 mL) minced fresh coriander; 3 tbsp (50 mL) water; 2 tbsp (25 mL) each vegetable oil and lime juice; 1 tbsp (15 mL) fish sauce or soy sauce; 2 cloves garlic, minced; 1 green onion, minced; 1 tsp (5 mL) granulated sugar; and generous splash hot pepper sauce. **Makes about ¾ cup (175 mL).**

Grilled Chicken Salad

This light but filling salad is perfect anytime.

4	small boneless skinless chicken breasts (1 lb/500 g total)	4
8 oz	green beans, trimmed	250 g
2	large tomatoes, cut into 8 wedges each	2
4 cups	torn Boston or Bibb lettuce	1 L
⅓ cup	pitted black olives	75 mL

DRESSING:

¼ cup	extra-virgin olive oil	50 mL
2 tbsp	white wine vinegar	25 mL
2 tsp	lemon juice	10 mL
1 tsp	granulated sugar	5 mL
½ tsp	herbes de Provence or dried thyme	2 mL
½ tsp	paprika	2 mL
¼ tsp	each salt and pepper	1 mL

❯ DRESSING: In jar, shake oil, vinegar, lemon juice, sugar, herbes de Provence, paprika, salt and pepper. Pour 3 tbsp (50 mL) into bowl; add chicken and turn to coat. Let stand for 10 minutes. *(Make-ahead: Cover and refrigerate for up to 8 hours.)*

❯ Place chicken on greased grill over medium-high heat; close lid and grill, turning once, until no longer pink inside, about 12 minutes. Slice thinly.

❯ Meanwhile, in pan of boiling salted water, cover and blanch beans until tender-crisp, about 2 minutes. Drain; chill in cold water. Drain well.

❯ In large bowl, toss together beans, tomatoes, lettuce, olives and remaining dressing; divide among plates. Arrange chicken alongside.

Makes 4 servings. PER SERVING: about 301 cal, 28 g pro, 17 g total fat (3 g sat. fat), 11 g carb, 3 g fibre, 67 mg chol, 425 mg sodium. % RDI: 6% calcium, 16% iron, 15% vit A, 37% vit C, 32% folate.

Grilled Turkey Breast

Oil, salt and pepper are the essentials, but add crumbled dried sage and Dijon mustard to the oil if you like.

1½ lb	boneless turkey breast	750 g
2 tsp	extra-virgin olive oil	10 mL
Pinch	each salt and pepper	Pinch

❯ Brush turkey with oil; sprinkle with salt and pepper. Place on greased grill over medium heat; close lid and grill, turning twice, until juices run clear when turkey is pierced, about 40 minutes. Let stand for 10 minutes; slice. *(Make-ahead: Wrap and refrigerate for up to 24 hours.)*

Makes 6 servings. PER SERVING (WITHOUT SKIN): about 136 cal, 23 g pro, 4 g total fat (1 g sat. fat), 0 g carb, 0 g fibre, 54 mg chol, 50 mg sodium. % RDI: 1% calcium, 8% iron, 2% folate.

TIP

● Because tomatoes are soft, they are rarely sold fully ripe. So buy tomatoes a few days ahead of making Grilled Chicken Salad and let them ripen at room temperature. You can speed up the process by enclosing them in a paper bag with an apple or a banana. Works every time, thanks to the ethylene gas these fruits emit.

Stuffed Portobello Mushrooms

When your family and friends include vegetarians, portobello mushrooms are an incredibly delicious alternative to the usual burgers, steaks or chops. But beware – these fungi are so good that meat eaters may prefer them!

4	large portobello mushrooms (1 lb/500 g)	4
2 tbsp	vegetable oil	25 mL
1 cup	shredded Gouda or Gruyère cheese	250 mL
½ cup	fresh bread crumbs	125 mL
¼ cup	chopped fresh parsley	50 mL
¼ cup	toasted almonds, chopped	50 mL
¼ cup	drained oil-packed sun-dried tomatoes, chopped	50 mL
2 tbsp	minced fresh chives or green onions	25 mL
¼ tsp	pepper	1 mL

❯ Remove stems from mushrooms and reserve for another use, such as stock. Brush mushrooms all over with oil.

❯ In bowl, combine cheese, bread crumbs, parsley, almonds, sun-dried tomatoes, chives and pepper; set aside.

❯ Place mushrooms, gill side down, on greased grill over medium-high heat; close lid and grill just until juices start to release, about 4 minutes.

❯ Turn mushrooms and spoon cheese filling evenly over gills. Close lid and grill until cheese is melted and mushrooms are tender, about 4 minutes.

Makes 4 servings. PER SERVING: about 254 cal, 11 g pro, 20 g total fat (6 g sat. fat), 10 g carb, 2 g fibre, 33 mg chol, 291 mg sodium. % RDI: 22% calcium, 10% iron, 8% vit A, 20% vit C, 13% folate.

Balsamic Dressed Greens

6 cups	torn mixed greens or torn arugula	1.5 L
2 tbsp	balsamic vinegar	25 mL
1 tbsp	extra-virgin olive oil	15 mL
¼ tsp	each salt and pepper	1 mL

❯ In salad bowl, toss together greens, vinegar, oil, salt and pepper.

Makes 4 servings. PER SERVING: about 52 cal, 1 g pro, 4 g total fat (trace sat. fat), 4 g carb, 1 g fibre, 0 mg chol, 164 mg sodium. % RDI: 5% calcium, 4% iron, 18% vit A, 18% vit C, 31% folate.

Grilled Peanut Tofu Salad

This dish entertains your mouth! It's crunchy, crisp, fresh, soft and nicely coated with peanut sauce.

⅓ cup	natural peanut butter	75 mL
¼ cup	lime juice	50 mL
2	cloves garlic, minced	2
2 tbsp	each liquid honey and soy sauce	25 mL
½ tsp	each salt and pepper	2 mL
1	pkg (454 g) firm tofu	1
1 tbsp	vegetable oil	15 mL
8 cups	torn leaf lettuce	2 L
2 cups	shredded carrots	500 mL
1 cup	bean sprouts	250 mL
2	green onions, thinly sliced	2
¼ cup	chopped roasted peanuts	50 mL

❯ In bowl, whisk together peanut butter, lime juice, garlic, 2 tbsp (25 mL) hot water, honey, soy sauce and half each of the salt and pepper.

❯ Cut tofu horizontally into 4 slices; pat dry. Brush with oil; sprinkle with remaining salt and pepper. Place on greased grill over medium-high heat; close lid and grill, turning once, until grill-marked, about 10 minutes. Cut each into quarters.

❯ Arrange lettuce on 4 plates. Top each with 4 pieces tofu, carrots, then bean sprouts. Drizzle with dressing; sprinkle with green onions and chopped peanuts.

Makes 4 servings. PER SERVING: about 386 cal, 21 g pro, 24 g total fat (3 g sat. fat), 32 g carb, 7 g fibre, 0 mg chol, 844 mg sodium. % RDI: 30% calcium, 36% iron, 177% vit A, 58% vit C, 63% folate.

GREAT GLAZES

Instead of store-bought barbecue sauce, try out this pair of glazes when grilling or roasting chops, pork tenderloins, salmon fillets, chicken parts, burgers or steaks. Just remember to apply the glaze in the last few minutes of grilling or roasting so the sweetness in the sauce doesn't burn. Each glaze makes enough for about 1½ lb (750 g).

BALSAMIC HONEY GLAZE

● In saucepan, bring 1¼ cups (300 mL) balsamic vinegar and ½ cup (125 mL) liquid honey to boil over medium-high heat. Boil until reduced to ¾ cup (175 mL), about 15 minutes. Mix 1 tsp (5 mL) cornstarch with 1 tbsp (15 mL) cold water; stir into glaze and boil until thickened, about 1 minute. Let cool. **Makes about ¾ cup (175 mL).**

BOURBON MUSTARD GLAZE

● In saucepan, bring ⅔ cup (150 mL) orange juice; ¼ cup (50 mL) strained apricot jam; and dash hot pepper sauce to boil over medium-high heat. Boil until reduced to ⅔ cup (150 mL), about 5 minutes. In small bowl, stir together 3 tbsp (50 mL) bourbon or rye whisky; 1 tbsp (15 mL) each grainy mustard and water; and 2 tsp (10 mL) cornstarch. Stir into glaze and boil until thickened, about 2 minutes. Let cool. **Makes about ¾ cup (175 mL).**

CHAPTER 10

Make It Tonight...
for Company

Asparagus Gruyère Tart

Simple to make and stunning to look at, this tart is a vegetarian option for suppers, lunches and brunches.

2	bunches (1 lb/500 g each) thin asparagus, trimmed	2
1	pkg (450 g) butter puff pastry, thawed but still cold	1
2 tbsp	Dijon mustard	25 mL
1½ cups	shredded Gruyère cheese	375 mL
½ tsp	coarsely cracked pepper	2 mL
1	egg	1
1 tbsp	milk	15 mL

> Line 2 rimless baking sheets with parchment paper or leave ungreased. Set aside.

> In steamer or on rack in saucepan, cover and steam asparagus until tender-crisp, about 3 minutes. Chill in cold water; pat dry.

> Unroll each pastry sheet onto prepared pan. Spread evenly with mustard, leaving 1-inch (2.5 cm) border. Arrange asparagus, side by side and alternating ends, on mustard; sprinkle with cheese and pepper.

> In small bowl, beat egg with milk; lightly brush over pastry border. Bake in top and bottom thirds of 450°F (230°C) oven, rotating and switching pans halfway through, until puffed and golden and cheese is bubbly, about 18 minutes. *(Make-ahead: Set aside for up to 6 hours.)* Cut each into 6 pieces; serve warm or cool.

Makes 12 servings. PER SERVING: about 228 cal, 8 g pro, 14 g total fat (7 g sat. fat), 17 g carb, 2 g fibre, 46 mg chol, 211 mg sodium. % RDI: 15% calcium, 11% iron, 12% vit A, 10% vit C, 37% folate.

COMPANY ON A WEEKNIGHT? ARE YOU CRAZY?

Not at all – the trick is planning. First off, keep it simple: choose a make-ahead or freeze-ahead dish, a barbecue main or a slow cooker entrée. Then do the following to make it a nice, relaxing evening.

● Serve a dish you're comfortable making. It's perfectly fine to use your recipes over and over. When you get tired of them, try new ones. Who knows? You could become famous for your roasted salmon or cranberry-glazed pork chops.

● Get your prep done early. Shop ahead of time, and wash and trim vegetables and salad ingredients.

● Serve a starter. Soup or salad are both good. While guests are enjoying them, the main course and sides can simmer, grill or roast away.

● Enlist helpers. Get the rest of the household to set the table and deal with beverages, ice and glasses before dinner. One guest or family member can pick up plates and serve during dinner. Nobody to help? Do this the night before or rely on your invitees. When a guest asks how she/he can help, point her/him to the table or the drinks area. This is not an admission of incompetence – it's a sign of hospitality.

● Preheat plates, bowls and platters. Warm plates and bowls in microwave on high for about 3 minutes with a bowl containing 1 cup (250 mL) water. The boiling water warms everything nicely. Warm platters in an oven that's been heated and turned off.

● Make dessert ahead. Or serve fresh fruit with a rich sauce. See page 213 for inspiration.

● Enjoy your company. People come to talk and have a good time, not for a flawless performance.

● Wash up tomorrow. Stack dishes neatly and save them for the night after. Hit the hay – you've earned it!

Smoked Trout Spread

Whole grain crackers and rye flatbreads are particularly well suited to the Nordic flavour of this dip.

10 oz	skinless boneless smoked trout	300 g
4 oz	light cream cheese, softened	125 g
3 tbsp	light mayonnaise	50 mL
1 tbsp	prepared horseradish	15 mL
2 tsp	lemon juice	10 mL
Pinch	each salt and cayenne pepper	Pinch
¼ cup	minced green onions	50 mL

> In food processor, whirl together trout, cream cheese, mayonnaise, horseradish, lemon juice, salt and cayenne pepper until smooth. Add all but 2 tsp (10 mL) of the green onions; pulse just until blended. *(Make-ahead: Refrigerate in airtight container for up to 2 days.)*

> Scrape into serving dish; garnish with remaining green onions.

Makes 2½ cups (625 mL). PER 2 TBSP (25 mL): about 48 cal, 5 g pro, 3 g total fat (1 g sat. fat), 1 g carb, 0 g fibre, 16 mg chol, 344 mg sodium. % RDI: 1% calcium, 1% iron, 2% vit A, 2% vit C, 1% folate.

Herbed Feta Dip

Serve this creamy dip with an assortment of vegetables. It's especially popular for family entertaining occasions, as kids never seem to tire of vegetables and dip.

¾ cup	finely crumbled feta cheese	175 mL
½ cup	each light sour cream and light mayonnaise	125 mL
2 tbsp	minced fresh parsley	25 mL
1 tbsp	minced fresh oregano (or ½ tsp/2 mL dried)	15 mL
1	small clove garlic, minced	1
Dash	hot pepper sauce	Dash

> In bowl, mash together feta cheese, sour cream, mayonnaise, parsley, oregano, garlic and hot pepper sauce. Cover and refrigerate for 1 hour. *(Make-ahead: Refrigerate for up to 24 hours.)*

Makes 1½ cups (375 mL). PER 1 TBSP (15 mL): about 31 cal, 1 g pro, 3 g total fat (1 g sat. fat), 1 g carb, 0 g fibre, 6 mg chol, 84 mg sodium. % RDI: 3% calcium, 1% iron, 1% vit A, 1% folate.

TIP
• If your crudité selection includes carrots, slice them on a slight diagonal for easy scooping.

Mussels in Fennel Tomato Sauce

A pot of mussels, a crusty baguette and a bottle of wine: the recipe for a fun, relaxed evening.

2 lb	mussels	1 kg
1	can (14 oz/398 mL) tomatoes	1
1 tbsp	extra-virgin olive oil	15 mL
1	each onion and stalk celery, diced	1
2	cloves garlic, minced	2
Half	bulb fennel, diced	Half
1 tsp	each dried basil and oregano	5 mL
1	bay leaf	1
½ tsp	salt	2 mL
¼ tsp	pepper	1 mL
¼ cup	white wine or sodium-reduced chicken stock	50 mL
1 tbsp	tomato paste	15 mL
¼ cup	chopped fresh parsley	50 mL

❯ Scrub mussels, removing any beards. Discard any that do not close when tapped. Set aside. Reserving juice, drain and dice tomatoes. Set aside.

❯ In Dutch oven or large saucepan, heat oil over medium heat; fry onion, celery, garlic, fennel, basil, oregano, bay leaf, salt and pepper, stirring occasionally, until onion is softened, 5 minutes.

❯ Add tomatoes, reserved juice, wine and tomato paste; bring to boil. Reduce heat; simmer until reduced by half, about 5 minutes.

❯ Add mussels; cover and steam over medium-high heat, stirring once, until mussels open, about 5 minutes. Discard bay leaf and any mussels that do not open. Stir in parsley.

Makes 4 servings. PER SERVING: about 141 cal, 10 g pro, 5 g total fat (1 g sat. fat), 14 g carb, 3 g fibre, 18 mg chol, 587 mg sodium. % RDI: 7% calcium, 26% iron, 12% vit A, 50% vit C, 23% folate.

Maple Soy– Glazed Salmon

A quick broil at the end gives this salmon a golden, glazed finish. This recipe multiplies easily for a party.

4	salmon fillets (about 6 oz/175 g each)	4
¼ cup	maple syrup	50 mL
2 tsp	each sodium-reduced soy sauce and lime juice	10 mL
1	jalapeño pepper, seeded and minced	1
1	small clove garlic, minced	1
Pinch	pepper	Pinch

❯ Place salmon in shallow dish. In bowl, combine maple syrup, soy sauce, lime juice, jalapeño pepper, garlic and pepper; pour half over salmon and turn to coat. Cover and refrigerate for 30 minutes, turning once.

❯ Place salmon on parchment paper– or foil-lined rimmed baking sheet. Roast in 450°F (230°C) oven, brushing halfway through with remaining marinade, until fish flakes easily when tested, about 10 minutes. Broil until glazed, about 3 minutes.

Makes 4 servings. PER SERVING: about 330 cal, 30 g pro, 17 g total fat (3 g sat. fat), 14 g carb, trace fibre, 84 mg chol, 172 mg sodium. % RDI: 3% calcium, 6% iron, 2% vit A, 12% vit C, 21% folate.

Mushroom Pork Medallions for Two

You can replace the pork tenderloin with 12 oz (375 g) boneless skinless chicken breast, cut crosswise into ½-inch (1 cm) thick slices. But when it's just two, do splurge on the pork tenderloin.

1	pork tenderloin (about 12 oz/375 g)	1
¼ tsp	each salt and pepper	1 mL
1 tbsp	vegetable oil	15 mL
1	onion, sliced	1
2 cups	button or quartered mushrooms	500 mL
Half	small sweet red pepper, sliced	Half
3	cloves garlic, minced	3
1 tsp	crumbled dried sage	5 mL
1¼ cups	sodium-reduced chicken stock	300 mL
1 tbsp	all-purpose flour	15 mL
2	green onions, sliced	2

> Slice pork into 8 equal rounds; sprinkle with half each of the salt and pepper.

> In large skillet, heat oil over medium-high heat; brown pork, turning once, about 2 minutes. Transfer to plate.

> Drain off any fat from pan. Add onion, mushrooms, red pepper, garlic, sage and remaining salt and pepper; sauté until onion and mushrooms are golden, about 5 minutes.

> Add stock and bring to boil; boil for 2 minutes. Whisk flour with 2 tbsp (25 mL) water; whisk into sauce. Return pork to pan; simmer until sauce is thickened, juices run clear when pork is pierced and just a hint of pink remains inside, about 4 minutes. Sprinkle with green onions.

Makes 2 or 3 servings. PER EACH OF 3 SERVINGS: about 234 cal, 30 g pro, 8 g total fat (1 g sat. fat), 10 g carb, 2 g fibre, 67 mg chol, 504 mg sodium. % RDI: 3% calcium, 19% iron, 8% vit A, 67% vit C, 14% folate.

LEFTOVER SAFETY

• Always refrigerate or freeze any leftovers within 2 hours of serving.

• Carve large cuts of meat into slices and store in serving-size packets.

• Cover and refrigerate cooked rice within 1 hour of cooking; keep leftover rice for no longer than 24 hours.

• Transfer large quantities of thick food, such as stew or chili, to several shallow uncovered containers for quicker cooling in the refrigerator.

• Label and date wrapped leftovers in your fridge and eat within 3 days.

• Check the refrigerator once a week and discard old leftovers.

Stuffed Pork Tenderloin

One average tenderloin serves two or three. Double this quick recipe for more guests and do the same for the potato salad. In cold weather, grill the tenderloin on an indoor grill or grill pan. Cover with a domed lid or upside-down foil roasting pan to simulate the barbecue.

1	pork tenderloin (about 12 oz/375 g)	1
2 tbsp	grated Parmesan cheese	25 mL
2 tbsp	minced fresh parsley	25 mL
¼ tsp	each salt and pepper	1 mL
⅓ cup	minced drained oil-packed sun-dried tomatoes	75 mL

> Cut pork lengthwise almost but not all the way through; open like book. Sprinkle with Parmesan cheese, parsley, salt and pepper. Sprinkle sun-dried tomatoes down centre. Fold pork over filling; secure with toothpicks.

> Place on greased grill over medium-high heat; close lid and grill, turning occasionally, until juices run clear when pork is pierced and just a hint of pink remains inside, about 18 minutes. Transfer to cutting board; tent with foil and let stand for 5 minutes. Remove toothpicks and slice.

Makes 2 or 3 servings. PER EACH OF 3 SERVINGS: about 190 cal, 30 g pro, 6 g total fat (2 g sat. fat), 3 g carb, 1 g fibre, 65 mg chol, 339 mg sodium. % RDI: 6% calcium, 14% iron, 4% vit A, 27% vit C, 5% folate.

Warm Potato Salad

4	potatoes (2 lb/1 kg), peeled (if desired) and cubed	4
¼ cup	extra-virgin olive oil	50 mL
2 tbsp	wine vinegar	25 mL
1 tbsp	Dijon mustard	15 mL
½ tsp	salt	2 mL
¼ tsp	pepper	1 mL
½ cup	each diced celery and sweet green pepper	125 mL
2 tbsp	chopped fresh basil or parsley	25 mL

> In saucepan of boiling salted water, cover and cook potatoes until tender, about 10 minutes. Drain and transfer to bowl; let cool for 10 minutes.

> Meanwhile, in small bowl, whisk together oil, vinegar, mustard, salt and pepper; pour over potatoes. Add celery, green pepper and basil. Toss together.

Makes 4 servings. PER SERVING: about 274 cal, 3 g pro, 14 g total fat (2 g sat. fat), 36 g carb, 3 g fibre, 0 mg chol, 750 mg sodium. % RDI: 3% calcium, 6% iron, 2% vit A, 50% vit C, 11% folate.

Gremolada Rack of Lamb

Frenched refers to the way meat is prepared: the end of each rib bone is scraped clean to within 1 inch (2.5 cm) of the eye of the raw meat. It's a restaurant preparation worth doing for guests at home. Frozen imported racks of lamb are often frenched.

2	racks of lamb, frenched (about 1¼ lb/625 g each)	2
¼ tsp	each salt and pepper	1 mL
GREMOLADA:		
½ cup	minced fresh parsley	125 mL
2 tbsp	extra-virgin olive oil	25 mL
4 tsp	grated lemon rind	20 mL
½ tsp	ground coriander	2 mL
2	cloves garlic, minced	2
¼ tsp	each salt and pepper	1 mL

❯ GREMOLADA: In bowl, mix together parsley, oil, lemon rind, coriander, garlic, salt and pepper.

❯ Trim any outside fat from lamb; sprinkle with salt and pepper. Press gremolada onto rounded side. Place, gremolada side up, in roasting pan. *(Make-ahead: Cover and refrigerate for up to 12 hours.)*

❯ Roast in 450°F (230°C) oven for 10 minutes. Reduce heat to 325°F (160°C); roast until meat thermometer registers 145°F (63°C) for medium-rare, about 15 minutes longer. (Or grill over medium heat for 20 minutes.)

❯ Transfer to cutting board and tent with foil; let stand for 5 minutes before carving between bones.

Makes 4 servings. PER SERVING: about 253 cal, 24 g pro, 16 g total fat (5 g sat. fat), 2 g carb, 1 g fibre, 89 mg chol, 337 mg sodium. % RDI: 3% calcium, 17% iron, 4% vit A, 20% vit C, 5% folate.

THE WELL-STOCKED KITCHEN
ESSENTIAL SPICES AND HERBS

• Solo spices: salt, peppercorns to grind (worth the effort), cinnamon, paprika, cumin, ginger, dry mustard, and hot pepper flakes or cayenne

• Spice combos: chili powder, curry powder, Montreal steak spice, Cajun seasoning, five-spice powder and zaatar (the latest up-and-comer)

• Solo herbs: thyme, basil, oregano, sage, rosemary, dillweed, mint and bay leaves

• Herb combos: dried Italian herb seasoning and herbes de Provence

• Handy additions: ground nutmeg, coriander seeds, allspice, cloves and fennel seeds

HOW TO STORE
Keep herbs and spices in a cool, dark spot – near the stove is a definite no-no. Try a drawer; label the tops of the jars and arrange alphabetically. Use them lavishly and renew every six months.

HOW TO BUY
For dried herbs, buy leaves, not powdered. In season, use fresh herbs, usually about three times the amount of dried called for.

Asian-Seasoned Steak with Cucumber Radish Pickle

Even if a dish is for entertaining, you can still think healthy. Red meat is one of the best sources of iron.

3 tbsp	each oyster sauce and sodium-reduced soy sauce	50 mL
4 tsp	each minced gingerroot, granulated sugar and sesame oil	20 mL
½ tsp	hot pepper sauce	2 mL
4	cloves garlic, minced	4
1	top sirloin grilling steak, 1 inch (2.5 cm) thick (about 2 lb/1 kg)	1
2 tsp	toasted sesame seeds	10 mL

CUCUMBER RADISH PICKLE:

3 cups	sliced English cucumber	750 mL
2 cups	thinly sliced radishes	500 mL
1 tsp	salt	5 mL
2 tbsp	rice vinegar or white wine vinegar	25 mL
1 tbsp	granulated sugar	15 mL
1 tsp	sesame oil	5 mL
¼ tsp	hot pepper sauce	1 mL

> In shallow bowl, whisk together oyster sauce, soy sauce, ginger, sugar, sesame oil, hot pepper sauce and garlic. Reserve ⅓ cup (75 mL) to heat and serve with steak; add steak to remaining marinade, turning to coat. Cover and refrigerate for 4 hours. *(Make-ahead: Refrigerate for up to 24 hours.)*

> CUCUMBER RADISH PICKLE: In colander, toss together cucumber, radishes and salt; let stand for 15 minutes. Shake off liquid and pat dry; place in bowl. Add vinegar, sugar, sesame oil and hot pepper sauce; toss to coat.

> Place steak on greased grill or in greased grill pan; close lid for barbecue and grill over medium-high heat, turning once, until medium-rare, about 16 minutes, or until desired doneness. Transfer to cutting board and tent with foil; let stand for 5 minutes before slicing and arranging on platter.

> Heat reserved marinade; drizzle over steak. Sprinkle with sesame seeds. Serve with Cucumber Radish Pickle.

Makes 6 to 8 servings. PER EACH OF 8 SERVINGS: about 193 cal, 22 g pro, 8 g total fat (2 g sat. fat), 8 g carb, 1 g fibre, 51 mg chol, 547 mg sodium. % RDI: 3% calcium, 19% iron, 1% vit A, 15% vit C, 10% folate.

Pecan-Crusted Chicken Cutlets

This is not a new recipe, but it's one that never fails to please guests. Other nuts, especially walnuts, are good for the crust, too.

¼ cup	all-purpose flour	50 mL
½ tsp	each salt and pepper	2 mL
1	egg	1
¼ cup	milk	50 mL
1¼ cups	finely chopped pecans or walnuts	300 mL
4	small boneless skinless chicken breasts (about 4 oz/125 g each)	4
2 tbsp	vegetable oil	25 mL
1¼ cups	sodium-reduced chicken stock	300 mL
2 tbsp	Dijon mustard	25 mL
2 tsp	chopped fresh parsley	10 mL
2 tsp	butter	10 mL
2 tsp	liquid honey	10 mL

> In shallow bowl, whisk together flour and half each of the salt and pepper. In separate bowl, whisk egg with milk. Pour pecans into third bowl.

> Slice chicken in half horizontally to make 8 cutlets; sprinkle with remaining salt and pepper. Dip cut side of chicken into flour mixture; dip into egg mixture then pecans. Set aside.

> In large skillet, heat 1 tbsp (15 mL) of the oil over medium-low heat; fry chicken, pecan side down, in batches and adding more oil if necessary, until pecans begin to darken and crisp, about 2 minutes. Turn and fry until chicken is no longer pink inside, about 4 minutes. Transfer to platter. Cover and keep warm.

> Drain any fat from skillet. Add chicken stock and bring to boil, scraping up brown bits from bottom of pan. Boil until reduced to about ½ cup (125 mL), about 5 minutes. Whisk in mustard, parsley, butter and honey. Serve with chicken.

Makes 4 servings. PER SERVING: about 479 cal, 32 g pro, 33 g total fat (5 g sat. fat), 15 g carb, 3 g fibre, 121 mg chol, 715 mg sodium. % RDI: 6% calcium, 14% iron, 6% vit A, 2% vit C, 12% folate.

Turkey Scaloppine with Leafy Salad

Scaloppine made from turkey or chicken are always tender. The salad is a fresh twist and a crunchy contrast to the turkey's crisp coating.

2½ cups	dry bread crumbs	625 mL
⅓ cup	grated Parmesan cheese	75 mL
2 tbsp	minced fresh parsley	25 mL
2 tsp	dried thyme	10 mL
⅓ cup	10% cream or milk	75 mL
4	turkey or chicken scaloppine (about 1 lb/500 g)	4
3 tbsp	vegetable oil	50 mL
4 cups	torn mixed salad greens	1 L
1 tbsp	extra-virgin olive oil	15 mL
2 tsp	lemon juice	10 mL
½ tsp	each salt and pepper	2 mL
	Lemon wedges	

❯ In shallow dish, combine bread crumbs, cheese, parsley and thyme. Pour cream into second shallow dish. Dip scaloppine into cream, letting excess drip back into dish. Press into bread-crumb mixture, turning to coat both sides. Place on rimmed baking sheet.

❯ In large skillet, heat 2 tbsp (25 mL) of the vegetable oil over medium-high heat; fry scaloppine, turning once, in batches and adding remaining vegetable oil as necessary, until golden, about 4 minutes.

❯ Meanwhile, in large bowl, toss salad greens, olive oil, lemon juice, salt and pepper. Serve salad on scaloppine. Garnish with lemon wedges.

Makes 4 servings. PER SERVING: about 587 cal, 39 g pro, 24 g total fat (6 g sat. fat), 53 g carb, 3 g fibre, 71 mg chol, 1,123 mg sodium. % RDI: 32% calcium, 46% iron, 16% vit A, 23% vit C, 34% folate.

TIP
● If thin scaloppine are unavailable, make your own with thick turkey cutlets or slices of turkey breast. Place between sheets of plastic wrap and, with flat side of meat mallet, pound to scant ¼-inch (5 mm) thickness.

Tilapia and Tomato Sauce

You can brown the fish fillets and simmer them in the tomato sauce until they're done, or fry them completely in the skillet for 8 minutes and serve with the sauce spooned over top.

3 tbsp	extra-virgin olive oil (approx)	50 mL
1	onion, sliced	1
3	cloves garlic, minced	3
1	sweet red pepper, sliced	1
1 tsp	dried oregano	5 mL
½ tsp	ground cumin	2 mL
½ tsp	each salt and pepper	2 mL
½ tsp	hot pepper sauce	2 mL
1	can (28 oz/796 mL) diced tomatoes	1
2 tbsp	chopped fresh coriander	25 mL
2 tbsp	orange juice	25 mL
1 tbsp	lime juice	15 mL
4	tilapia or catfish fillets	4

❯ In shallow Dutch oven, heat 1 tbsp (15 mL) of the oil over medium heat; fry onion, garlic, red pepper, oregano, cumin, half each of the salt and pepper, and the hot pepper sauce, stirring often, until vegetables are very tender, about 15 minutes.

❯ Add tomatoes; bring to boil. Reduce heat and simmer until thickened and reduced to about 2 cups (500 mL), about 20 minutes. Stir in coriander, orange juice and lime juice. *(Make-ahead: Let cool completely; refrigerate in airtight container for up to 2 days.)*

❯ Meanwhile, in large skillet, heat remaining oil over medium-high heat. Sprinkle fish with remaining salt and pepper; fry, turning once, in batches and adding more oil if necessary, until browned, 4 minutes. Nestle into hot sauce; simmer until fish flakes easily when tested, 4 minutes.

Makes 4 servings. PER SERVING: about 274 cal, 28 g pro, 13 g total fat (2 g sat. fat), 15 g carb, 3 g fibre, 63 mg chol, 617 mg sodium. % RDI: 9% calcium, 24% iron, 14% vit A, 132% vit C, 23% folate.

Swiss Cheese Fondue

Fully ripened cheese and good-quality wine make the best fondue. Kirsch (cherry eau-de-vie) is the most traditional flavouring, but plum eau-de-vie (*pflümli*, *pruneau* or Slivovitz) and apple brandy, such as Calvados, are also recommended.

1	clove garlic	1
2 cups	dry white wine	500 mL
1 lb	Emmenthal cheese, shredded (4 cups/1 L)	500 g
1 lb	Gruyère cheese, shredded (4 cups/1 L)	500 g
2 tbsp	cornstarch	25 mL
¼ tsp	pepper	1 mL
Pinch	grated nutmeg	Pinch
2 tbsp	kirsch	25 mL
2	baguettes, cut in 1-inch (2.5 cm) cubes	2
1	each apple and pear, cored and cubed	1

> Cut small slits in garlic clove; rub clove all over inside of fondue pot. Pour in all but 2 tbsp (25 mL) of the wine; bring to simmer over medium heat on stove top.

> Add Emmenthal and Gruyère cheeses; stir with wooden spoon until melted. Dissolve cornstarch in remaining wine; stir into fondue pot along with pepper and nutmeg. Bring to simmer, stirring; simmer for 1 minute. Stir in kirsch.

> Place over medium-low heat of fondue burner on table, stirring often and adjusting heat as necessary to maintain low simmer. Serve with bread, apple and pear cubes to skewer and dip into cheese mixture.

Makes 6 servings. PER SERVING: about 665 cal, 32 g pro, 28 g total fat (15 g sat. fat), 66 g carb, 4 g fibre, 83 mg chol, 868 mg sodium. % RDI: 77% calcium, 22% iron, 23% vit A, 5% vit C, 48% folate.

VARIATIONS

Garlic Fondue

● Instead of rubbing the pot with garlic, add 3 cloves garlic, thinly sliced, to white wine at beginning of cooking.

True Canadian Cheese Fondue

● Omit garlic. Substitute 1⅓ lb (670 g) Oka cheese, shredded (5½ cups/1.375 L), and 12 oz (375 g) extra-old Cheddar cheese, shredded (3 cups/750 mL) for Emmenthal and Gruyère cheeses. Along with pepper and nutmeg, stir in 1½ tsp (7 mL) Dijon mustard, 1 tsp (5 mL) Worcestershire sauce and pinch cayenne pepper. Substitute 1 tbsp (15 mL) whisky for kirsch.

Raclette

Classic meets modern in this selection of ingredients that you can prepare ahead. There's about 3 oz (90 g) cheese per person, but heartier appetites (and cheese lovers) may want to have 5 oz (150 g), which would increase the total to 2½ lb (1.25 kg).

1½ lb	raclette cheese	750 g
1½ lb	cooked sausage (such as knackwurst) or cured sausage (such as smoked turkey or kielbasa)	750 g
2 cups	drained pickles (such as cornichons, gherkins and cocktail onions)	500 mL
1	bunch broccoli, cut into florets	1
1	can (14 oz/398 mL) whole baby corn	1
24	small new potatoes (about 3 lb/1.5 kg)	24
	Paprika and pepper	

> Scrape away most of the tough rind from cheese. Thinly slice cheese into 3½-inch (9 cm) squares or cut to fit raclette pan. Arrange on serving plate.

> Diagonally cut sausages into ½-inch (1 cm) thick slices; arrange on separate serving plate. Place pickles in bowls.

> In large saucepan of boiling salted water, cover and cook broccoli until tender-crisp, 2 to 3 minutes. With slotted spoon, transfer to bowl of cold water to chill; drain and pat dry. Transfer to serving bowl.

> Drain and rinse corn; pat dry. Place in serving bowl. *(Make-ahead: Cover all prepared ingredients and refrigerate for up to 24 hours.)*

> In same saucepan of boiling salted water, cover and cook potatoes just until tender, 16 to 18 minutes; drain well. *(Make-ahead: Let cool; refrigerate for up to 24 hours. Reheat in microwave at high for 4 to 6 minutes.)* Transfer to cloth napkin–lined heatproof bowl; fold napkin over potatoes to keep warm.

> To serve, choose one of the following.

• **FOR THE PURIST:** Quarter potatoes; place on plate. Place 1 slice cheese in raclette tray; broil under raclette broiler until melted and bubbly, about 2 minutes. Scrape over potatoes. Sprinkle with paprika and pepper to taste. Add pickles.

• **FOR VARIETY:** Arrange piece each of sausage, broccoli and baby corn in raclette tray; top with cheese and broil under raclette broiler.

• **FOR ACTION:** Chop potatoes; place in raclette tray. Top with cheese and broil under raclette broiler while grilling sausage on top portion of raclette grill.

Makes 8 servings. PER SERVING: about 800 cal, 40 g pro, 48 g total fat (24 g sat. fat), 57 g carb, 5 g fibre, 127 mg chol, 1,597 mg sodium. % RDI: 79% calcium, 21% iron, 31% vit A, 103% vit C, 33% folate.

TIP
• Use top level of raclette grill to keep potatoes warm in a covered heatproof dish.

Shrimp and Pea Risotto

With a bag of shrimp and another of shelled edamame or peas in the freezer, you're ready to roll out a very smart little supper. The shrimp thaw quickly in cold water.

1 tbsp	extra-virgin olive oil	15 mL
1	onion, finely diced	1
2	cloves garlic, minced	2
1 tsp	grated lemon rind	5 mL
¼ tsp	each salt and pepper	1 mL
1 cup	arborio or other short-grain rice	250 mL
¼ cup	dry white wine or sodium-reduced chicken stock	50 mL
2½ cups	hot sodium-reduced chicken stock	625 mL
10 oz	peeled deveined large raw shrimp	300 g
1 cup	frozen peas or frozen shelled edamame	250 mL
2 tbsp	chopped fresh mint or parsley	25 mL

❯ In large saucepan, heat oil over medium heat; fry onion, garlic, lemon rind, salt and pepper, stirring occasionally, until softened, about 3 minutes.

❯ Add rice, stirring to coat. Add wine; boil until wine is evaporated, about 1 minute.

❯ Stir in stock and bring to boil. Reduce heat to low; cover and simmer, stirring once, for 10 minutes. Stir vigorously for 15 seconds. Cover and simmer for 5 minutes.

❯ Stir in shrimp and peas; cover and simmer until shrimp are pink, peas are tender and rice is creamy and slightly firm to the bite, about 3 minutes. Sprinkle with mint.

Makes 4 servings. PER SERVING: about 338 cal, 22 g pro, 5 g total fat (1 g sat. fat), 49 g carb, 3 g fibre, 108 mg chol, 652 mg sodium. % RDI: 6% calcium, 21% iron, 11% vit A, 10% vit C, 15% folate.

CHAPTER 11

Make It Tonight...
Breakfast for Dinner

Turkey Potato Patties

This recipe is quick to put together if you have leftover mashed potatoes. If you don't, follow the tip. Serve with poached eggs, salsa and a salad.

1	egg	1
1½ cups	diced cooked turkey or chicken	375 mL
1 cup	mashed potatoes	250 mL
¼ cup	dry bread crumbs	50 mL
1	green onion, finely chopped	1
2 tbsp	finely chopped fresh parsley	25 mL
2 tsp	Dijon mustard	10 mL
¼ tsp	each dried thyme and sage	1 mL
¼ tsp	each salt and pepper	1 mL
1 tbsp	vegetable oil (approx)	15 mL

> In bowl, beat egg; mix in turkey, potatoes, bread crumbs, green onion, parsley, mustard, thyme, sage, salt and pepper. Form into eight ½-inch (1 cm) thick patties. *(Make-ahead: Cover and refrigerate for up to 8 hours.)*

> In large skillet, heat oil over medium heat; fry patties, turning once, reducing temperature if browning too quickly and adding more oil if necessary, until patties are crusty and golden, about 6 minutes.

Makes 4 servings. PER SERVING: about 184 cal, 14 g pro, 7 g total fat (1 g sat. fat), 16 g carb, 1 g fibre, 73 mg chol, 401 mg sodium. % RDI: 4% calcium, 11% iron, 3% vit A, 8% vit C, 8% folate.

TIP
• To make mashed potatoes, peel and cube 2 potatoes. In saucepan of boiling salted water, cover and cook potatoes until tender, about 12 minutes. Drain and mash with potato masher.

EQUIPMENT
THE THREE MUST-HAVE KNIVES

1. CHEF'S KNIFE
2. SERRATED BREAD KNIFE
3. PARING KNIFE

FIND THE PERFECT CHEF'S KNIFE
This is the most important knife to have in your kitchen. Here's what you need to know to find the right one for you.
• Look for one with a forged blade rather than a lighter, less-dense stamped blade.
• A blade 8 inches (20 cm) long is ideal for home cooks. Get a longer one if you're tall and will use it professionally.
• The blade should extend from the tip of the knife right through the handle, where it's known as the tang.
• The handle can be metal, wood or moulded plastic – choose one that's comfortable to hold.
• A good chef's knife is a lifetime investment – buy quality and you'll only need to buy once.

HOW TO WASH AND STORE
Always hand-wash knives to avoid dulling the blade and damaging wooden handles. Store in a wooden block, in a drawer in a wooden knife insert or on a magnetic strip. Never store knives loose in a drawer, where edges can be dulled and an unsuspecting helper can get cut.

KEEP THEM SHARP
A butcher's steel is not a sharpener, but it will help maintain your knife's sharp edge. To use, hold the knife blade at a 20-degree angle and draw the knife along the length of the steel, angling with your wrist to ensure the entire length of the blade is honed. Six to eight strokes on each side should suffice. Have your knives sharpened regularly by a professional sharpener – cookware shops often offer this service.

180

Zucchini Pancakes

Top with sour cream or Feta Tomato Cream
(recipe, this page).

4 cups	coarsely grated zucchini (about 6, or 1 lb/500 g total)	1 L
1 tsp	salt	5 mL
2	green onions, minced	2
2	eggs, beaten	2
1 cup	buttermilk	250 mL
2 tbsp	vegetable oil	25 mL
⅔ cup	cornmeal	150 mL
½ cup	all-purpose flour	125 mL
1 tsp	granulated sugar	5 mL
¼ tsp	each baking soda and pepper	1 mL
2 tbsp	butter (approx)	25 mL

❯ In colander, toss zucchini with salt; let stand
for 20 minutes. Squeeze out as much liquid as
possible; transfer zucchini to bowl. Stir in green
onions, eggs, buttermilk and oil; set aside.

❯ In large bowl, whisk together cornmeal, flour,
sugar, baking soda and pepper. Pour zucchini
mixture over top; stir just until blended.

❯ In large skillet, heat half of the butter over
medium heat. Spoon heaping 2 tbsp (25 mL)
batter for each pancake into pan; flatten and
spread with back of spoon. Fry, adding more
butter if necessary, until bottoms are golden,
about 2 minutes.

❯ Turn and fry until edges are golden, about
2 minutes. Place on paper towel–lined baking
sheet. (Make-ahead: Let cool and stack between
waxed paper; refrigerate in airtight container for
up to 2 days. Reheat on baking sheet in 325°F/160°C
oven, about 8 minutes.)

Makes 4 servings. PER SERVING: about 335 cal, 9 g pro, 16 g total
fat (5 g sat. fat), 38 g carb, 3 g fibre, 113 mg chol, 518 mg sodium. % RDI:
10% calcium, 13% iron, 13% vit A, 10% vit C, 28% folate.

Feta Tomato Cream

1 cup	grape or cherry tomatoes	250 mL
½ cup	crumbled feta cheese (about 2½ oz/75 g)	125 mL
¼ cup	plain Balkan-style yogurt	50 mL
1 tbsp	chopped fresh mint	15 mL
1 tbsp	extra-virgin olive oil	15 mL
2 tsp	lemon juice	10 mL
Pinch	each salt and pepper	Pinch

❯ Quarter tomatoes; place in small bowl. In food
processor, blend feta cheese, yogurt, mint,
oil, lemon juice, salt and pepper. Scrape over
tomatoes; stir to blend. (Make-ahead: Cover and
refrigerate for up to 6 hours.)

Makes 1¼ cups (300 mL). PER 1 TBSP (15 mL): about 20 cal, 1 g
pro, 2 g total fat (1 g sat. fat), 1 g carb, 0 g fibre, 4 mg chol, 43 mg sodium.
% RDI: 2% calcium, 1% iron, 1% vit A, 2% vit C, 1% folate.

Ricotta Crêpes

These heavenly cheese-filled crêpes are perfect for brunch or dinner.

3 tbsp	butter, melted	50 mL
1	onion, finely chopped	1
2 cups	ricotta cheese	500 mL
2	egg yolks	2
1 tsp	finely chopped fresh basil (or ½ tsp/2 mL dried)	5 mL
¼ tsp	each salt and pepper	1 mL
Pinch	nutmeg	Pinch
	Crêpes (recipe, this page)	

> In small skillet, heat 1 tsp (5 mL) of the butter over medium heat; cook onion until softened, about 1 minute. Let cool. In bowl, combine onion, cheese, egg yolks, basil, salt, pepper and nutmeg.

> Spoon 2 tbsp (25 mL) of the cheese mixture onto centre of each crêpe; fold in half, then in half again, handkerchief-style. Transfer to parchment paper–lined or greased rimmed baking sheet. Brush with remaining butter. *(Make-ahead: Cover and refrigerate for up to 2 days or freeze in airtight container for up to 2 weeks.)*

> Bake in 350°F (180°C) oven until filling is hot and edges are crisp and golden, about 7 minutes.

Makes 16 crêpes, or 8 servings. PER SERVING: about 353 cal, 15 g pro, 23 g total fat (13 g sat. fat), 22 g carb, 1 g fibre, 206 mg chol, 319 mg sodium. % RDI: 19% calcium, 12% iron, 24% vit A, 33% folate.

Crêpes

Dress these crêpes up with almost any sweet or savoury filling. For dessert, spread with raspberry or apricot jam, or chocolate hazelnut spread. Heat and crisp them the same way as the Ricotta Crêpes.

1⅓ cups	all-purpose flour	325 mL
¼ tsp	salt	1 mL
4	eggs	4
1½ cups	milk	375 mL
¼ cup	butter, melted	50 mL

> In bowl, whisk flour with salt. In small bowl, whisk together eggs, milk and 2 tbsp (25 mL) of the butter; whisk into flour mixture until smooth. Cover and refrigerate for 1 hour. Strain through fine sieve into bowl.

> Heat 8-inch (20 cm) crêpe pan or skillet over medium heat. For each crêpe, brush pan with some of the remaining butter; pour scant ¼ cup (50 mL) of the batter into centre of pan, swirling pan to coat. Cook, turning once, until golden, about 1 minute. Transfer to plate. *(Make-ahead: Layer between waxed paper, wrap in plastic wrap and refrigerate for up to 3 days or freeze in airtight container for up to 1 month.)*

Makes 16 crêpes. PER CRÊPE: about 93 cal, 3 g pro, 5 g total fat (3 g sat. fat), 9 g carb, trace fibre, 56 mg chol, 81 mg sodium. % RDI: 3% calcium, 4% iron, 5% vit A, 13% folate.

Spinach, Ham and Cheese Strata

This strata is great for a group at brunch, lunch or supper. You can assemble it a day ahead, so it's suited to busy times.

1	loaf sourdough bread	1
1	pkg (10 oz/300 g) frozen spinach, thawed and squeezed dry	1
6	green onions, thinly sliced	6
1½ cups	shredded Swiss cheese	375 mL
1 cup	diced ham or smoked turkey	250 mL
8	eggs	8
2½ cups	milk	625 mL
1 tbsp	Dijon mustard	15 mL
¼ tsp	each salt and pepper	1 mL

❯ Cut bread into 1-inch (2.5 cm) cubes to make about 12 cups (3 L). In large bowl, stir together bread, spinach, onions, cheese and ham. Spoon into greased 13- x 9-inch (3 L) glass baking dish.

❯ In bowl, whisk together eggs, milk, mustard, salt and pepper; pour over bread mixture and let stand for 20 minutes, pressing occasionally. *(Make-ahead: Cover and refrigerate for up to 24 hours.)*

❯ Bake in 375°F (190°C) oven until puffed and golden, about 45 minutes.

Makes 8 servings. PER SERVING: about 383 cal, 25 g pro, 15 g total fat (7 g sat. fat), 37 g carb, 3 g fibre, 220 mg chol, 828 mg sodium. % RDI: 33% calcium, 20% iron, 35% vit A, 7% vit C, 47% folate.

Smoked Turkey French Toast Sandwiches

Instead of frying these fabulous sandwiches, we bake them – it's so much less work.

8	slices granary or whole grain bread	8
¼ cup	Russian-style mustard	50 mL
8	thin slices Gruyère cheese (about 6 oz/175 g)	8
1	tomato, sliced	1
1	ripe avocado, peeled, pitted and sliced	1
4	thin slices sweet onion	4
8 oz	shaved smoked turkey	250 g
2	eggs	2
½ cup	milk	125 mL
Pinch	each salt and pepper	Pinch

❯ Spread 1 side of each bread slice with mustard. On half of the slices, arrange cheese, tomato, avocado, onion and turkey. Top with remaining bread, mustard side down.

❯ In shallow dish, whisk together eggs, milk, salt and pepper. Dip each sandwich into egg mixture, turning to soak well. Place on parchment paper–lined or greased rimmed baking sheet; pour any remaining egg mixture over top. *(Make-ahead: Cover and refrigerate for up to 2 hours.)*

❯ Bake in 375°F (190°C) oven, turning once, until golden, about 25 minutes.

Makes 4 servings. PER SERVING: about 626 cal, 37 g pro, 31 g total fat (12 g sat. fat), 54 g carb, 8 g fibre, 166 mg chol, 1,364 mg sodium. % RDI: 49% calcium, 31% iron, 25% vit A, 18% vit C, 38% folate.

Sausage and Potato Omelette

This thick omelette has it all – tomatoes, spinach, potatoes and sausage. While it's cooking, there's time to toss a salad and warm whole grain rolls.

2	mild Italian sausages (6 oz/175 g), thinly sliced	2
1 tbsp	extra-virgin olive oil	15 mL
1	small onion, chopped	1
1 cup	grape or cherry tomatoes	250 mL
1	potato, peeled (if desired) and diced	1
6	eggs	6
¼ tsp	each salt and pepper	1 mL
¼ cup	packed shredded fresh spinach	50 mL
1	green onion, thinly sliced	1
½ cup	shredded mozzarella cheese (optional)	125 mL

❯ In 9-inch (23 cm) cast-iron ovenproof skillet, brown sausages over medium-high heat. With slotted spoon, transfer to paper towel–lined plate. Drain fat from pan.

❯ In same pan, heat oil over medium heat; fry onion, tomatoes and potato, stirring occasionally, until potato is tender, about 12 minutes. Return sausage to skillet.

❯ Meanwhile, in bowl, whisk together eggs, salt and pepper; stir in spinach and green onion. Pour into skillet and stir to combine. Sprinkle with mozzarella (if using).

❯ Cover and cook over medium-low heat until bottom and side are firm but top is still slightly runny, about 10 minutes.

❯ Broil until golden and set, about 3 minutes. Cut into wedges.

Makes 4 servings. PER SERVING: about 288 cal, 17 g pro, 19 g total fat (6 g sat. fat), 12 g carb, 1 g fibre, 300 mg chol, 508 mg sodium. % RDI: 6% calcium, 13% iron, 16% vit A, 15% vit C, 24% folate.

EQUIPMENT
SPLATTER SCREEN

Skillets rarely have lids because moisture makes fried food soggy. When frying foods that tend to splatter, especially over high heat, a wire mesh antisplash lid placed over the skillet will help control fat spatters without making the food soggy. It also keeps the cook and the stove clean.

Folded Salsa Omelette

Here's a time-saver: replace homemade salsa with 1 to 2 cups (250 to 500 mL) store-bought salsa.
We recommend the chunky variety.

8	eggs	8
Pinch	each salt and pepper	Pinch
4 tsp	butter (approx)	20 mL
½ cup	shredded Cheddar cheese	125 mL
SALSA:		
1⅓ cups	cherry tomatoes, quartered	325 mL
⅓ cup	chopped sweet green pepper	75 mL
⅓ cup	finely chopped red onion	75 mL
4 tsp	chopped fresh coriander or parsley	20 mL
1 tbsp	vegetable oil	15 mL
1 tbsp	white wine vinegar	15 mL
¼ tsp	each salt and pepper	1 mL

> SALSA: In bowl, mix tomatoes, green pepper, onion, coriander, oil, vinegar, salt and pepper; set aside.

> In bowl, whisk together eggs, 2 tbsp (25 mL) water, salt and pepper just until blended but not frothy.

> In 8-inch (20 cm) omelette pan or skillet, melt 1 tsp (5 mL) of the butter over medium heat. Pour one-quarter of the egg mixture into skillet; cook until almost set, gently lifting edge to allow any uncooked eggs to flow underneath, 3 minutes.

> Spoon ⅓ cup (75 mL) of the salsa onto half of the omelette; sprinkle 2 tbsp (25 mL) of the cheese over salsa. Fold uncovered half over top; cook for 2 minutes. Slide onto plate. Repeat with remaining ingredients, adding more butter as necessary. Serve with remaining salsa.

Makes 4 servings. PER SERVING: about 285 cal, 17 g pro, 22 g total fat (9 g sat. fat), 5 g carb, 1 g fibre, 399 mg chol, 397 mg sodium. % RDI: 14% calcium, 11% iron, 28% vit A, 33% vit C, 29% folate.

THE WELL-STOCKED KITCHEN
ESSENTIALS FOR COOL, DARK STORAGE

Remember, under the sink is too warm and moist. Keep these foods dry and cool for best results.
- Onions
- Garlic
- Potatoes: regular and sweet (store separately from onions and garlic)
- Rutabaga
- Winter squash (in season)

Zucchini Red Pepper Omelettes

If the family arrives home at different times, leave the zucchini mixture, eggs and cheese ready in the fridge so the latecomers can have a fresh omelette.

8	eggs	8
¼ tsp	each salt and pepper	1 mL
4 tsp	butter (approx)	20 mL
FILLING:		
1 tbsp	vegetable oil	15 mL
1	small onion, diced	1
1	small zucchini (about 4 oz/125 g), cubed	1
½ tsp	dried oregano	2 mL
½ cup	sliced roasted red peppers	125 mL
1 cup	crumbled feta cheese	250 mL

> FILLING: In skillet, heat oil over medium heat; fry onion, zucchini and oregano, stirring occasionally, until tender, about 6 minutes. Stir in red peppers. Transfer to small bowl; set aside.

> In bowl, whisk eggs, salt, pepper and 2 tbsp (25 mL) water just until blended but not frothy.

> In 8-inch (20 cm) omelette pan or skillet, melt 1 tsp (5 mL) of the butter over medium heat. Add one-quarter of the zucchini mixture and one-quarter of the egg mixture. Make figure eight with spatula to combine. Sprinkle with one-quarter of the cheese. Cook until almost set, gently lifting edge with spatula to allow any uncooked eggs to flow underneath, about 3 minutes.

> Fold in half; cook for 2 minutes. Slide onto plate. Repeat with remaining ingredients, adding more butter as necessary.

Makes 4 servings. PER SERVING: about 329 cal, 19 g pro, 26 g total fat (12 g sat. fat), 7 g carb, 1 g fibre, 417 mg chol, 767 mg sodium. % RDI: 23% calcium, 13% iron, 36% vit A, 70% vit C, 34% folate.

Pancetta and Egg Pita Pizzas

A whole wheat pita is the base for a nest of caramelized onions cupping a sunny-side-up egg. Use fresh pitas because they are easy to split in half.

5 oz	sliced pancetta or bacon, chopped	150 g
5 cups	thinly sliced onions (4 large)	1.25 L
3	cloves garlic, minced	3
1 tsp	dried rosemary, crumbled	5 mL
½ tsp	salt	2 mL
¼ tsp	pepper	1 mL
¼ cup	minced fresh parsley	50 mL
2	whole wheat pitas	2
2 tbsp	extra-virgin olive oil	25 mL
4	eggs	4

> In large skillet, fry pancetta over medium-high heat until crisp, about 5 minutes. Using slotted spoon, transfer to paper towel–lined plate.

> Drain off all but 1 tbsp (15 mL) fat from pan. Fry onions, garlic, rosemary, salt and pepper over medium heat, stirring, until onions are golden, 18 minutes. Stir in parsley and pancetta.

> Meanwhile, split each pita in half around edge into rounds; place, cut side up, on large rimmed baking sheet. Brush with oil. Bake in 400°F (200°C) oven until beginning to crisp, about 5 minutes.

> Top each pita round with heaping ¼ cup (50 mL) of the onion mixture; spread onions to form well large enough to hold egg. Crack 1 egg into each well. Bake until whites are firm and yolks are soft, about 15 minutes.

Makes 4 servings. PER SERVING: about 350 cal, 14 g pro, 20 g total fat (5 g sat. fat), 30 g carb, 5 g fibre, 197 mg chol, 673 mg sodium. % RDI: 7% calcium, 17% iron, 10% vit A, 23% vit C, 33% folate.

Gratin of Hard-Cooked Eggs

This creamy casserole – shared by *Canadian Living* reader Edie Warner of Winnipeg – fits the bill for breakfast and supper.

2 tbsp	butter	25 mL
3 tbsp	all-purpose flour	50 mL
1½ cups	milk	375 mL
Pinch	each salt, pepper and nutmeg	Pinch
1¼ cups	shredded Gruyère, Cheddar or Swiss cheese	300 mL
6	hard-cooked eggs	6
4	green onions	4
1¼ cups	frozen peas	300 mL
½ cup	fresh bread crumbs	125 mL

❯ In saucepan, melt butter over medium heat; stir in flour and cook, stirring and without browning, for 2 minutes. Gradually whisk in milk; add salt, pepper and nutmeg. Bring to boil; reduce heat and simmer for 2 minutes. Remove from heat; stir in 1 cup (250 mL) of the cheese until melted.

❯ Halve eggs lengthwise; chop onions into pea-size pieces. Arrange eggs, cut side up, in greased 6-cup (1.5 L) gratin or casserole dish; sprinkle with peas and onions. Pour sauce over top; sprinkle with bread crumbs and remaining cheese. *(Make-ahead: Cover and refrigerate for up to 6 hours.)*

❯ Bake in 450°F (230°C) oven until bubbly and slightly browned, 25 to 30 minutes.

Makes 6 servings. PER SERVING: about 288 cal, 18 g pro, 18 g total fat (10 g sat. fat), 13 g carb, 2 g fibre, 229 mg chol, 237 mg sodium. % RDI: 34% calcium, 11% iron, 27% vit A, 7% vit C, 27% folate.

TIP

● To hard-cook eggs, place in single layer in saucepan wide enough to fit number of eggs. Add enough cold water to come 1 inch (2.5 cm) over tops of eggs. Cover and bring to boil over high heat. Remove from heat; let stand for 20 minutes. Drain off water; chill eggs in cold water.

CHAPTER 12

Make It Tonight...
Side Dishes and Salads

Lemon Brussels Sprouts

We toss tender-crisp vegetables, such as beans, asparagus and these sprouts, with lemon juice just before serving to keep their green colour vibrant.

8 cups	brussels sprouts (about 2 lb/1 kg), trimmed and halved	2 L
¼ cup	butter, softened	50 mL
2 tsp	grated lemon rind	10 mL
4 tsp	lemon juice	20 mL
Pinch	each salt and pepper	Pinch

> In large saucepan of boiling salted water, cover and simmer brussels sprouts until tender-crisp, about 6 minutes. Drain and return to pan.

> Add butter, lemon rind and juice, salt and pepper; heat, tossing, until butter is melted.

Makes 8 servings. PER SERVING: about 89 cal, 3 g pro, 6 g total fat (4 g sat. fat), 9 g carb, 4 g fibre, 15 mg chol, 287 mg sodium. % RDI: 3% calcium, 9% iron, 12% vit A, 102% vit C, 26% folate.

Asparagus with Creamy Lemon Sauce

Choose firm asparagus stalks with deep green or purplish closed tips. To keep asparagus fresh, store in refrigerator in plastic bag with woody ends wrapped in damp paper towel. Use within two days of purchase or, better still, within two days of picking!

3 tbsp	light mayonnaise	50 mL
2 tsp	lemon juice	10 mL
1 tsp	minced fresh chives or green onion	5 mL
Pinch	each granulated sugar, salt and pepper	Pinch
1 lb	asparagus	500 g

> In small bowl, whisk together mayonnaise, 2 tsp (10 mL) water, lemon juice, chives, sugar, salt and pepper; set sauce aside.

> Break woody ends off asparagus. Cover and steam on rack above 1 inch (2.5 cm) boiling water until tender-crisp, about 3 minutes for thin stalks or up to 7 minutes for thick stalks. Drain and arrange on plate; drizzle with sauce.

Makes 4 servings. PER SERVING: about 55 cal, 2 g pro, 4 g total fat (1 g sat. fat), 4 g carb, 2 g fibre, 4 mg chol, 87 mg sodium. % RDI: 2% calcium, 6% iron, 8% vit A, 12% vit C, 54% folate.

VARIATION

Asparagus with Creamy Mustard Sauce
● Replace lemon juice with 1 tsp (5 mL) Dijon mustard. Replace chives with parsley.

Roasted Cauliflower Salad

This is not your usual pasta, potato or grain salad but rather one that features the mellow flavour of roasted cauliflower. Anchovies, capers, olives and raisins add a touch of sun-drenched Sicily.

1 tsp	fennel seeds	5 mL
8 cups	cauliflower florets (1 large head)	2 L
¼ cup	extra-virgin olive oil	50 mL
¼ tsp	each salt and pepper	1 mL
2 tbsp	lemon juice	25 mL
1 tsp	anchovy paste	5 mL
½ cup	Kalamata olives, pitted and quartered	125 mL
¼ cup	golden raisins	50 mL
2 tbsp	capers, drained and rinsed	25 mL

> Using mortar and pestle or bottom of pot, crush fennel seeds.

> In large bowl, toss cauliflower with 2 tbsp (25 mL) of the oil, fennel seeds, salt and pepper; spread on large rimmed baking sheet. Roast in 450°F (230°C) oven until golden and tender-crisp, about 20 minutes. Let cool.

> In serving bowl, whisk together remaining oil, lemon juice and anchovy paste. Cut cauliflower into ¼-inch (5 mm) thick slices or bite-size pieces; add to bowl. Add olives, raisins and capers. Toss to combine. *(Make-ahead: Cover and refrigerate for up to 24 hours.)*

Makes 8 servings. PER SERVING: about 128 cal, 2 g pro, 10 g total fat (1 g sat. fat), 9 g carb, 4 g fibre, 0 mg chol, 448 mg sodium. % RDI: 3% calcium, 5% iron, 75% vit C, 20% folate.

HOW TO WASH AND STORE GREENS, HERBS AND VEGETABLES

SALAD GREENS, CELERY AND HERBS Wash before storing – you're more likely to go to the bother of making a salad for supper if the greens are ready. Separate leaves or stalks and swish in cool water. Repeat, especially for sandy herbs and greens, such as coriander and spinach. Spin dry, lay out in single layer on dry towels and roll loosely. Enclose in plastic bag and store in crisper.

BROCCOLI, BOK CHOY, BEANS, SPINACH, SWISS CHARD AND BRUSSELS SPROUTS Wrap in tea towels, enclose in a plastic bag and store in the crisper. Before cooking, dunk in a sinkful of cool water; swish leafy or sandy vegetables to remove dirt. Avoid soaking vegetables.

CARROTS, BEETS OR ANY VEGETABLES WITH TOPS Remove tops – use beet greens as a vegetable, like spinach. Wrap in tea towel, enclose in a plastic bag and store in the crisper. Before cooking carrots, peel and trim. For beets, scrub with vegetable brush to remove dirt. Cook with root and base of stems; scrape off peel, root and top bit when beets are fork-tender.

LEEKS Trim off dark green parts and root end. Slit from root end to close to pale green part. Swish, white ends up, in cool water, separating layers to ensure that none of the sand in which they grew remains between the layers.

Steamed Vegetables

Because water-soluble vitamins can't escape into the boiling liquid, steamed vegetables retain more nutrients and minerals than boiled ones. Steaming is suitable for small quantities because the steam can quickly cook each piece. Place steamer at least 1 inch (2.5 cm) above boiling water.

> **Asparagus**
PREP: Snap off woody ends; peel thick stems if desired
Time: 3 minutes (thin stalks) to 7 minutes (thick stalks)

> **Beets**
PREP: Cut off tops; keep whole and unpeeled until after cooking
Time: 40 minutes

> **Bok Choy**
PREP: Trim and chop coarsely, or halve if small
Time: 5 minutes

> **Broccoli**
PREP: Cut into florets; peel and slice stalks
Time: 7 minutes

> **Brussels Sprouts**
PREP: Trim off wilted or coarse outer leaves; cut thin end off stem and score shallow X in bottom
Time: 10 minutes

> **Cabbage**
PREP: Remove coarse outer leaves, then quarter and remove core; shred finely or cut into wedges
Time: 10 to 12 minutes

> **Carrots or Parsnips**
PREP: Peel and cut into coins, sticks or chunks
Time: 15 minutes

> **Cauliflower**
PREP: Cut into florets
Time: 10 minutes

> **Green Beans**
PREP: Cut off stem end
Time: 10 minutes

> **New Potatoes**
PREP: Scrub well; cut if large
Time: 30 minutes

EQUIPMENT
STEAMERS 101
VEGETABLE STEAMER
A collapsible basket made of perforated, interleaved panels that stands out of the water on three little legs and expands to fit inside saucepans between 5 inches (12 cm) and 9 inches (23 cm) in diameter. A central stem can be used to lift out the steamer or removed to accommodate a whole cauliflower or artichokes.

POT STEAMERS
If you are purchasing a new set of pots, a set with a steamer is a worthwhile investment. Or look for one with a perforated bottom and concentric ridges to fit over pots of various sizes.

CHINESE STEAMING POTS
An alternative to a wok and bamboo steamer combo is a lightweight aluminum or stainless-steel set consisting of a water pot base and two or three stackable steaming trays with a domed lid. Unlike a flat lid, the domed style directs condensed water droplets down the side and prevents them from dripping into the food.

Corn on the Cob

Choose your favourite way to cook husked cobs of corn. Any of the following yield tender, sweet corn ready for topping and crunching.
- Boil or steam for 8 to 10 minutes.
- Grill over medium-high heat for 10 to 15 minutes.
- Microwave at high for about 10 minutes.

CREATIVE CORN TOPPINGS

You can brush cooked corn on the cob with butter or olive oil and season with salt and pepper. Or get creative and dress them up with one of these butter, mayonnaise or olive oil toppings. **Each topping makes about ⅓ cup (75 mL), enough for 6 cobs of corn.**

PESTO Butter
> Mix together ¼ cup (50 mL) butter, softened; 2 tbsp (25 mL) grated Parmesan cheese; 1 clove garlic, minced; and 1 tbsp (15 mL) minced fresh basil.

PROVENÇALE Butter
> Mix together ¼ cup (50 mL) butter, softened; 1 tbsp (15 mL) Dijon mustard; and ¾ tsp (4 mL) herbes de Provence.

INDIAN-SPICED Olive Oil with Butter
> Mix together 2 tbsp (25 mL) extra-virgin olive oil; 2 tbsp (25 mL) butter, softened; 1 tbsp (15 mL) minced fresh coriander; 1 tsp (5 mL) curry paste; and ½ tsp (2 mL) lemon juice.

MEDITERRANEAN Olive Oil
> Mix together 3 tbsp (50 mL) extra-virgin olive oil; 4 tsp (20 mL) minced sun-dried tomatoes; ½ tsp (2 mL) dried thyme; and pinch each salt and pepper.

SMOKY ORANGE Mayonnaise
> Mix together ¼ cup (50 mL) light mayonnaise; 2 tsp (10 mL) barbecue sauce; and 1 tsp (5 mL) each chopped chipotle pepper and grated orange rind.

LEMON PEPPER Mayonnaise
> Mix together ¼ cup (50 mL) light mayonnaise; 1 tsp (5 mL) each grated lemon rind and lemon juice; and ½ tsp (2 mL) pepper.

Eggplant Stacks with Tomato, Onions and Asiago

This handsome side dish can also serve as a vegetarian main.

2	small slim eggplants (about 8 oz/250 g total)	2
2	cloves garlic, minced	2
2 tbsp	extra-virgin olive oil	25 mL
¾ tsp	each salt and pepper	4 mL
1	small sweet onion	1
2	large tomatoes	2
¾ tsp	dried Italian herb seasoning	4 mL
½ cup	shredded Asiago cheese	125 mL
½ cup	shredded mozzarella cheese	125 mL

❯ Trim off both ends of eggplants; cut into ½-inch (1 cm) thick slices. In 13- x 9-inch (3.5 L) metal cake pan, toss together eggplant, garlic and half each of the oil, salt and pepper; arrange in single layer in pan. Broil 6 inches (15 cm) from heat, turning once, until golden, about 6 minutes.

❯ Meanwhile, cut onion and tomatoes into ¼-inch (5 mm) thick slices. Separate and lay onion rings then tomatoes over eggplant, sprinkling each layer with Italian herb seasoning and remaining salt, pepper and oil. Bake in 400°F (200°C) oven until bubbly and beginning to brown, about 20 minutes.

❯ Sprinkle with Asiago and mozzarella cheeses; broil until golden, about 1 minute. Transfer to serving dish.

Makes 4 servings. PER SERVING: about 211 cal, 8 g pro, 15 g total fat (6 g sat. fat), 14 g carb, 3 g fibre, 24 mg chol, 620 mg sodium. % RDI: 19% calcium, 7% iron, 12% vit A, 33% vit C, 13% folate.

TECHNIQUE
CHOPPING

Sounds simple, doesn't it? But mastering this technique guarantees less prep time and more cooking and eating time. You need a sharp chef's knife and a big chopping board to contain the mess. Space makes a big difference.

TO CHOP AN ONION, SHALLOT, GARLIC CLOVE OR OTHER ROUND VEGETABLE:
• Peel, keeping root end intact. On cutting board, cut in half lengthwise (root to stem); place cut sides down. With round knuckles and keeping fingertips curled under on other hand, hold root end of one half firmly on board. With knife held horizontally, make 2 or 3 cuts through stem end, almost but not all the way through to root, depending on thickness desired.

• With knife held vertically and keeping vegetable steady, cut lengthwise from stem end almost but not all the way through to root end, into same-size thick slices.

• With tip of knife constantly on board, slice across vegetable with rocking motion, moving curled fingers away from blade and toward root end while chopping, finishing with and discarding root.

TIP: Generally, dicing refers to cutting a food into ⅛- to ¼-inch (3 to 5 mm) cubes, and cubing refers to cutting it into ½-inch (1 cm) cubes. Chopping denotes a slightly coarser, more irregular cut.

TIP

• To make in a gratin dish, as in our photo, layer broiled eggplant in dish with remaining vegetables, seasonings and oil. Bake as directed. Sprinkle with cheese and continue baking until cheese is melted and golden.

Tri-Colour Pepper Sauté

Red and yellow peppers take three to six weeks longer than green to develop sweetness and change colour. No wonder they taste so good! Maximize their use in recipes when they're in season.

4	sweet peppers (red, yellow and green)	4
2 tbsp	extra-virgin olive oil	25 mL
2	cloves garlic, minced	2
1	shallot (or half small onion), finely chopped	1
¼ tsp	each salt and pepper	1 mL
1 tbsp	white balsamic or wine vinegar	15 mL

❯ Seed, core and cut sweet peppers into ½-inch (1 cm) wide strips.

❯ In large skillet, heat oil over medium heat; fry garlic and shallot until softened, about 2 minutes.

❯ Add sweet peppers, salt and pepper; fry, stirring often, until tender-crisp, about 7 minutes.

❯ Add vinegar; cook, stirring, just until evaporated, about 1 minute.

Makes 4 servings. PER SERVING: about 100 cal, 1 g pro, 7 g total fat (1 g sat. fat), 10 g carb, 2 g fibre, 0 mg chol, 146 mg sodium. % RDI: 1% calcium, 5% iron, 18% vit A, 253% vit C, 9% folate.

TECHNIQUE
JULIENNING

It may seem fancy, but it's just a French cooking term for cutting food into matchstick-shaped pieces or strips. These strips can vary in size and length from matchstick- to pinky-size. This technique is particularly suited to long vegetables, such as carrots and parsnips, but can be used for celery, squash, sweet potatoes, potatoes and apples. The secret is to create a flat base so the object to be julienned is steady on the cutting board.

TO JULIENNE A CARROT, PARSNIP OR OTHER LONG VEGETABLE:

• Peel vegetable.
• Cut crosswise into 2-inch (5 cm) lengths. Trim thin strip off 1 side to create flat side. Place on flat side and cut lengthwise into about ⅛-inch (3 mm) thick slices.
• Stack slices; cut lengthwise into about ⅛-inch (3 mm) thick matchstick-size strips.

Lightened-Up "Creamed" Spinach

The rich, decadent taste and creamy texture of the original isn't lost in this healthier version of the classic spinach side dish.

¼ cup	light or regular herbed cream cheese	50 mL
2 tbsp	milk	25 mL
2 tsp	lemon juice	10 mL
Pinch	each salt and pepper	Pinch
Pinch	nutmeg	Pinch
1	bag (10 oz/284 g) spinach, cooked and drained	1

❯ In skillet or saucepan, whisk together cream cheese, milk, lemon juice, salt, pepper and nutmeg over medium-low heat until melted and smooth.

❯ Finely chop spinach; add to cheese sauce and cook, stirring, until blended and hot, about 2 minutes.

Makes 2 or 3 servings. PER EACH OF 3 SERVINGS: about 70 cal, 5 g pro, 4 g total fat (2 g sat. fat), 5 g carb, 2 g fibre, 13 mg chol, 204 mg sodium. % RDI: 14% calcium, 23% iron, 77% vit A, 17% vit C, 60% folate.

HOW TO COOK SPINACH

Trim ends of stems, and coarse veins if desired, from 1 bag fresh spinach (bag sizes vary slightly). Rinse spinach; shake off excess water. In large saucepan or Dutch oven, cover and steam spinach over medium-high heat, with just the water clinging to leaves and stirring once, until wilted, about 5 minutes. In sieve, press out liquid. *(Make-ahead: Let cool; cover and refrigerate for up to 24 hours.)* **One 10-oz (284 g) bag makes about 1½ cups (375 mL), enough for 2 or 3 servings.**

Pan-Roasted Cherry Tomatoes

Cherry tomatoes and their diminutive counterparts, grape tomatoes, are juicier and zestier year-round than larger tomatoes.

1 tbsp	extra-virgin olive oil	15 mL
4 cups	cherry tomatoes	1 L
1	clove garlic, minced	1
1 tsp	dried Italian herb seasoning	5 mL
¼ tsp	salt	1 mL
Pinch	each granulated sugar and hot pepper flakes	Pinch
2	green onions, sliced	2
2 tsp	balsamic or wine vinegar	10 mL

> In large skillet, heat oil over medium-high heat; fry tomatoes, garlic, Italian herb seasoning, salt, sugar, hot pepper flakes and green onions, stirring occasionally, until tomatoes are shrivelled, about 5 minutes. Stir in vinegar.

Makes 4 servings. PER SERVING: about 63 cal, 2 g pro, 4 g total fat (1 g sat. fat), 7 g carb, 2 g fibre, 0 mg chol, 152 mg sodium. % RDI: 2% calcium, 5% iron, 13% vit A, 32% vit C, 9% folate.

VARIATION

Pan-Roasted Cherry Tomatoes with Corn and Zucchini

● Replace dried Italian herb seasoning with ½ tsp (2 mL) each paprika and dried oregano. Add 1 small zucchini, cut into 1-inch (2.5 cm) pieces, and ½ cup (125 mL) frozen corn kernels, thawed. Replace balsamic vinegar with cider vinegar.

Shaved Zucchini with Asiago

Thinly sliced raw zucchini makes a lovely side dish or a light antipasto on its own or on a platter alongside olives, roasted red peppers and prosciutto.

1	zucchini (8 oz/250 g)	1
¼ tsp	salt	1 mL
Pinch	pepper	Pinch
⅓ cup	shaved Asiago cheese	75 mL
2	leaves fresh basil, shredded	2
1 tbsp	lemon juice	15 mL
1 tbsp	extra-virgin olive oil	15 mL

> Using mandoline or sharp knife, cut zucchini diagonally into paper-thin slices. Overlapping slightly, arrange on small flat plate. *(Make-ahead: Cover and set aside for up to 6 hours.)*

> Sprinkle with salt and pepper, then cheese and basil; drizzle with lemon juice and oil.

Makes 4 to 6 servings. PER EACH OF 6 SERVINGS: about 49 cal, 2 g pro, 4 g total fat (1 g sat. fat), 2 g carb, 1 g fibre, 5 mg chol, 149 mg sodium. % RDI: 5% calcium, 1% iron, 2% vit A, 7% vit C, 4% folate.

Vinaigrette Cabbage Salad

This useful little keeper will last for up to seven days in the refrigerator. It's a fantastic side dish for everything from stews to grilled meat.

2 tbsp	vegetable oil	25 mL
2 tbsp	cider vinegar or white wine vinegar	25 mL
2 tsp	Dijon mustard	10 mL
2 tsp	granulated sugar	10 mL
½ tsp	each celery seeds, salt and pepper	2 mL
1	clove garlic, minced	1
6 cups	shredded green cabbage	1.5 L
1	carrot, shredded	1
2	green onions, chopped	2

> In large bowl, whisk together oil, vinegar, mustard, sugar, celery seeds, salt, pepper and garlic. Add cabbage, carrot and green onions; toss to coat. Let stand for 15 minutes before serving. *(Make-ahead: Cover and refrigerate for up to 1 week.)*

Makes 6 servings. PER SERVING: about 74 cal, 1 g pro, 5 g total fat (trace sat. fat), 8 g carb, 2 g fibre, 0 mg chol, 232 mg sodium. % RDI: 4% calcium, 6% iron, 39% vit A, 42% vit C, 16% folate.

Rapini

There is nothing subtle about rapini! We invite you to enjoy its pleasant bitterness and bold taste. You may just become a convert. This particular recipe is delicious tossed with hot pasta and a generous sprinkle of freshly grated Parmesan cheese.

1	bunch rapini (about 1 lb/500 g)	1
3 tbsp	extra-virgin olive oil	50 mL
3	cloves garlic, sliced	3
¼ tsp	hot pepper flakes	1 mL
¼ tsp	salt	1 mL

> Trim off tough bottoms about ¼ inch (5 mm) from base of rapini stalks. In deep skillet of boiling salted water, cover and cook stalks until tender, about 6 minutes; drain and pat dry.

> In same skillet, heat oil over medium heat; fry garlic and hot pepper flakes until garlic begins to brown, about 2 minutes. Add rapini and salt; heat through, tossing rapini to coat.

Makes 4 servings. PER SERVING: about 130 cal, 4 g pro, 10 g total fat (1 g sat. fat), 6 g carb, 2 g fibre, 0 mg chol, 396 mg sodium. % RDI: 23% calcium, 13% iron, 32% vit A, 55% vit C, 4% folate.

VARIATION

Rapini with Sun-Dried Tomatoes and Pine Nuts

● In skillet, toast 2 tbsp (25 mL) pine nuts over low heat until light brown, about 5 minutes. Add to pan of cooked rapini along with 3 tbsp (50 mL) chopped sun-dried tomatoes; heat through.

TIP

● Rapini (also called raab and broccoli rabe) looks like thin broccoli with clusters of buds. Like broccoli and turnip, it is part of the cruciferous family of vegetables. It has an assertive but pleasant bitter taste that is somewhat mellowed by cooking. Choose bunches with plump, moist stems and dark green leaves with no trace of yellow. Rapini will keep in the refrigerator for about 4 days wrapped in towels and enclosed in a plastic bag or inside a perforated crisper bag. Wash just before cooking.

NEVER MAKE DRESSING AGAIN

Say goodbye to the salad dressing aisle with these simple make or shake versions. Or do as they do in Italy: drizzle greens with a 3:1 ratio of extra-virgin olive oil to wine vinegar, then sprinkle with sea salt and grind a bit of fresh black pepper over top. *Bellissimo!*

Two-Minute Oil and Vinegar Dressing

On a busy day after work and school, making a salad may seem like the last thing you want to do. But if the lettuce is washed and waiting and there's a superior homemade dressing in the fridge, chances are you will make that salad. Here is a classic dressing to have on hand. One-third cup (75 mL) is enough to dress 6 to 8 cups (1.5 to 2 L) salad greens, which serves four.

2	cloves garlic, quartered	2
½ tsp	salt	2 mL
½ cup	canola or extra-virgin olive oil	125 mL
¼ cup	wine vinegar	50 mL
2 tsp	Dijon mustard	10 mL
Pinch	each granulated sugar and pepper	Pinch

> On cutting board and using fork, crush garlic with salt. In jar, shake together garlic, oil, vinegar, mustard, sugar and pepper until blended. *(Make-ahead: Refrigerate for up to 1 week.)*

Makes about ¾ cup (175 mL). PER 1 TBSP (15 mL): about 83 cal, trace pro, 9 g total fat (1 g sat. fat), trace carb, 0 g fibre, 0 mg chol, 107 mg sodium.

Creamy Lemon Dill Dressing

This is wonderfully thick and tangy, but if you prefer a thinner dressing, stir in 2 tbsp (25 mL) milk. Either way, it's perfect for tossing with salad greens, whether all at once to dress 12 cups (3 L) or in smaller salads to suit your family. It's also delicious as a dip.

⅓ cup	each light sour cream and light mayonnaise	75 mL
2 tbsp	chopped fresh dill (or 1 tsp/5 mL dried dillweed)	25 mL
4 tsp	lemon juice	20 mL
2 tsp	Dijon mustard	10 mL
¼ tsp	each salt and pepper	1 mL

> In small bowl, whisk together sour cream, mayonnaise, dill, lemon juice, mustard, salt and pepper. *(Make-ahead: Refrigerate in airtight container for up to 5 days.)*

Makes ¾ cup (175 mL) PER 1 TBSP (15 mL): about 29 cal, 1 g pro, 2 g total fat (2 g sat. fat), 1 g carb, 0 g fibre, 3 mg chol, 114 mg sodium. % RDI: 1% calcium, 1% iron, 2% vit C.

VARIATION

Creamy Blue Cheese Dressing

● Omit dill. Replace lemon juice with 1 tbsp (15 mL) wine vinegar. Stir in ¼ cup (50 mL) crumbled blue cheese and 1 tbsp (15 mL) chopped fresh chives.

Shaker Dressings

Shake up these dressings in screw-top jars. They're excellent tossed with warm cooked vegetables, such as potatoes, green beans, asparagus or carrots, or with cool salad greens or fresh tomatoes. They're also delicious drizzled over grilled fish, poultry or chops.

Mustard Honey Vinaigrette

❯ In jar, shake together ¾ cup (175 mL) vegetable oil; ⅓ cup (75 mL) wine vinegar; 2 tbsp (25 mL) Dijon mustard; 2 tbsp (25 mL) liquid honey; and ¼ tsp (1 mL) each salt and pepper. *(Make-ahead: Refrigerate for up to 2 weeks. Shake well before using.)*

Makes 1⅓ cups (325 mL). PER 1 TBSP (15 mL): about 76 cal, 0 g pro, 8 g total fat (1 g sat. fat), 2 g carb, 0 g fibre, 0 mg chol, 46 mg sodium. % RDI: 1% iron.

Oregano Vinaigrette

❯ In jar, shake together ⅓ cup (75 mL) each extra-virgin olive oil and vegetable oil; 3 tbsp (50 mL) red wine vinegar; 2 tbsp (25 mL) water; 2 tsp (10 mL) Dijon mustard; 1 clove garlic, minced; 1 tsp (5 mL) dried oregano; and ½ tsp (2 mL) each salt and pepper. *(Make-ahead: Refrigerate for up to 3 days. Shake well before using.)*

Makes about 1 cup (250 mL). PER 1 TBSP (15 mL): about 81 cal, 0 g pro, 9 g total fat (1 g sat. fat), trace carb, 0 g fibre, 0 mg chol, 80 mg sodium. % RDI: 1% iron.

Cranberry Shallot Dressing

❯ In jar, shake together ½ cup (125 mL) frozen cranberry concentrate, thawed; ¼ cup (50 mL) each vegetable oil, water and wine vinegar; 2 tsp (10 mL) grainy or Dijon mustard; 2 small shallots, minced; and ½ tsp (2 mL) each salt and pepper. *(Make-ahead: Refrigerate for up to 3 days. Shake well before using.)*

Makes about 1 cup (250 mL). PER 1 TBSP (15 mL): about 49 cal, trace pro, 3 g total fat (trace sat. fat), 5 g carb, trace fibre, 0 mg chol, 80 mg sodium. % RDI: 1% iron, 12% vit C.

Lemon Thyme Dressing

❯ In jar, shake together ¾ cup (175 mL) vegetable oil; 1 tbsp (15 mL) grated lemon rind; ¼ cup (50 mL) lemon juice; 1 tsp (5 mL) dried thyme; and ¼ tsp (1 mL) each salt and pepper. *(Make-ahead: Refrigerate for up to 2 weeks. Shake well before using.)*

Makes 1 cup (250 mL). PER 1 TBSP (15 mL): about 92 cal, 0 g pro, 10 g total fat (1 g sat. fat), trace carb, 0 g fibre, 0 mg chol, 36 mg sodium. % RDI: 1% iron, 3% vit C.

Party Spinach Salad with Snow Peas and Almonds

This is a great party salad – you can prepare all the ingredients early, then toss them together at serving time. For an easy weeknight supper, simply cut the recipe in half.

1	bag (10 oz/284 g) spinach, trimmed and torn	1
1 cup	snow peas, trimmed and thinly sliced	250 mL
1	can (8 oz/227 g) sliced water chestnuts, drained and rinsed	1
1	sweet red pepper, thinly sliced	1
½ cup	slivered almonds, toasted	125 mL
1	green onion, thinly sliced diagonally	1
GINGER DRESSING:		
¼ cup	vegetable oil	50 mL
2 tbsp	soy sauce	25 mL
2 tbsp	rice vinegar	25 mL
2	cloves garlic, minced	2
1 tsp	minced gingerroot (or pinch ground ginger)	5 mL
¼ tsp	pepper	1 mL

❯ GINGER DRESSING: In jar, shake together oil, soy sauce, vinegar, garlic, ginger and pepper. Set aside. *(Make-ahead: Refrigerate for up to 1 week.)*

❯ Arrange spinach in large bowl. Top with snow peas, water chestnuts and red pepper. *(Make-ahead: Cover bowl with damp towel and plastic wrap. Refrigerate for up to 2 hours.)*

❯ Add dressing; toss to coat. Garnish with almonds and green onion.

Makes 6 to 8 servings. PER EACH OF 8 SERVINGS: about 140 cal, 4 g pro, 11 g total fat (1 g sat. fat), 9 g carb, 3 g fibre, 0 mg chol, 289 mg sodium. % RDI: 5% calcium, 13% iron, 31% vit A, 73% vit C, 35% folate.

TIP

• Toast almonds in dry skillet over medium heat for about 5 minutes. Swirl nuts in pan as they darken to keep them from burning.

Creamy Cucumber Salad

This Scandinavian-inspired salad is easy to prepare and full of lively accents. Salting and draining the cucumber is essential to prevent a watery salad.

3 cups	thinly sliced peeled English cucumber	750 mL
1 tsp	salt	5 mL
½ cup	thinly sliced red onion	125 mL
¼ cup	light or regular sour cream	50 mL
1 tbsp	chopped fresh dill (or 1 tsp/5 mL dried dillweed)	15 mL
1 tbsp	white wine vinegar	15 mL
1 tsp	granulated sugar	5 mL

> In colander, sprinkle cucumber with salt; let stand to drain for 30 minutes. Pat dry.

> Meanwhile, soak onion in cold water for 15 minutes; drain and pat dry.

> In bowl, whisk together sour cream, dill, vinegar and sugar. Add cucumber and onion; toss to coat.

Makes 4 servings. PER SERVING: about 38 cal, 2 g pro, 1 g total fat (1 g sat. fat), 6 g carb, 1 g fibre, 2 mg chol, 302 mg sodium. % RDI: 4% calcium, 1% iron, 1% vit A, 7% vit C, 7% folate.

Green Bean and Sweet Onion Salad

Here's a bright, crisp salad tossed with a sassy jalapeño dressing.

4 cups	green beans (about 8 oz/250 g), trimmed	1 L
½ cup	thinly sliced sweet onion, such as Vidalia or Spanish	125 mL
2 tbsp	toasted slivered almonds	25 mL
JALAPEÑO DRESSING:		
1	jalapeño pepper (or 1 tsp/5 mL minced pickled jalapeño)	1
¼ cup	extra-virgin olive oil	50 mL
2 tbsp	wine vinegar	25 mL
½ tsp	each salt and pepper	2 mL

> In large pot of boiling salted water, cover and cook green beans until tender-crisp, about 3 minutes. Drain and chill in cold water. Drain and pat dry.

> JALAPEÑO DRESSING: Wearing rubber gloves, seed and mince jalapeño. In large bowl, whisk together jalapeño, oil, vinegar, salt and pepper.

> Add green beans and onion; toss to coat. *(Make-ahead: Cover and refrigerate for up to 8 hours.)* Sprinkle with almonds.

Makes 4 servings. PER SERVING: about 187 cal, 3 g pro, 16 g total fat (2 g sat. fat), 10 g carb, 3 g fibre, 0 mg chol, 516 mg sodium. % RDI: 5% calcium, 11% iron, 9% vit A, 27% vit C, 17% folate.

CHAPTER 13

Make It Tonight... Sweets and Treats

Raspberry Rhubarb Sundaes

Sundaes are decadent, right? Not always. This one certainly tastes sinful, but it's loaded with healthy fruit and nuts and lightened up with frozen yogurt instead of rich ice cream.

¼ cup	slivered almonds	50 mL
8	scoops vanilla frozen yogurt (4 cups/1 L)	8
RASPBERRY RHUBARB SAUCE:		
3 cups	chopped fresh rhubarb	750 mL
1 cup	frozen raspberries	250 mL
½ cup	granulated sugar	125 mL

❯ RASPBERRY RHUBARB SAUCE: In large microwaveable bowl, toss together chopped rhubarb, raspberries and granulated sugar; cover and microwave at high for 10 minutes or until rhubarb is tender but chunky. (Or combine in saucepan and bring to boil; simmer over medium heat for 15 minutes.) Let cool.

❯ Meanwhile, in small skillet, toast almonds over medium heat until lightly browned, about 5 minutes. Set aside.

❯ Place 1 scoop of the frozen yogurt in each of 4 dishes or glasses; top with half of the rhubarb sauce. Repeat layers. Sprinkle with almonds.

Makes 4 servings. PER SERVING: about 481 cal, 11 g pro, 15 g total fat (7 g sat. fat), 80 g carb, 4 g fibre, 19 mg chol, 122 mg sodium. % RDI: 34% calcium, 6% iron, 6% vit A, 20% vit C, 10% folate.

VARIATION

Strawberry Peach Sundaes

● Omit Raspberry Rhubarb Sauce and almonds. In saucepan, combine 2 cups (500 mL) sliced peeled peaches or nectarines, ¼ cup (50 mL) granulated sugar and pinch cinnamon; bring to boil over medium heat. Reduce heat and simmer, stirring gently once or twice, until peaches are tender, about 10 minutes. Add 1 cup (250 mL) sliced strawberries; let cool. In 4 glasses or bowls, alternately layer sauce and frozen yogurt. Garnish with 4 whole strawberries or go crazy and replace strawberries with blackberries, blueberries or raspberries.

Sundae Sauces

Both homemade sauces are easy to make and so much more delectable than store-bought. The caramel is gooey; the chocolate, wickedly rich.

CARAMEL SAUCE:

1½ cups	granulated sugar	375 mL
⅔ cup	whipping cream	150 mL
¼ cup	butter	50 mL

➤ In heavy saucepan over medium heat, stir sugar with ⅓ cup (75 mL) water until sugar is dissolved; brush down side of pan with pastry brush dipped in cold water. Bring to boil; boil vigorously, without stirring but brushing down side of pan, until dark amber, about 6 minutes.

➤ Standing back and averting face, add cream; whisk until smooth. Whisk in butter until smooth. Let cool. *(Make-ahead: Refrigerate in airtight container for up to 1 week; rewarm to liquefy.)*

Makes 1½ cups (375 mL). PER 2 TBSP (25 mL): about 173 cal, trace pro, 8 g total fat (5 g sat. fat), 25 g carb, 0 g fibre, 29 mg chol, 44 mg sodium. % RDI: 1% calcium, 8% vit A.

CHOCOLATE SAUCE:

1 cup	whipping cream	250 mL
2 tbsp	corn syrup	25 mL
6 oz	bittersweet chocolate, chopped	175 g

➤ In small saucepan, bring cream and corn syrup to boil; remove from heat. Add chocolate; whisk until smooth. Let stand until thickened, about 15 minutes. *(Make-ahead: Refrigerate in airtight container for up to 1 week; rewarm to liquefy.)*

Makes 1⅔ cups (400 mL). PER 2 TBSP (25 mL): about 139 cal, 1 g pro, 11 g total fat (7 g sat. fat), 10 g carb, 1 g fibre, 23 mg chol, 10 mg sodium. % RDI: 2% calcium, 4% iron, 6% vit A.

Pineapple with Kirsch Syrup

This is a delicious twist on fresh fruit for dessert. It is especially recommended after a meal of Swiss Cheese Fondue (recipe, page 176).

½ cup	granulated sugar	125 mL
⅓ cup	kirsch or orange juice	75 mL
1	golden pineapple, peeled and cored	1

➤ In small saucepan, bring sugar, kirsch and 2 tbsp (25 mL) water to boil over medium-high heat, swirling to dissolve sugar. Let cool. *(Make-ahead: Refrigerate in airtight container for up to 2 days.)*

➤ Cut pineapple into bite-size pieces; place in large glass bowl. *(Make-ahead: Cover and refrigerate for up to 4 hours.)* Add half of the syrup; toss. Divide among dessert dishes; pass remaining syrup.

Makes 8 servings. PER SERVING: about 115 cal, trace pro, trace total fat (0 g sat. fat), 25 g carb, 1 g fibre, 0 mg chol, 1 mg sodium. % RDI: 1% calcium, 1% iron, 55% vit C, 5% folate.

Sabayon

Sabayon (or *zabaglione* in Italian) is a luscious, foamy custard that is made by whisking together egg yolks, sugar and wine over gently simmering water. It's lovely poured over fresh fruit (especially berries), cake or ice cream – and is simply delicious all by itself.

4	egg yolks	4
½ cup	fruity white wine (such as Riesling) or dry Marsala	125 mL
¼ cup	granulated sugar	50 mL

> In large heatproof bowl over saucepan of gently simmering water, whisk together egg yolks, wine and sugar until thick enough to mound softly on spoon, 5 to 7 minutes. Serve immediately.

Makes 2 cups (500 mL), or 6 servings. PER SERVING: about 83 cal, 2 g pro, 4 g total fat (1 g sat. fat), 9 g carb, 0 g fibre, 136 mg chol, 6 mg sodium. % RDI: 2% calcium, 4% iron, 6% vit A, 8% folate.

Creamy Orange Honey Dip with Fruit

This light dessert is elegant enough for company and simple to whip up for the cook. Garnish with strips of orange rind, if desired. And don't forget to set out sturdy skewers for spearing the fruit.

1 cup	light sour cream	250 mL
2 tbsp	thawed orange juice concentrate	25 mL
1 tbsp	liquid honey	15 mL
	Strip orange rind (optional)	
	Assorted fresh fruit (such as cubed watermelon, cantaloupe, honeydew melon, strawberries and grapes)	

> In small bowl, combine sour cream, orange juice concentrate and honey. *(Make-ahead: Cover and refrigerate for up to 24 hours.)*

> Place in centre of large serving plate; garnish with orange rind (if using). Arrange fruit around dip.

Makes 1¼ cups (300 mL). PER 1 TBSP (15 ML) WITHOUT FRUIT: about 20 cal, 1 g pro, 1 g total fat (trace sat. fat), 3 g carb, 0 g fibre, 2 mg chol, 11 mg sodium. % RDI: 2% calcium, 1% vit A, 5% vit C, 1% folate.

Creamy Rice Pudding

The hint of spice adds just the right amount of flavour to this ever-popular simple dessert. You can add 2 tbsp (25 mL) golden raisins or cranberries, or garnish with a sprinkle of toasted sliced almonds. If you want to serve it cold, place plastic wrap directly on surface of warm pudding and refrigerate; stir in ¼ cup (50 mL) milk before serving.

2 tbsp	butter	25 mL
½ cup	short-grain rice	125 mL
¼ tsp	ground cardamom or cinnamon	1 mL
¼ tsp	cinnamon	1 mL
2½ cups	milk	625 mL
2 tbsp	granulated sugar	25 mL
1 tsp	finely grated orange rind	5 mL

> In small saucepan, melt butter over medium heat. Add rice, cardamom and cinnamon; stir to coat.

> Stir in milk and sugar; bring to boil. Reduce heat, cover and simmer, stirring often, until most of the liquid is absorbed and rice is tender, about 25 minutes.

> Stir in orange rind. Serve warm.

Makes 4 servings. PER SERVING: about 241 cal, 7 g pro, 9 g total fat (5 g sat. fat), 34 g carb, trace fibre, 30 mg chol, 135 mg sodium. % RDI: 17% calcium, 2% iron, 13% vit A, 2% vit C, 4% folate.

VARIATION

Coconut Rice Pudding
● Replace milk with 1 can (400 mL) coconut milk and ¾ cup (175 mL) milk.

DESSERT DRESS-UPS

You don't have to be a pastry chef or buy from a high-end bakery to serve stylish desserts.

● Sauces dress up scoops of good-quality ice cream, frozen yogurt and sorbet. Chocolate Sauce or Caramel Sauce (recipes, page 213) are handy to keep in the fridge. For a quick raspberry sauce (the kind restaurants call *coulis*), purée a package of frozen raspberries in syrup and press through a sieve to remove the seeds. Add a splash of raspberry liqueur or kirsch if you like. Serve over peaches and ice cream for a classic peach Melba. It's also lovely over fresh strawberries.

● For a vanilla crème anglaise, or pouring custard, let high-quality vanilla ice cream melt. Stir in a little vanilla or rum if you like.

● Buy little squirt bottles. Any of the sauces above are attractive on a square or a plate of ice cream and fruit. Drizzle over or around the dessert – you don't need much to make a great impression.

● Bananas to the rescue: Melt a couple spoonfuls of butter in a skillet; add about the same amount of brown sugar and let melt together. Add chunks of firm but ripe bananas (1 small banana per person) and turn to coat with sauce. Stir in some rum if you like and spoon out of the pan before the bananas soften. Serve immediately over scoops of vanilla or chocolate ice cream.

● Dust on some icing sugar. It's amazing how a fine shower of this sweet stuff over a homemade brownie or crumble elevates the ordinary to chic. Use a small fine sieve – carefully fill with a spoonful of icing sugar, place over the dessert and tap lightly so the icing sugar snows down evenly and delicately.

Buttermilk Panna Cotta with Strawberry Coulis

Buttermilk adds a slight tartness to this creamy, custardlike Italian dessert. The bright red coulis made from frozen berries couldn't be easier to make.

1 tbsp	unflavoured gelatin	15 mL
1 cup	whipping cream	250 mL
⅓ cup	granulated sugar	75 mL
2 tsp	vanilla	10 mL
1 cup	buttermilk	250 mL

STRAWBERRY COULIS:

1	pkg (425 g) frozen strawberries in syrup, thawed	1

> In small saucepan, sprinkle gelatin over 2 tbsp (25 mL) of the cream; let stand for 5 minutes. Stir over medium-low heat until dissolved.

> In separate saucepan, heat together remaining cream, sugar and vanilla over medium heat until steaming; remove from heat. Stir in gelatin mixture and buttermilk. Pour into six 6-oz (175 mL) ramekins. Cover and refrigerate until set, about 4 hours. *(Make-ahead: Refrigerate for up to 2 days.)*

> STRAWBERRY COULIS: In food processor, whirl strawberries until smooth; press through fine strainer into bowl. Run knife around edge of each ramekin; turn out onto dessert plate. Drizzle coulis attractively onto plate.

Makes 6 servings. PER SERVING: about 236 cal, 4 g pro, 14 g total fat (9 g sat. fat), 24 g carb, 0 g fibre, 52 mg chol, 61 mg sodium. % RDI: 7% calcium, 2% iron, 13% vit A, 53% vit C, 6% folate.

MEASURING UP

Follow either the metric or the imperial measures throughout a recipe, not a combination. And use the right cup for the job: there are different ones for dry ingredients and for wet.

• Dry ingredient measures come in sets of different sizes: ¼ cup (50 mL), ⅓ cup (75 mL), ½ cup (125 mL) and 1 cup (250 mL).

• Liquid ingredient glass measuring cups have a spout and are marked on the outside.

• Measuring spoons are used for both dry and liquid ingredients and come in four sizes: ¼ tsp (1 mL), ½ tsp (2 mL), 1 tsp (5 mL) and 1 tbsp (15 mL).

DRY INGREDIENTS

• Lightly spoon dry ingredients into dry measure.

• Do not pack down or tap measure on counter (except for brown sugar, which should be packed enough to keep cup shape when dumped out).

• Fill measure until heaping. Then, working over canister, push straight edge of knife across top of measure.

LIQUID INGREDIENTS

• Place liquid measuring cup on counter. Pour in liquid to desired level, then bend down to check measurement at eye level.

• If liquid doesn't come exactly to desired mark on outside, pour off a little or add a little as needed.

Crispy Ice-Cream Sandwiches

Everyone's favourite treat of crispy rice squares gets even better with ice cream, chocolate and sprinkles.

2 cups	vanilla ice cream	500 mL
8 oz	semisweet chocolate, chopped	250 g
¼ cup	coloured sprinkles	50 mL
RICE CRISP SQUARES:		
5 cups	marshmallows (about 40)	1.25 L
¼ cup	butter	50 mL
1 tsp	vanilla	5 mL
5 cups	rice crisp cereal	1.25 L

> Line bottom of 13- x 9-inch (3.5 L) metal cake pan with parchment paper; grease sides. Set aside.

> RICE CRISP SQUARES: In large saucepan, melt marshmallows with butter over medium-low heat, stirring constantly, until smooth, about 5 minutes. Remove from heat; stir in vanilla.

> Add half of the cereal; stir until combined. Add remaining cereal; stir to coat completely. Scrape into greased bowl; let cool enough to handle, about 5 minutes. With greased hands, press into prepared pan; let cool completely.

> Run knife around edges of pan; remove from pan and peel off paper. Cut crosswise in half. Spread 1 half evenly with ice cream; top with remaining half. Wrap in plastic wrap; freeze in airtight container until firm, about 4 hours. Cut into 6 squares; cut each in half diagonally.

> Meanwhile, in heatproof bowl over saucepan of hot (not boiling) water, melt chocolate; let cool. Dip 1 corner of triangle halfway into chocolate; smooth with knife. Place coloured sprinkles on waxed paper; press chocolate edge into sprinkles. Wrap individually in plastic wrap; freeze in airtight container until firm, at least 4 hours. *(Make-ahead: Freeze for up to 2 days.)*

Makes 12 servings. PER SERVING: about 297 cal, 3 g pro, 11 g total fat (7 g sat. fat), 47 g carb, 1 g fibre, 22 mg chol, 197 mg sodium. % RDI: 3% calcium, 16% iron, 6% vit A, 6% folate.

Toffee Chocolate Chip Cookie Ice-Cream Sandwiches

The addition of chopped chocolate bars makes chocolate chip cookies irresistible. You can stop with the cookies or make them into these luscious ice-cream sandwiches.

2½ cups	vanilla, chocolate or butterscotch ice cream, slightly softened	625 mL
1 cup	toffee bits, finely chopped pecans or chocolate sprinkles	250 mL
TOFFEE CHOCOLATE CHIP COOKIES:		
½ cup	butter, softened	125 mL
½ cup	granulated sugar	125 mL
¼ cup	packed brown sugar	50 mL
1	egg	1
1½ tsp	vanilla	7 mL
1½ cups	all-purpose flour	375 mL
½ tsp	baking soda	2 mL
¼ tsp	salt	1 mL
4	bars (each 39 g) chocolate-covered toffee, chopped	4
1 cup	semisweet chocolate chips	250 mL
½ cup	chopped pecans	125 mL

> Line rimless baking sheets with parchment paper or grease; set aside.

> **TOFFEE CHOCOLATE CHIP COOKIES:** In large bowl, beat butter with granulated and brown sugars until fluffy. Beat in egg and vanilla. In separate bowl, whisk together flour, baking soda and salt; stir into butter mixture in 2 additions. Stir in toffee bars, chocolate chips and pecans.

> Roll dough by heaping tablespoonfuls (15 mL) into twenty 1¾-inch (4.5 cm) balls. Place, 2 inches (5 cm) apart, on prepared pans. Flatten to ½-inch (1 cm) thickness, rounding edges with fingers. Bake in top and bottom thirds of 350°F (180°C) oven, rotating and switching pans halfway through, until edges are golden, about 12 minutes. Transfer to racks; let cool completely. *(Make-ahead: Store in airtight container for up to 5 days or freeze for up to 2 weeks.)*

> Spread about ¼ cup (50 mL) ice cream on bottom of each of 10 cookies; top ice cream with second cookie. Roll sides in toffee bits.

> Wrap cookies individually in plastic wrap; freeze in airtight container until firm, about 4 hours. *(Make-ahead: Freeze for up to 5 days.)*

Makes 10 sandwiches. PER SANDWICH: about 570 cal, 6 g pro, 32 g total fat (16 g sat. fat), 68 g carb, 3 g fibre, 80 mg chol, 308 mg sodium. % RDI: 8% calcium, 16% iron, 19% vit A, 18% folate.

Super Fudgy Brownie Hearts

Delight a classroom full of kids, an office full of coworkers, or the friends and family you adore with the ultimate brownie – moist, fudgy and cut into hearts or simple bars.

7 oz	unsweetened chocolate, chopped	210 g
1 cup	butter	250 mL
4	eggs	4
2¼ cups	granulated sugar	550 mL
1½ tsp	vanilla	7 mL
1 cup	all-purpose flour	250 mL
¼ tsp	salt	1 mL

> Line 13- x 9-inch (3.5 L) metal cake pan with parchment paper, leaving overhang on long sides for handles; set aside.

> In heatproof bowl over saucepan of hot (not boiling) water, melt chocolate with butter, stirring occasionally. Let cool for 5 minutes.

> In large bowl, beat eggs with sugar until pale and thickened; stir in vanilla. Pour chocolate mixture over top. Sift flour with salt over chocolate; fold in until blended. Scrape into prepared pan.

> Bake in centre of 350°F (180°C) oven until cake tester inserted in centre comes out with a few moist crumbs clinging, about 30 minutes. Let cool in pan on rack for 10 minutes.

> Using parchment paper, lift brownies from pan onto cutting board. Using 1¾-inch (4.5 cm) heart-shaped cookie cutter, cut out brownies, rinsing and drying cutter between cuts. (Or cut into bars, wiping knife clean between cuts.)

> Place on parchment or waxed paper–lined tray; cover loosely with plastic wrap. Let cool completely. *(Make-ahead: Store in airtight container for up to 5 days.)*

Makes about 30 pieces. PER PIECE: about 99 cal, 1 g pro, 6 g total fat (4 g sat. fat), 12 g carb, 1 g fibre, 25 mg chol, 53 mg sodium. % RDI: 1% calcium, 3% iron, 4% vit A, 2% folate.

TIPS

• **Rinsing and drying your cookie cutter or knife between cuts ensures clean edges.**

• **Refrigerate brownie scraps in airtight container for up to 2 weeks (or freeze for longer storage) and use to top ice cream. They're so delicious that you might want to label the container "liver" so the pieces are still around at sundae time!**

Blueberry Streusel Muffins

For this Canadian favourite, fresh wild blueberries are best. Out of season you can stir frozen wild berries straight from the freezer into the batter. That way they won't colour it.

2 cups	all-purpose flour	500 mL
1 cup	packed brown sugar	250 mL
¾ tsp	baking soda	4 mL
½ tsp	salt	2 mL
1	egg	1
1 cup	buttermilk	250 mL
¼ cup	butter, melted	50 mL
1 tsp	vanilla	5 mL
½ tsp	grated lemon rind	2 mL
1 cup	fresh or frozen wild blueberries	250 mL
STREUSEL:		
⅓ cup	packed brown sugar	75 mL
¼ cup	slivered almonds	50 mL
¼ cup	all-purpose flour	50 mL
¼ tsp	grated nutmeg	1 mL
2 tbsp	butter, melted	25 mL

❯ Line muffin cups with paper liners or grease; set aside.

❯ STREUSEL: In bowl, stir together brown sugar, almonds, flour and nutmeg. Drizzle with butter; toss with fork. Set aside.

❯ In large bowl, whisk flour, sugar, baking soda and salt. In separate bowl, whisk egg, buttermilk, butter, vanilla and lemon rind. Pour over dry ingredients; stir twice. Sprinkle with blueberries; stir just until dry ingredients are moistened.

❯ Spoon into prepared muffin cups; sprinkle with streusel. Bake in centre of 375°F (190°C) oven until tops are firm to the touch, about 25 minutes. *(Make-ahead: Let cool in pan for 2 minutes. Transfer to rack and let cool completely. Store in airtight container for up to 1 day. Or wrap individually in plastic wrap; freeze in airtight container for up to 2 weeks.)*

Makes 12 muffins. PER MUFFIN: about 264 cal, 4 g pro, 8 g total fat (4 g sat. fat), 45 g carb, 1 g fibre, 265 mg sodium. % RDI: 5% calcium, 12% iron, 6% vit A, 15% folate.

Mocha Snacking Cake

This tender, moist cake is terrific on its own, dusted with icing sugar or dressed up with ice cream or whipped cream and berries. If you don't have strong brewed coffee, make it with 2 tbsp (25 mL) instant coffee.

⅔ cup	butter, softened	150 mL
1½ cups	granulated sugar	375 mL
2	eggs	2
1 tsp	vanilla	5 mL
1⅔ cups	all-purpose flour	400 mL
¾ cup	cocoa powder	175 mL
1 tsp	each baking soda and baking powder	5 mL
¼ tsp	salt	1 mL
1⅓ cups	strong brewed coffee, cooled	325 mL

> Grease sides of 8-inch (2 L) square metal cake pan; line bottom with parchment or waxed paper. Set aside.

> In large bowl, beat butter with sugar until fluffy; beat in eggs, 1 at a time, just until incorporated. Stir in vanilla.

> In separate bowl, sift together flour, cocoa, baking soda, baking powder and salt; add to butter mixture alternately with coffee, making 2 additions of dry ingredients and 1 of coffee. Beat until almost smooth. Scrape into prepared pan; spread evenly.

> Bake in 350°F (180°C) toaster oven or in centre of oven until cake tester inserted in centre comes out clean, 45 to 50 minutes. Let cool in pan on rack. *(Make-ahead: Wrap in plastic wrap and store for up to 3 days. Or overwrap with heavy-duty foil and freeze for up to 2 weeks.)*

Makes 12 servings. PER SERVING: about 275 cal, 4 g pro, 12 g total fat (7 g sat. fat), 41 g carb, 2 g fibre, 63 mg chol, 283 mg sodium. % RDI: 2% calcium, 13% iron, 11% vit A, 19% folate.

THE WELL-STOCKED KITCHEN
ESSENTIAL BAKING SUPPLIES

- <u>Sugar</u>: granulated, brown and icing
- <u>Liquid sweeteners</u>: honey and corn syrup
- <u>Flour</u>: all-purpose, whole grain and cake-and-pastry
- <u>Leaveners</u>: baking powder and baking soda
- <u>Cornstarch</u>
- <u>Vanilla</u>: preferably pure vanilla extract
- <u>Spices</u>: cinnamon and nutmeg
- <u>Chocolate</u>: cocoa powder, chocolate chips, bittersweet and unsweetened chocolate
- <u>Dried fruit</u>: raisins, and dried cranberries and blueberries
- <u>Nuts</u>: slivered almonds, and pecan and walnut halves
- <u>Rolled oats</u>: large-flake

Layered Apple Cake

This cake – more like a square than a cake – is classy enough for company, yet homey. And it's a snap to make.

2 cups	graham cracker crumbs	500 mL
½ cup	butter, melted	125 mL
3 tbsp	packed brown sugar	50 mL
CAKE:		
½ cup	butter, softened	125 mL
1 cup	packed brown sugar	250 mL
1	egg	1
1 tsp	vanilla	5 mL
1½ cups	all-purpose flour	375 mL
1 tsp	each cinnamon and baking powder	5 mL
½ tsp	salt	2 mL
½ cup	milk	125 mL
2 cups	diced peeled apples	500 mL

❯ Grease 9-inch (2.5 L) square metal cake pan; set aside.

❯ In bowl, mix together crumbs, butter and brown sugar; set aside 1 cup (250 mL) for topping. Press remaining crumb mixture into prepared pan. Bake in centre of 350°F (180°C) oven until firm, about 10 minutes.

❯ CAKE: Meanwhile, in large bowl, beat butter with sugar until fluffy; beat in egg and vanilla. In separate bowl, whisk flour, cinnamon, baking powder and salt; stir into butter mixture alternately with milk, making 2 additions of dry ingredients and 1 of milk. Fold in apples. Spread evenly over crust. Sprinkle reserved crumb mixture over top.

❯ Bake in centre of 350°F (180°C) oven until cake tester inserted in centre comes out clean, about 1 hour. Let cool; cut into squares. *(Make-ahead: Cover and store for up to 2 days.)*

Makes 9 servings. PER SERVING: about 500 cal, 5 g pro, 24 g total fat (14 g sat. fat), 68 g carb, 2 g fibre, 86 mg chol, 473 mg sodium. % RDI: 7% calcium, 19% iron, 21% vit A, 2% vit C, 20% folate.

Lunch Box Cereal Bars

One substitute for the dried berry fruit mix is a combination of equal amounts of raisins, dried cranberries, dried cherries and dried blueberries. These are available at bulk food stores and most supermarkets.

2½ cups	toasted oat cereal rounds	625 mL
2 cups	mixed dried berry fruit or trail mix	500 mL
1 cup	cornflakes	250 mL
1 cup	rice crisp cereal	250 mL
½ cup	sweetened shredded coconut	125 mL
⅔ cup	packed brown sugar	150 mL
⅓ cup	butter	75 mL
⅓ cup	corn syrup	75 mL
¼ cup	liquid honey	50 mL
¼ tsp	salt	1 mL
½ tsp	vanilla	2 mL

❯ Grease 13- x 9-inch (3.5 L) metal cake pan; set aside.

❯ In large heatproof bowl, stir together oat cereal rounds, dried berry fruit mix, cornflakes, rice crisp cereal and coconut.

❯ In saucepan, combine brown sugar, butter, corn syrup, honey and salt; bring to boil over medium-high heat, stirring often. Boil, stirring constantly, until foamy, about 2 minutes. Remove from heat; stir in vanilla. Let stand for 1 minute. Pour over cereal mixture; stir until evenly coated.

❯ Scrape into prepared pan. Using greased spatula, press firmly into even layer. Let cool completely. Cut into 18 bars. *(Make-ahead: Layer between waxed paper in airtight container and store for up to 3 days or freeze for up to 2 weeks.)*

Makes 18 bars. PER BAR: about 174 cal, 1 g pro, 5 g total fat (3 g sat. fat), 34 g carb, 2 g fibre, 11 mg chol, 144 mg sodium. % RDI: 3% calcium, 9% iron, 4% vit A, 2% folate.

Lemon Buttermilk Cupcakes

Cake-and-pastry flour, which is lower in gluten than all-purpose flour, gives these cupcakes a fine, tender texture. Sift the flour before measuring.

½ cup	butter	125 mL
1¼ cups	granulated sugar	300 mL
2	eggs	2
1½ tsp	finely grated lemon rind	7 mL
2 cups	sifted cake-and-pastry flour	500 mL
1½ tsp	baking powder	7 mL
½ tsp	baking soda	2 mL
¼ tsp	salt	1 mL
1¼ cups	buttermilk	300 mL
LEMON GLAZE:		
1½ cups	icing sugar	375 mL
½ tsp	finely grated lemon rind	2 mL
¼ cup	lemon juice	50 mL

❯ Line muffin cups with paper liners or grease; set aside.

❯ In large bowl, beat butter with sugar until light and fluffy; beat in eggs, 1 at a time, beating well after each addition. Stir in lemon rind.

❯ In separate bowl, whisk together flour, baking powder, baking soda and salt. Stir into butter mixture alternately with buttermilk, making 3 additions of dry ingredients and 2 of buttermilk. Spoon into prepared muffin cups.

❯ Bake in centre of 350°F (180°C) oven until cake tester inserted in centre comes out clean, 16 to 20 minutes. Transfer to rack. Let cool completely. *(Make-ahead: Store in single layer in airtight container for up to 2 days or freeze for up to 2 weeks.)*

❯ LEMON GLAZE: In small bowl, whisk sugar and lemon rind and juice; spoon over cupcakes.

Makes 18 cupcakes. PER CUPCAKE: about 198 cal, 2 g pro, 6 g total fat (4 g sat. fat), 35 g carb, trace fibre, 35 mg chol, 153 mg sodium. % RDI: 3% calcium, 7% iron, 5% vit A, 3% vit C, 8% folate.

SIFTING

- All-purpose flour does not require sifting.

- Sift cake-and-pastry flour before measuring.

- Sift cocoa powder and icing sugar after measuring to eliminate lumps.

Plum Hazelnut Crumble

Enjoy warm or cool with frozen yogurt or ice cream.

6 cups	sliced plums (or part nectarines), about 2¼ lb (1.125 kg) whole fruit	1.5 L
⅓ cup	packed brown sugar	75 mL
2 tbsp	all-purpose flour	25 mL
¼ tsp	cinnamon	1 mL
1 tbsp	icing sugar	15 mL
HAZELNUT CRUMBLE:		
¾ cup	hazelnuts	175 mL
¾ cup	all-purpose flour	175 mL
½ cup	packed brown sugar	125 mL
½ cup	cold butter	125 mL

❯ Grease 8-inch (2 L) square glass baking dish; set aside.

❯ HAZELNUT CRUMBLE: On rimmed baking sheet, toast hazelnuts in 350°F (180°C) oven until fragrant, about 10 minutes. Briskly rub nuts in tea towel to remove as much of the skins as possible.

❯ In food processor, finely chop nuts. Pulse in flour, sugar and butter until in fine crumbs with a few larger pieces. (Or with knife, chop nuts. In bowl, mix nuts, flour and sugar; cut in butter with pastry blender or 2 knives.) Set aside.

❯ In large bowl, toss plums, brown sugar, flour and pinch of the cinnamon. Spread in prepared dish. Sprinkle with Hazelnut Crumble. Bake in centre of 350°F (180°C) oven until topping is crisp and filling is tender and bubbly, about 40 minutes. Serve warm or let cool on rack.

❯ In small bowl, whisk icing sugar with remaining cinnamon; sprinkle over crumble.

Makes 6 to 8 servings. PER EACH OF 8 SERVINGS: about 394 cal, 4 g pro, 21 g total fat (8 g sat. fat), 52 g carb, 4 g fibre, 36 mg chol, 126 mg sodium. % RDI: 5% calcium, 12% iron, 14% vit A, 15% vit C, 13% folate.

Quick Apple Rhubarb Turnover

We recommend butter puff pastry sold boxed in rolls in the freezer section of your supermarket.

2	large apples, peeled, cored and thinly sliced	2
1 cup	chopped rhubarb	250 mL
¼ cup	granulated sugar	50 mL
2 tbsp	all-purpose flour	25 mL
1 tsp	lemon juice	5 mL
¼ tsp	cinnamon	1 mL
Half	pkg (450 g pkg) butter puff pastry	Half
1	egg yolk	1
2 tsp	granulated sugar	10 mL

❯ Line rimmed baking sheet with parchment paper or grease; set aside.

❯ In large bowl, toss together apples, rhubarb, sugar, flour, lemon juice and cinnamon.

❯ Unroll pastry onto prepared pan. Spoon apple mixture lengthwise along half of the pastry, leaving ½-inch (1 cm) border uncovered. Whisk egg yolk with 1 tsp (5 mL) water; lightly brush some over border. Using parchment paper to lift, fold uncovered pastry over filling; with fork, press edges to seal. Brush top with egg yolk mixture. Cut 4 evenly spaced 2-inch (5 cm) slashes on top; sprinkle with sugar.

❯ Bake in centre of 375°F (190°C) oven until golden and filling is tender, about 40 minutes.

Makes 6 servings. PER SERVING: about 439 cal, 6 g pro, 23 g total fat (4 g sat. fat), 54 g carb, 3 g fibre, 51 mg chol, 144 mg sodium. % RDI: 4% calcium, 14% iron, 3% vit A, 7% vit C, 18% folate.

INDEX

ABOUT OUR NUTRITION INFORMATION

To meet nutrient needs each day, moderately active women 25 to 49 need about 1,900 calories, 51 g protein, 261 g carbohydrate, 25 to 35 g fibre and not more than 63 g total fat (21 g saturated fat). Men and teenagers usually need more. Canadian sodium intake of approximately 3,500 to 4,500 mg daily should be reduced. Percentage of recommended daily intake (% RDI) is based on the highest recommended intakes (excluding those for pregnant and lactating women) for calcium, iron, vitamins A and C, and folate. Figures are rounded off. They are based on the first ingredient listed when there is a choice and do not include optional ingredients or those with no specified amounts.

ABBREVIATIONS

cal = calories

pro = protein

carb = carbohydrate

sat. fat = saturated fat

chol = cholesterol

CREDITS

PHOTOGRAPHY

— **Michael Alberstat:** pages 28, 94, 123 and 224

— **Susan Ashukian:** page 219

— **Hasnain Dattu:** pages 15 and 81

— **Yvonne Duivenvoorden:** front cover; pages 16, 21, 22, 25, 36, 41, 42, 44, 47, 62, 68, 74, 88, 93, 103, 107, 108, 115, 126, 145, 157, 160, 165, 183, 184, 189, 196, 201, 202, 205, 209, 227 and 228; back cover

— **Geoff George:** back flap (Elizabeth Baird)

— **Kevin Hewitt:** page 118

— **Edward Pond:** pages 138, 175 and 221; back flap (Test Kitchen staff)

— **David Scott:** page 18

FOOD STYLING

— **Julie Aldis:** pages 183 and 189

— **Donna Bartolini:** pages 15, 22, 36, 42, 62, 115, 123, 160, 221 and 224

— **Carol Dudar:** page 28

— **Lucie Richard:** pages 18, 44, 47, 94, 145, 165, 201, 202 and 228

— **Claire Stancer:** pages 21, 25, 41, 74, 81, 88, 107, 196 and 205

— **Claire Stubbs:** front cover; pages 16, 68, 93, 103, 108, 118, 126, 157, 184, 209 and 227; back cover

— **Rosemarie Superville:** page 175

PROPS STYLING

— **Maggi Jones:** page 175

— **OK Props:** page 183

— **Oksana Slavutych:** front cover; pages 15, 16, 18, 21, 22, 25, 28, 36, 41, 42, 44, 47, 62, 68, 74, 81, 88, 93, 94, 103, 107, 108, 115, 118, 123, 126, 145, 157, 160, 165, 184, 189, 196, 201, 202, 205, 209, 221, 224, 227 and 228; back cover

— **Mollie Wilkins/Judy Inc.:** page 219

TRANSCONTINENTAL BOOKS
1100 René-Lévesque Boulevard West
24th Floor
Montreal, Que. H3B 4X9
Tel.: 514 340-3587
Toll-free: 1-866-800-2500
www.canadianliving.com

Bibliothèque et Archives nationales du Québec and Library and
Archives Canada cataloguing in publication

Baird, Elizabeth, 1939-
Make It Tonight: Delicious, No-Fuss Dinner Solutions for Every Cook
At head of title: Canadian Living
ISBN 978-0-9738355-6-4
1. Cookery. 2. Quick and easy cookery. I. Title. II. Title: Canadian Living.

TX714.B34 2007   641.5   C2007-941271-8

Project editor: Christina Anson Mine
Production manager: Marie-Suzanne Menier
Copy editors: Miriam Osborne, Valérie Quintal
Indexer: Gillian Watts
Front and back covers: photography, Yvonne Duivenvoorden;
food styling, Claire Stubbs; props styling, Oksana Slavutych
Cover design: Michael Erb
Graphic concept and layout: orangetango

Printed in Canada
© Transcontinental Books, 2007
Legal deposit — 3rd quarter 2007
National Library of Quebec
National Library of Canada
ISBN 978-0-9738355-6-4

We acknowledge the financial support of our publishing activity
by the Government of Canada through the BPDIP program of the
Department of Canadian Heritage, as well as by the Government
of Quebec through the SODEC program Aide à la promotion.

Transcontinental Books

For information on special rates for corporate libraries
and wholesale purchases, please call 1-866-800-2500.